Star Speak

By the same author:

The Unkindest Cuts: The Scissors and the Cinema
Susan Hayward: The Divine Bitch
Down the Yellow Brick Road: The Making of The Wizard of Oz
The Golden Age of "B" Movies
Hollywood on Ronald Reagan: Friends and Enemies Discuss Our
  President, The Actor
Hollywood on Hollywood: Tinsel Town Talks
Blackface to Blacklist: Al Jolson, Larry Parks and "The Jolson Story"

StarSpeak
Hollywood on Everything

Doug McClelland

FABER AND FABER   BOSTON AND LONDON

Published by Faber and Faber, Inc.

50 Cross Street
Winchester, MA 01890

Printed in the United States

Library of Congress Cataloging-in-Publication Data
McClelland, Doug.
  StarSpeak : Hollywood on everything.
   1. Moving-picture industry—United States.
2. Moving-pictures—United States—Biography. I. Title.
PN1993.5.U6M32 1987   791.43'0973   86-29877
ISBN 0-571-12981-1 (pbk.)

This book is dedicated to

Charlie Earle
Jim Meyer
Eduardo Moreno

The best of friends

Categories

Foreword

When the evolution—revolution?—from silent to talking pictures began in the late 1920s, one skeptical studio executive shrugged, "Who would want to hear movie actors talk?"

As it turned out, just the whole world.

By the early 1930s, some of the theater's most acclaimed plays were being brought to new verbal life by Hollywood folk, and some of the most gifted dramatists had begun turning out dialogue especially for the extraordinary denizens of the glamour capital. The public became fascinated not only with what movieland's vivid personalities had to say as characters in *reel* life, but what they had to say as characters in *real* life. Stories came to matter not really all that much, though; audiences in the greatest number ever wanted to see STARS.

This golden age continued for 20 years, until the big studios were forced to give up their theater-owning monopoly (which had assured them of bookings for their films) and television reared its ominous antenna. Wide-screen innovations and Marilyn Monroe perambulations temporarily recalled the retreating movie audience. But things were never really the same in Tinsel Town again.

Since then, trends have come and gone, many very successful, but they were still only trends, things of passing interest. Spectacle, sexual explicitness, violence, horror, science fiction, the Brat Pack—these have been the basic formulae of the more profitable films in recent decades.

Increasingly, it was television stars who captured the more sedentary public's keenest attention, though a movie star still popped up here and there to intrigue a younger and younger audience.

It was a new Hollywood.

Through everything, however, there has been one constant: Hollywood has continued to speak—professionally and personally.

If its celluloid images have influenced generations, so have its real-life ones. With rare exceptions such as the elusive, maybe image-perpetuating Greta Garbo, Hollywood people fell in love with the sound of their own voices very early, and, with a fidelity unique for that fickle city of few angels, they have retained this devotion.

The closing of a script at day's end never silenced those toiling in film, as this book of their pithy, occasionally ribald off-camera dialogue proves. Collected here are the most revealing of their own quotations, the wittiest of their ripostes, the strongest of their opinions, the brightest of their anecdotes over six decades. Some of the more than 1,000 comments included were made in books, magazines and newspapers; others on television and even radio. Still others were imparted more informally, sometimes simply over cocktails to this writer-editor.

Just about everybody who was anybody in Hollywood (or thought they were) is present, along with the newer names in "the cinema firma*mint*," as Jean Hagen's shrilly ignorant silent screen queen put it in *Singin' in the Rain*. Stars, as well as lesser players, directors, producers, moguls, writers, cameramen, costume designers, agents, even gossip columnists—their own words of sometimes controversial wisdom are all preserved on these pages.

"Speech," wrote one Mathurin Mondo, "is the supreme art of man."

Maybe even of movie stars.

I am indebted to George Zeno for the color portrait of Marilyn Monroe on the front cover of this book.

Special thanks for their help on *StarSpeak* to Charlie Earle, Jim Meyer, Eduardo Moreno and my editor, Douglas Hardy.

My gratitude also to Patrick Agan, Sarah Alpern, John Cocchi, Kirk Crivello, George Dean, Maeve Druesne, Richard Hegedorn, Beverly Linet, Eleanor O'Sullivan, James Robert Parish, Bea Smith, Jorge Tablada and Lou Valentino.

Doug McClelland

Fall, 1986

StarSpeak

Acting

I finished *Strategic Air Command* with Jimmy Stewart on a Friday night, winding up with some highly dramatic emotional scenes. The next morning—studios were working Saturdays then—I was swept into a key comedy scene in a new picture, *A Woman's World*. I was playing opposite Cornel Wilde, whom I had never met. I was so confused and tired after the long, harrowing schedule on *Air Command* that I simply gave up. I dropped my arms, turned to my secretary and asked, "Who am I?" Everyone laughed, but I wasn't joking.

June Allyson

❏

I don't dig this brooding, analytical stuff. I just danced, and I just acted.

Fred Astaire

❏

The Hollywood studios amaze me! Each is like an entire city. Come the revolution, we could all live right at any one of them. They even have their own printing presses. Everything is on such a gigantic scale, everything but the acting. Funny, that must be the one side that is toned down, made smaller so as not to appear exaggerated.

Fay Bainter

❏

When I go to the movies—which is seldom these days—I see such restraint, such blank pusses, that I wonder if these actors know what they're doing. There's a (very fine) line between underacting and not acting at all. And not acting is what a lot of actors are guilty of. It amazes me how some of these little numbers with dreamy looks and a dead pan are getting away with it.

I've even seen a couple of them with Oscars in their hands. I'd hate to see them on stage with a dog act. There's a marvelous quote from Shelley Winters, who said, "I love Bette Davis because she's not afraid to be bad." That's the truth. When Bette's good, she's real good. When she's bad, she's awful ... but at least she's not afraid to bat an eyelash.

Joan Blondell

I have no respect for acting. Acting is the expression of the neurotic impulse. It's a bum's life ... You get paid for doing nothing and it means nothing. Acting is fundamentally a childish thing to pursue. Quitting acting—that is the mark of maturity.

Marlon Brando

George Raft and Gary Cooper once played a scene in front of a cigar store, and it looked like the wooden Indian was overacting.

George Burns

Robert Taylor had to do all the work in *Camille* while Garbo stood still and was photographed in front of a black velvet curtain. He earned his salary, by Christ. While Garbo's own lighting man made sure the cameraman was photographing her through gauze, poor Robert Taylor had to go all around the bleeding furniture, had marks to hit, lights to find and lines to speak, just so he could get over to Garbo who would whisper, "I'm dying," and the critics would say she was a great actress. Put her up on a stage with Paul Scofield or Maggie Smith and Garbo would disappear into the woodwork.

Michael Caine

I learned a lot from that lady (Susan Hayward). I learned more about my trade, about presence in front of the camera, by watching her. She acted like it was nothing, with no effort.

Rory Calhoun

Larry Olivier is not an actor. He's a chameleon. He wears all that make-up and all those costumes and just disguises himself. Half the time you don't even know it's him.

Bette Davis

John Wayne actually got angry at me when I abandoned my tough-guy image to play the tormented artist Vincent van Gogh in *Lust for Life*. I remember we were at a party and Wayne motioned for me to come out on the back porch. "Why are you playing a weak, sniveling guy?" he said. He was really furious at me. It was like I was not being true to my people. I said, "Duke, we're *actors*. We just create the illusion of these big macho guys. You know, John, you really didn't win all those wars." But we obviously didn't see eye-to-eye. He actually thought he was John Wayne.

Kirk Douglas

If I weren't doing what I'm doing now, the actress thing, I'd be in an asylum, I'm sure of it.

Mia Farrow

During the shooting of *Mrs. Miniver*, Dame May Whitty had a "two-shot" with young actor Richard Ney, who later married the star, Greer Garson. She asked the handsome new-to-Hollywood actor to react so that the next line would make more sense. Richard replied, "Of course, Dame May. I shall do as you say, but I think my way is better." The titled English actress looked down her nose. "Young man, you haven't *got* a way!"

Joan Fontaine

Dustin Hoffman's perfectionism? If you argue with him on something, he wants his point and he wants his way. Finally, if you say, "All right, we'll do it *your* way," he'll say, "No—I don't want to do it my way until you *like* doing it my way." It's not enough to *give in* to him, you have to *like* what he wants, too!

Teri Garr

Brando? Actors like him are good but on the whole I do not enjoy actors who seek to commune with their armpits, so to speak.

Greer Garson

There was a time when I dreamed of being a great actress. Now I'd rather have a short role with long eyelashes than a long role with no eyelashes.

Paulette Goddard

The most important thing in acting is honesty. Once you've learned to fake that, you're in!

Samuel Goldwyn

Take Joan Collins. She's common, she can't act—yet she's the hottest female property around these days. If that doesn't tell you something about the state of our industry today, what does?

Stewart Granger

I think Grace Kelly was the finest actress I ever worked with. Forgive me, Ingrid, Kate, Audrey and all the others. But Grace had something extraordinary. She was so very, very relaxed in front of the camera. When we did *To Catch a Thief*, you know, she was quite young. Had someone else played it, her role could have been unpleasant—a spoiled, silly little girl. But the way Grace played her, you liked her.

Cary Grant

The hard part was not playing all those roles that Marlon Brando and all those guys were doing. That's the easy way to act. You just hide behind all those wonderful characters.

George Hamilton

Greer Garson
"Method" the pits

Katharine Hepburn
On Tracy's purity

❏

I fought acting till I discovered I had to do it. With acting, I have always felt that I had a big ball of string attached to my head. It lets me run around just far enough to do things like writing short stories and poems and songs. Then all of a sudden it pulls me up and puts me down on a stage and I have to act. I'm like the man with the talent in the Bible. It isn't the talent I wanted but I can't bury it.

Signe Hasso

❏

Spencer (Tracy) was like eating a baked potato. It's pure, of the earth, and it's dependable. For Spencer, acting was easy, living was difficult. No one really knows anybody, *truly* knows him. I don't know what his torment was.

Katharine Hepburn

❏

Actors are cattle. Disney probably has the right idea. He draws them and if he doesn't like them he tears them up.

Alfred Hitchcock

❏

I was never looked at. I was never able to be aggressive with a woman. When I started acting, I felt attractive for the first time.

Dustin Hoffman

❏

As for Orson Welles, he's got a secret. It's what he's saying. As long ago as *Jane Eyre*, which he played in English, he wouldn't tell the audience even then. To hell with 'em. They want to know what it's all about, let 'em go somewhere and read the book! Jerry Wald tried to get him to dub his lines in *Long Hot Summer*, but not only did he refuse the suggestion but he wouldn't even let Jerry get the Kingfish to dub them for him.

Nunnally Johnson

❏

Method acting's an abomination. The chief lesson young actors and actresses from these so-called modern schools learn is complete and unerring egotism. They are taught to relate everything to self. They care little for the words of the author, little for the dictates of the director, little for the efforts of the other actors in the play, and absolutely nothing for the audience . . . Marlon Brando has been known to place rubber stoppers in his ears so he cannot hear the words spoken by other players!

Boris Karloff

In America it is considered a lot more important to be a great Barney Miller than a great Hamlet.

Stacy Keach

Sometimes I really love being an actor, sometimes it seems really stupid to me. It's an odd way to make a living. I take it as seriously as I have to, but the reality is I'm not trained in the British Theater, and it's not in my blood and I'm not dying to have a massive coronary on stage doing *Hamlet*, you know? I don't *need* it. I need something creative. And maybe I need something in this general area. Naw, I think "need" is too strong. There are a lot of actors that have a *need* for acting. And whatever the psychological ramifications are that go along with that. I don't *need* it.

Michael Keaton

As for my leading ladies at MGM, the hardest thing was finding dancers who could also act and sing. Most of them couldn't even say hello.

Gene Kelly

I don't think anybody knew I could act until I put on a bathing suit (in *From Here to Eternity*).

Deborah Kerr

I am the incurable ham and Hollywood is a ham's paradise. I'm always acting even when I'm alone in a room. Then I go prancing about.

Charles Laughton

I am never satisfied with what I do. Each performance provides another glimpse or insight. I can remember only one moment in my career, during the long national tour of *Duel of Angels*, when I thought I had reached something like perfection. Those moments are rare.

Vivien Leigh

John Barrymore was wonderful in *Midnight*. He had his wife, Elaine Barrie, in the picture and she kept an eye on him. When we'd been shooting about three weeks, Elaine came to me and said, "You know, John thinks this is a wonderful picture—he read the script last night." This was my introduction to idiot cards, flying back and forth all over the place for John. We had this one scene where he had to walk down a narrow corridor, and with the cameras and lights and things, there was just no room for idiot cards. So I said, "John, I'm afraid you're going to have to learn this." He said, "Oh? Do you want me to recite the soliloquoy from *Hamlet* for you?" and he did. So I said, "Then why the hell those idiot cards?" He said, "My dear fellow, why should I fill my mind with this shit just to forget it tomorrow morning?"

Mitchell Leisen

Why are there only a few people who can do what I do, and there's 25,000 competent actors to play *On Golden Pond*? Because comedy is tough! Comedy is beneath them! It's *low*. That's elitist crap! To be a great comedian, you have to be a great actor. But to be a fine dramatic actor, you don't have to also know comedy.

Jerry Lewis

I was forced into being an actress and I didn't want to be. If I had to do it all over again, I'd do it differently. I'd sit home and write lyrics and music.

Ida Lupino

❏

Elizabeth Taylor is still a primitive—sort of the Grandma Moses of acting.

Joseph L. Mankiewicz

❏

I never worried about typecasting. I always wanted to characterize. To me, it's the whole fun of acting. I like to imitate, maybe too much at times. These young actors, you don't find them fiddling around, putting on beards and so forth—and damn it, I think it takes a lot of the fun out of it. *Every* part is a character part.

Fredric March

❏

Upon being told by a country club he wanted to join that actors were not accepted:
   I'm no actor, and I've got 64 pictures to prove it.

Victor Mature

❏

I took up acting because it let me burn off energy. Besides, I wanted to beat the 40-hour-a-week rap. But, man, I didn't escape. Now I'm working *72* hours a week! Acting's a hard scene for me. Every script I get is an enemy I have to conquer.

Steve McQueen

❏

The main thing is, if you talk too much, the audience won't remember anything. So say something short and memorable.

Steve McQueen

❏

I don't understand this Method stuff. I remember Laurence Olivier asking Dustin Hoffman why he stayed up all night. Dustin, looking really beat, really bad, said it was to get into the scene being filmed that day, in which he was

Ida Lupino
Forced into acting

Steve McQueen
A hard scene

supposed to have been up all night. Olivier said, "My boy, if you'd learn how to act you wouldn't have to stay up all night."

Robert Mitchum

❏

In *The Exile* and in *Atlantis*, you will see the new Montez, the girl who has learned to act, Maria, your friend, who will get better and better now. Years will pass, and I will still get better. As an old lady I will be perfect, beloved and admired by all, like Ethel Barrymore, plus the Montez fire and cunning. Always I will get better. Never again will I *steenk* on the screen.

Maria Montez

❏

I'm an underrated actor ... because I play heroes and that really is acting. I'm scared witless most of the time.

Roger Moore

❏

I'm a terrier, because I was never naturally good at anything. And that includes acting.

Paul Newman

❏

Talking about preparation is all hogwash; it takes the mystery out of the movies. I don't want to know how some guy wore the same socks for months to prepare for a role; then when I see the movie that's all I can think about—dirty socks.

Sean Penn

❏

It was my voice and my voice alone that won me my first film role in *The Invisible Man* in 1933. I was between Broadway roles, and my agent suggested I take a test for a motion picture, *A Bill of Divorcement*. I knew nothing about movies, and I went through the test reluctantly. I didn't get the part—it went to John Barrymore. But my agent called a few months later and said he had a Hollywood contract for me to star in *The Invisible Man*. I was puzzled by this, and demanded to know how a poor test could result in a contract. My agent said, "I must admit there was a certain amount of laughter at your performance, but they were looking for a voice, not an actor."

Claude Rains

❏

The greatest performance I have ever seen was given by Tallulah Bankhead in the test she made to play Amanda Wingfield in *The Glass Menagerie*. Karl Freund photographed the test. He cried. She was dying to do that role. The first day, she was kneeling—the light reflecting in her eyes—as she hemmed the daughter's dress. And when she spoke a certain line, there was just the right catch in her voice. She *was* that woman! She had promised not to drink; she could not keep her promise. Jack Warner said, "Errol Flynn is enough." It cost a fortune to do an Errol Flynn picture because he was always drunk. And thanks to Errol Flynn, Tallulah lost the part. It was so, so sad.

Irving Rapper

❏

When I was a contract player at Universal, I used to go over to the set where they were filming *Inherit the Wind* and watch Spencer Tracy and Fredric March. March was a real working actor. You could see his craft right out there on his face. And Tracy just glided through it. I couldn't figure it out. Then one day there was Tracy walking right in front of me. He turned around and said, "Who are you? Why are you always hanging around?" I said, "I'm an actor." And he looked at me and said, "An actor, huh?", and did that great wink. "Just remember not to ever let anyone catch you at it."

Burt Reynolds

❏

Bette Davis was and is every inch a lady—polite, mannerly, gracious, even self-effacing. But by today's standards she could never have gotten a job in a high school production of *East Lynne*. I know it's goatish of me to say it, but Miss Davis was, when I played with her (in *Kid Galahad*), not a very gifted amateur and employed any number of jarring mannerisms that she used to form an image. In her early period Miss Davis played the image, and not herself, and certainly not the character provided by the author.

Edward G. Robinson

Claude Rains
The voice of success

Burt Reynolds
Never caught at it

Norma Shearer
Preferred male role

□

Scarlett O'Hara is going to be a thankless and difficult role. The part I'd like to play is Rhett Butler.

Norma Shearer

□

Someone asked Spencer Tracy if he got tired of playing himself all the time. He said, "Who do you want me to play? Humphrey Bogart?" I feel it's all right to bring your own style to a character.

James Stewart

□

I had no trouble playing any kind of role. My problems began when I had to be myself.

Gene Tierney

□

14

Acting is not an important job in the scheme of things. Plumbing is.

Spencer Tracy

❏

In the States, they never place the same amount of emphasis on the voice. Actors are willing to gain 50 pounds or pull a tooth for a part, but they don't do the voice. Acting here is mostly physical. I'm appalled by half of the voices I hear. It's amazing that women in New York spend thousands of dollars on their hair, their face, their clothes, and then they talk *like this*.

Kathleen Turner

❏

John Ford taught me what to do in front of the movie camera. He taught me not to *act* but to *react*.

John Wayne

❏

Best movie actors are animals. And next are children. Children get nearer to being true and honest and that's the essential thing in movie acting. Older actors can learn a lot from children. Greatest thing I have ever seen was a scene between Jack Barrymore and child actress Virginia Weidler. Barrymore was drinking a cup of tea. Virginia was speaking her lines, and half-way through her speech Jack raised his cup. Virginia said, "Excuse me, Mr. Barrymore. You shouldn't do that during my speech." Barrymore was terrified.

Orson Welles

❏

I like girls. They're all fine by me—until they become actresses. Suddenly, they're machines. A combination IBM calculator and McCormick reaper.

Richard Widmark

❏

Fredric March was able to do a very emotional scene with tears in his eyes and pinch my fanny at the same time.

Shelley Winters

❏

Acting is like sex. You should do it and not talk about it.

Joanne Woodward

Addiction

After Richard's (Dick Powell) death I had a very rough period when I took to drinking too much wine. I still have a hard time watching his movies, but then I'd wake up in the middle of the night hearing his voice coming from the television set I'd forgotten to turn off. For a moment I'd think he hadn't died at all. It was all a nightmare.

June Allyson

❏

It's criminal for someone to say, "that's a man's smoke" or "he drank like a man." Some people I know who are alcoholics now weren't strong at all . . . weren't manly at all . . . they were just able to drink a lot of whiskey. It doesn't mean a thing as far as manhood goes. When I was asked to go on television and say, "I'm an alcoholic," I jumped at the chance. A lot of people said it took a lot of courage. It didn't take any courage for me because I didn't have anything to lose. To me, it's like seeing a bunch of people driving down to a bridge that's out and they don't know it because they can't see it. I say, "Look, if you go driving down there at 60 miles an hour and don't stop, you'll go right in the river." I feel it's my responsibility to do that. It can happen to anybody. It took me 25 years to become an alcoholic and that's a long time because I have a hell of a constitution.

Dana Andrews

❏

I went completely out of control. I had several serious car accidents, one which landed me in the hospital for six months. I almost died from that. All because of alcohol. I'm not ashamed of my past. I'm very proud of the fact that I'm not in an institution. As a matter of fact, I was declared insane because of the disease of alcoholism. Everything in my life was closing in on me: my lover died of cancer, my businesses had all gone bankrupt, I was no longer wanted in the film industry. The bottle was my only escape. I was in and out of jails, hospitals and institutions. I slept in doorways on Skid Row. I hate to admit it but I was a drunk. And a mean drunk. If you had taken a drink out of my hand at that time, I would have broken your arm. I was a mess. The Salvation Army took me in, and Alcoholics Anonymous. If it were not for those organizations, I would not be sitting here.

Robert Arthur

Cocaine habit-forming? It certainly is not. I've been using it for years.

Tallulah Bankhead

I lay in bed, suddenly awake, staring at it. An enormous white crab slowly crawling across the ceiling. I thought, this can't be the DTs. Can you get the DTs when you're only 30?

Diana Barrymore

When we did *The Great Profile*, John Barrymore was at the nadir of his life, dissipated but somehow handsome still. I remember he had a male nurse named Karl with him all the time. At one point we had to shoot in a nearby theater location where we shared a kitchen. I noticed that Karl brought him one Coke after another all day long. When I saw that the cooking rum in the kitchen was disappearing, I knew what was happening. Mr. Barrymore was in a fog most of the time—no, make that in another world. But when he faced the cameras he came to life. It was amazing.

Anne Baxter

I was all messed up in my head, and I was hopeless, just like a lot of kids today who see their idols assassinated, who get their heads opened up when they go to Chicago to protest. So like a lot of them, I turned to drugs. People go into drugs, whether they're rich or poor, when you take their hope, their potency, their manhood away from them. When I got my potency back, I came out of it. I didn't have any dramatic, rolling-on-the-floor withdrawal symptoms. I just started studying acting. It made me feel as though I could be something, mean something.

Robert Blake

❏

The trouble with the world is that everybody in it is three drinks behind.

Humphrey Bogart

❏

I don't hate my mother or my father now. I've learned that alcoholism is a disease. I hated them at times when I was a kid. I thought it was my fault when they got drunk. I felt it was because they didn't love me. It's common for kids to feel that way. I wish they had had Al-Anon in those days, which is for the families and children of alcoholics.

Carol Burnett

❏

Some sections of the press suggested that it was Elizabeth (Taylor) who drove me to drink. Poor dear, she had nothing to do with it. I began drinking when success came to me, about the age of 22. It never affected me badly. I didn't have a hangover until I was 45. But it did get me into scrapes. I used to fight, physically, a lot.

Richard Burton

❏

I was sitting in the front row of a Cocaine Anonymous meeting and I was a total mess—sweaty, stinky, my skin was all broken out. And I just decided it was over. It was over. I had been given a great gift (acting ability) and I wasn't going to go to my grave in regret. I've been clean ever since that day.

Gary Busey

❏

I think I'll get out of these wet clothes and into a dry martini.

Charles Butterworth

❏

The leading lady of *Angels with Dirty Faces* was lovely, talented Ann Sheridan. So much to offer—and a three-pack-a-day smoker. She just didn't eat because cigarettes killed her appetite. One day a well-known doctor came on the *Angels* set, and I asked him to lunch, inviting Annie to join us. At the table she lit a cigarette immediately. She ordered ham and eggs, took one little bit of the ham, then lit another cigarette. The doctor said, "You know, time was when coronary thrombosis was a great new thing among women. Whenever it happened, it went up and down the land, doctor to doctor—'a female coronary!' Not lately. Cigarettes have done it." Annie said, "Oh, really?" and went right on smoking. Years later when the lung cancer hit, she didn't have much of a chance.

James Cagney

I happen to think marijuana is a fool's paradise, which got me drummed out of most of the parties around here where they pass it around like the brandy and cigars. So they think I'm square. The joke is that while they're turning up their noses at me for not touching the stuff, I'm doling out checks for institutions trying to hook them off it. How's that for a laugh?

Michael Caine

The best research for playing a drunk is being a British actor for 20 years.

Michael Caine

President Reagan and all members of his cabinet have agreed to take a drug test. Now if they'd only take the test we all want them to take: an IQ test.

Johnny Carson

Me? An alcoholic? How could I be? I'm a Phi Beta Kappa!

Jan Clayton

A lot of damage was done in a short period, and it's terrifically hard to undo it. There were rumors of alcoholism, of pill addiction—they were right on that one—even that I had a fatal disease. People who had hired me before no longer wanted me.

Rosemary Clooney

❑

For the past year I have been re-building myself after 20 years of reaching out for a glass or a pill to make me feel good—and there is no question that they did just that. Having a different woman all the time was part of the same system. And if a woman wasn't available, then the drug would eliminate the need for one. If one wasn't there, the other was. But the drugs began to have a dire effect—the effect of self-destruction.

Tony Curtis

❑

Marijuana should be legalized because I feel with young people it is the forbidden fruit element that attracts them. I came along a few years after the prohibition era so I was not part of that time, but certainly then the appeal was the forbidden fruit aspect. If pot is legalized I think the young might fall away from it.

Bette Davis

❑

I gave cigarettes up, darling, but you smoke. They aren't harmful. Listen, they spend millions of dollars on cancer research, and they come up with nothing, so they have to scare people somehow. Why don't they put on every bottle of Scotch "Drink this and you will get cirrhosis of the liver"? Why don't they write on every bottle of aspirin "Take 20 of these and they will kill you"? Smoke, darling.

Marlene Dietrich

❑

Gable had only one rule. He always quit at five—I think so he could start drinking. Gable was quite a drinker. In fact, most of the older actors were; and Gable did as well as any of them. Never, of course, on the set. He always came to work ready and clear. But in the evening he was a very heavy drinker. As a matter of fact, he told me once that if he couldn't drink he'd just as soon die.

Edward Dmytryk

❑

Until four years ago (1982), I drank my way through every movie I ever made. Who knows, I might have stopped drinking earlier if anyone had recognized my pain. But all they could see was that damn pretty face of mine. People didn't take me seriously. Even though I'd been seven years with Warner Brothers—seven years of shimmering up there on the screen as the number one teenage heartthrob—by the time it was over, I wasn't prepared for a thing. I'd been coddled, hadn't learned street smarts and didn't know anyone in the industry. And worse than that, my looks didn't mean a thing—in fact, they worked against me. Casting agents were on the hunt for Dustin Hoffman and Al Pacino types—they didn't want a surfer bum like me. The irony was I'd never been on a surfboard in my life.

Troy Donahue

I started taking drugs and alcohol when I was 15 years old. I started with marijuana. Then I began drinking. I was a real romantic, so I drank cognac. In my early 20s I took a lot of amphetamines. Then, later, I discovered coke. So, over the years, I managed to do about everything. I've since come to believe that drugs stunt your emotional growth. So, though I may have been 29, emotionally I was 15. In my early 30s it became worse and worse.

Richard Dreyfuss

I had everything. Working steadily with good parts. Then I started putting all my spare time in my arm. I'm not really sure why I started ... I was 17 ... In no time at all I was using whatever was available—mostly heroin, because I had the money to pay for it.

Bobby Driscoll

A blonde drove me to drink, and my one regret is that I never thanked her.

W.C. Fields

I make it a habit to keep a reasonable supply of medicinal stimulants on hand in case I encounter a venomous snake—which I also always keep on hand.

W.C. Fields

❏

Thou shalt not kill—anything less than a fifth.

W.C. Fields

❏

I don't drink now. I gave that up a few years ago, but I lived it up pretty good for a while. I remember John Barrymore saying to me one time, "Glenn, the only friends I have in this goddamned town are Haig & Haig."

Glenn Ford

❏

The bad habits are still around. They're just in the closet. The longest I ever quit smoking was five months, after the (double-bypass heart) operation. Drugs? I can't get them. I'm not sure if you had some on you I wouldn't accept. Speed was my drug. I don't like cocaine. I used to take Dexedrine. It makes you care about detail.

Bob Fosse

❏

I'm one-eighth Jewish and seven-eighths Irish, so I get drunk and feel guilty about it.

Zach Galligan

❏

Everything at MGM was competitive. Before MGM, I had enjoyed being myself. I had been judged by my talent. But in the movies, beauty was the standard of judgment, and this I definitely didn't have. Most people can work off extra pounds, but not me. They seemed to stick to me. I found the only way I could keep my weight down—and the only way I could go to sleep—was to take pills. For years I went to bed with pills and got up with pills.

Judy Garland

❏

Alcohol removes warts. Not from me—from whomever I'm with.

Jackie Gleason

❏

I'm no alcoholic. I'm a drunkard. There's a difference. A drunkard doesn't like to go to meetings.

Jackie Gleason

❏

I spent years drinking pretty good, but now I just drink wine with dinner.

Cary Grant

❏

There's an old expression: "Line the steps going up with velvet so you don't hurt your ass coming down." Well, during my 55 years, I've missed a couple of steps. Having fallen to the lowest rung in 1954, my wife had me committed to the state mental institute at Camarillo, California. Because I didn't know who I was. Or where I was. I was committed as a schizophrenic. But it was really booze that had done me in. Alcoholism was almost my dead end.

Billy Halop

❏

Booze is liquid suicide. I know booze can throw me down and kill me. Grass is better for you. I use a lot of it.

Sterling Hayden

❏

I never drink—well, maybe a glass of wine, at the most, a couple of times a month. Oh, I used to smoke and drink. When I was on Broadway I smoked so much my throat would close shut. I went to a doctor. He stuck the whole office down my throat trying to get it open. He told me he wouldn't be responsible for my throat if I continued to smoke. My mother had just died from cancer. That's it, I thought. I cut it off right then and there. I wouldn't be alive today if I hadn't stopped smoking 40 years ago.

Bob Hope

❏

My insecurities about holding my own on the London stage led to blazing rows with directors and heavy drinking. It was madness. Booze cuts off your feet, and I was just a drunken bore.

Anthony Hopkins

❏

I just drank a lot—out of boredom, pressure, frustration. Then a couple of years ago, I thought, "What on earth am I doing, drinking myself into oblivion? What kind of existence is that?" So I quit it. I'll have a couple of drinks now, but I don't slug it away anymore. It was disgusting. There's more to life than getting soused every night.

Rock Hudson

❏

I was in summer stock in New England when I had the breakdown about 10 years ago. I was in seven hospitals to get off drugs. I went down to 80 pounds, I didn't want to live. Then Father Peter McGuire found me and never let go. I became a Catholic. I went to work at the rectory, St. Anthony's Parish, Portsmouth, R.I., cooking and scrubbing floors. I had no money. I made $70 a week.

Betty Hutton

❏

Alcohol and drug abuse was a lifestyle everyone in Los Angeles was affecting at the time (the 1970s). *Everyone.* Plus my mother had ended up with a drinking problem, so I may have had a hereditary inclination. We're American Cherokee Indians—and don't give firewater to Indians, for God's sake. At any rate, I was always a social user—a pot smoker. I loved to smoke my reefer. In fact, that was probably the hardest thing to give up, smoking reefer. The coke really only became a problem when I became a heavy drinker. The two actually fed themselves. I realized I could drink more if I had a little coke and that if I had a drink it would be nice to have some coke to go with it. It was a great marriage—if you wanted to vegetate.

Don Johnson

❏

I smoked cigarettes until 15 years ago. Recently, I saw a film clip of me giving ballet lessons with a cigarette hanging from my mouth. Now what kind of fool was that?

Gene Kelly

What made me quit boozing? I saw myself on Geraldo Rivera's TV show. I saw it stone sober and I saw myself in *A Star is Born* at the same time. I realized it was my own life I was seeing on the screen. A rock 'n' roll star ruining himself drinking. I'll never touch it again, because I saw myself being lowered into my own coffin.

Kris Kristofferson

To each his own. At least I'm not a mainliner, and it's more fun getting high without a needle. At least you can get over booze.

Veronica Lake

I drink only beer and a little wine. Champagne? Oh, no. Champagne I only bathe in.

Hedy Lamarr

Both my children, but particularly my son, became involved with drugs. Malibu, where we lived in the 1960s, was a hotbed of youthful drug abuse —to these kids it was as common as bubble gum ... Everything was telling me to take my family and get away, so I did—to a tiny village in County Cork, Ireland. It was one of the last places on earth that was fairly drug free. We had a wonderful life. Anthony regained his health.

Angela Lansbury

I was spilling more than Dean Martin drinks.

Peter Lawford

Hedy Lamarr
Bathes in bubbly

Angela Lansbury
Fled drug scene

❏

On one occasion when Judy Garland and I embraced each other, I felt that it was such a unification of two great pill repositories it must have been a peak in pharmaceutical history. If Judy and I had married, she would have given birth to a sleeping pill instead of a child—we could have named it Barb-Iturate.

Oscar Levant

❏

Gail Russell died of alcoholism because she was deathly frightened of acting, but she had in her the makings of a great star. I think she had the most beautiful eyes I have ever seen, the most moving eyes. And she was immensely sensitive. Paramount had her under contract—like a horse. On *The Lawless*, I had absolute instructions from them not to let her have a drink. The first time I shot with her I had a long night-tracking shot. She couldn't remember a single line and it was three or four pages of important dialogue. And she grabbed me—her hands were icy cold, she was absolutely rigid—and she said, "Look, I don't want to be an actress. I'm not an actress. I can't act. I never had a director who gave me a scene this long before. I can't do it." And I said, "Oh, yes you can, and you *are* an actress." "No, I'm not, I've never kidded myself. I hate it, I'm frightened of it. Get me a drink and I'll be all right." So I said, "You know, I've been told not to get you a drink." She said, "Get me a drink!" I got her a drink and she did the scene.

Joseph Losey

❏

I used to take five or six needles a day. And when I took the cure they took it all away from me ... It was horrible, just horrible ... The drugs had me on the hook. I mean to dehook myself.

Bela Lugosi

❏

I'm not into drugs. I used to be ... In the old days everybody'd get stoned. People would be watching me perform, and they'd be going (takes a long, simulated drag), "Hey, those guys are pretty good!" It wasn't the drugs that bothered me. It was the way people acted on 'em. They behaved like blithering idiots, acid casualities.

Steve Martin

❏

I've smoked two joints in my life. Someone handed me cocaine at a party in a dish with a gold spoon. I thought it was Sweet 'n Low and put it in my coffee.

Shirley MacLaine

❏

My anger made me drink as an escape from reality, a way of forgetting. But you don't know when the medicinal effect ends and the poisoning begins ... This is my sixth year of sobriety. Overcoming alcoholism has been my greatest challenge and my greatest reward.

Mercedes McCambridge

❏

For my Oscar-winning role in *The Lost Weekend*, I prepared myself by studying drunks and derelicts. Didn't have to go far; half of my friends were boozers.

Ray Milland

❏

I thought I was dying. I thought I had mononucleosis or hypoglycemia. I didn't know what was wrong with me. Valium nearly killed me. I was taking five milligrams a day for 15 years.

Liza Minnelli

❏

I've been smoking shit for 40 years, and it never got to be a habit with me.

Robert Mitchum

❏

Montgomery Clift is the only person I know who's in worse shape than I am.

Marilyn Monroe.

❏

There are a lot of alcoholics like me who never disgraced themselves, never allow alcohol to interfere with their work or their relationships, who are slowly killing themselves.

Mary Tyler Moore

❏

I've tried pot and it doesn't move me, so I guess I tend toward booze. There's no question, though, that marijuana is less harmful than liquor, if it doesn't go beyond that. It doesn't make sense that I can go to a public bar for a couple of martinis and not get arrested, while those who choose to sit around minding their own business and smoking pot are risking a misdemeanor charge.

Paul Newman

❏

Take a moment to think what our children's environment would be like if radio stations decided not to play records with pro-drug messages, if movie studios refused to distribute pictures with gratuitous drug scenes and if television networks declined to air programs with casual and flippant remarks about drugs.

Paul Newman

❏

I still love to get high, I'd say, about four days a week. I think that's about average for an American. Last year on a raft trip I had a little flavor of the season—peach mescaline—but it was not like the hallucinatory state of the '60s. This was just kind of sunny. I don't advocate anything for anybody. But I choose always to be candid because I don't like the closet atmosphere of drugging. In other words, it ain't no big thing. You can wreck yourself with it, but Christ, you can wreck yourself with anything . . . My daughter knows all the drugs I do. She's seen me do 'em. She doesn't do any drugs. She's a vegetarian!

Jack Nicholson

❏

I became an alcoholic, but I think now I was born with the disease. I just lost control over my consumption and it started controlling my life. I made up my own world, lived in a fantasy environment and fell on my ass every time I went out on the stage. Now here's the truth—most people like me. They always have liked me and they don't want to see me destroy myself or make a fool of myself, so even the audiences made excuses. "This is not one of his good nights." "Tomorrow he'll be better." But I didn't get better. By the 1970s I was a zombie, and there were only three alternatives—get help, get sober or die.

Donald O'Connor

❏

I don't know anybody who drinks too much with consistency who's really very pleasant. To put it straightforwardly, I now consider that I was a fool at times when I drank. I took a couple of things from Alcoholic Anonymous. One was never to take a drink anymore, never. Not a sip. That's a rule for anybody who wants to quit drinking. The other thing was to call everybody I ever thought I had wronged and say so. I did that, including a couple of ex-wives who wholeheartedly agreed with me.

George Peppard

❏

I'm *afraid* to drink now. I'm *afraid* to use. Because I know it will kill me . . . The little voice says: "You did it last night, and you were *funny*. You gotta do it tonight!" The drug is subtle, seductive . . . You gotta *want* to quit. There's an old saying: "You can take the bottle away from a man a thousand times, but he only has to put it down once."

Richard Pryor

❏

It's an ongoing fight to stay sober. I thought I was fine and I was watching television one night and they had this big bust. They had all these giant rocks (chunks of cocaine) on the evidence table and I knew if someone had walked in the room that night with a rock, I would have smoked it. I kept thinking, "It's been three years, man. How can it be that close?" But that's the way it is, it's that close all the time.

Richard Pryor

❏

The music world has made it sound as if (drugs are) right there and the thing to do. Musicians that the young people like make no secret of the fact that they are users. And I must say this, that the motion picture industry has started down a road they'd been on before once, with alcohol abuse. I can remember when it was rather commonplace in films to portray drunk scenes and so forth as being humorous. And the motion picture industry decided some time ago that wasn't right for them to do ... and they stopped. And yet, recently, there have been some pictures in which there was a gratuitous scene in there just for a laugh about drug abuse that made it look kind of attractive and funny, not dangerous and sad. At a certain level of society in Hollywood, they have a dinner party and feel they have to put the drug out on the coffee table, as at a cocktail party. That has to be dealt with.

Ronald Reagan

I love MGM. I knew nothing of that assembly-line torture that they put Judy Garland through. No one ever gave me knock-out pills or stuck a needle in my behind, not as long as my mother was around. Judy didn't have a mother that cared, so she put her in the wrong hands.

Debbie Reynolds

Our two sons are at college where old movies are very popular today, particularly, it seems, the films of W.C. Fields. So I am going to please them by pasting a large photographic poster of that wacky gentleman on our playroom wall. Our house here on DeMille Drive was Mr. Fields' home until his death, and since I am sure his ghost prowls around at times I think he, too, will be pleased to see his picture on the wall. We are quite indebted to him, as we still have a nice pile of kindling wood made from endless whiskey crates that all but filled the basement when we bought the house. Every time we light a fire, I say, "Thank you, W.C."

Ann Richards

I was not promiscuous and I wasn't into drugs, real into drugs or alcohol. I mean, I experimented with all that, but I never abused it, I think. The way I rebelled was with my clothing.

Molly Ringwald

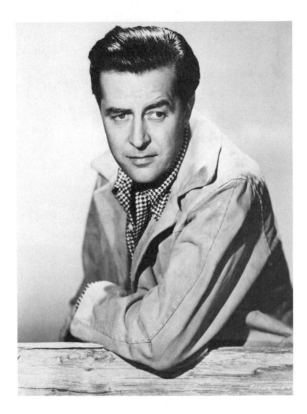

Ray Milland
Closely watched friends

Ann Richards
Grateful to Fields

❏

I'll have to use the word alcoholic because that's what I am. You don't get over alcoholism, you just don't drink. Getting into this business at such an early age contributed to my problems. I was pushed in and was playing opposite Ray Milland for $50 a week. I had been studying to be an artist and wasn't concerned about getting a movie career.

Gail Russell

❏

I realized that the only time in my life when I had screwed things up were those when I was doing a lot of drinking. I could go along for weeks drinking just a little now and then and be fine, but whenever I got drunk it was trouble.

Jane Russell

❏

My drinking got worse. The more successful I got, the worse the drinking became. I'd suffer blackouts and loss of memory. Life became a sort of hazy charade. The symptoms kept intensifying. I'd have these periods of violence, when I was drunk, about once every three months, then every two weeks and finally, a week or less apart. I busted up everything and everyone.

George C. Scott

❏

I think it wise never to drink before sundown. But I am only wise some of the time.

C. Aubrey Smith

❏

By the mid-1970s I was hiding bottles around the house and getting up in the middle of the night to drink and waking up in the morning to have a drink before breakfast. Sometimes I skipped breakfast. And lunch. Vodka has calories, and I was drinking a quart a day and starting to put on weight. I became careful not to drink before a show or an interview. I was sober on stage because I knew I could drink when I got back home. In this way, I thought I was handling it. Alcoholism could happen to other people, but not to me. I looked forward to leaving home and going on the road to do a show because I could drink more freely when I was alone in my room, without the family around.

Gale Storm

❏

I had my first whiskey sour at 14 and thought, "God, I've found a friend." Three years ago I thought our friendship was getting too steady, so I gave up.

Elaine Stritch

❏

For 35 years I couldn't go to sleep without at least two sleeping pills. And I'd always taken a lot of medication for pain. I'd had 19 major operations, and drugs had become a crutch. I wouldn't take them only when I was in pain. I was taking a lot of Percodan. I'd take Percodan and a couple of drinks before I went out. I just felt I had to get stoned to get over my shyness. Not being a drunk is the only way I'm going to stay alive. *Drunk* is a hard word, but I've had to face it. Somebody who drinks too much is a drunk. Somebody who takes too many pills is a junkie. There's no polite way to say it.

Elizabeth Taylor

❏

How can I tell my sons not to smoke pot when we go out and drink martinis and wreck our liver . . . when we smoke cigarettes and risk cancer. I'm more scared about LSD and the hard drugs. There are children of friends of mine who have blown their minds.

Elizabeth Taylor

❏

Doris Day is a great gal, the best pro I ever worked with. After two films, I had her drinking, smoking and saying naughty words.

Rod Taylor

❏

Anyone who stayed drunk for 25 years as I did would have to be in trouble. Hell, I used to take two-week lunch hours!

Spencer Tracy

❑

Cocaine, what a wonderful drug! Anything that makes you paranoid and impotent—mmm, give me some of *that!*

Robin Williams

❑

I've been sick all my life with fear. Of some imagined disaster that never did eventuate. When I was a child, I used to hide in the crooks of trees, just to be alone. When I became an actor I constantly felt I wasn't worthy, that I had no right to be a star. Naturally, I tried to find a way out. Alcoholism was the inevitable result. It took me more than 30 years to realize I was poisoning myself.

Robert Young

Age

My kids make fun of me. They say I started out as the girl next door, and now I'm the grandmother next door. And pretty soon I'll be the little old lady next door.

June Allyson

❑

Eighty is just a figure to me. Of course, each time I've renewed my driver's license, they've given me a five-year extension. Now I've gotten to the point where they give me three.

Fred Astaire

❑

I don't miss dancing a bit and don't work at it at all. I see no reason to try to be the oldest dancer in captivity. I don't want to break the record—and my neck along with it.

Fred Astaire

❑

The only thing that bothers me about growing older is that when I see a pretty girl now it arouses my memory instead of my hopes.

Milton Berle

❏

If a man, upon arising, fails to have a formidable challenge to overcome, he damn well better invent one, or suffer the consequences of getting old in a hurry.

Budd Boetticher

❏

I feel fortunate that at 90 I can do anything I could do when I was 89.

George Burns

❏

In Hollywood you are absolutely reproached for every wrinkle, for every year that passes. Look what they do to their older actresses. Look at Joan Crawford and that marvelous actress Bette Davis. They put axes or guns or butcher knives in their hands. It's monstrous.

Leslie Caron

❏

I'm not like Jane Fonda or any of these other women who say how fabulous they think it is to turn 40. I think it's a crock of shit. I'm not thrilled with it.

Cher

❏

One of my idols was always Ina Claire. When I was doing *Aren't We All?* in London I heard she was there and not well. So I went around to see her. It was shortly before she died, but there she was sitting up in bed looking blonde and beautiful in pink ruffles—and she was 91 or or 92! I said, "Ina, I just had my 81st birthday." "Oh," said Ina, "really? You beat me."

Claudette Colbert

❏

Quite old women hobble up to me nowadays on crutches and tell me they remember me from their childhood. One night a woman just stood there, her eyes full of tears, saying, "Oh, Miss Cooper," over and over again. I suppose I reminded her of something, though God knows what.

Gladys Cooper

They say you're lucky if you made it before 50, because after that roles register down. Women are there, like the chairs and tables, but there's no life force. They do not determine what occurs. They are only reactors. There is no power within them, no desire left, no needs that are beyond reach. They are passive. I'm not interested in such roles.

Colleen Dewhurst

I'm 53 years old and I am not in my prime. Actresses who say being over 50 is great are lying. I may look good, but I looked better at 32. No, it's not great being over 50. It's like going to the guillotine.

Angie Dickinson

Middle age is that time in a man's life when his daydreams center around a banker saying yes instead of a girl.

Jane Fonda

I believe in loyalty. I think when a woman reaches an age she likes, she should stick with it.

Eva Gabor

Remember, age is not important unless you are a cheese.

Helen Hayes

Jewelry takes people's minds off your wrinkles.

Sonja Henie

☐

Being 82 is getting up in the middle of the night as often as Burt Reynolds, but not for the same reason.

Bob Hope

☐

I know some good old gals in their 50s and 60s. All these women tell me, "Forty to 50. Those are the hot times." So far, you couldn't prove it by me. But hell, I'm only two years in.

Lauren Hutton

☐

To insist on staying young is to grow old with pessimism, like a wine which little by little turns to vinegar.

Grace Kelly

☐

When a man of 60 runs off with a young woman, I'm never surprised. I have a sneaking admiration for him. I wish him luck. After all, he's going to need it.

Deborah Kerr

☐

As long as you are curious, you defeat age.

Burt Lancaster

☐

I don't know how I got old. I was 35 years old yesterday. Here I am with five heart bypasses. I can't walk up a flight of stairs without panting for breath. Oh, the aches. My feet. My back. I won't get into it. But I'm 72 now, I'm not going to live much longer. I'd like to believe I'm choosy about what films I do, but I want to live well. Everything first class.

Burt Lancaster

❏

Zsa Zsa Gabor has discovered the secret of perpetual middle age.

Oscar Levant

❏

When my husband left, I was wild. It flabbergasted me. I realized I'm not so sophisticated after all. My husband had said an incredible thing to me: "I don't mind being a grandfather, but I don't want to be married to a grand-mother."

Viveca Lindfors

❏

I am never quite sure whether I am one of the cinema's elder statesmen, or just the oldest whore on the beat.

Joseph L. Mankiewicz

❏

One of the good things about getting older is that you find you're more interesting than most of the people you meet.

Lee Marvin

❏

People make me feel as though I am 100 years old because they are talking and writing about my age all the time. I think it could be aging to think about age. I never do on my own. In fact, one man sitting at a dinner party with me in Los Angeles said, "In New York they are always talking about how many times you have had your face lifted."

Merle Oberon

❏

I couldn't care less about the passage of time. If you're just a glamour girl it could be very hard on you. But I'm an actress who enjoys her work, so there's no problem. I can't wait to grow old. I'm going to be the nastiest old lady you ever saw!

Maureen O'Hara

Sonja Henie
A new wrinkle

Maureen O'Hara
Actress not glamour girl

42

❏

It isn't true that I don't trust anyone under 70.

Ronald Reagan

❏

I get a kick out of some of the stars out here in Hollywood. They're so afraid of growing old. There are two I'm thinking of who were five years older than I when we played on Broadway together. Now they say they're five years younger! How silly. Everybody has to grow old. So long as you do, you might as well try to grow old gracefully.

Barbara Stanwyck

❏

I'm 65 years old and I feel every goddamn day of it. I hate it when people say, "You're just beginning to live."

James Stewart

❏

Age in a woman means nothing. When I was 20 I had a sweetheart 70. She was superb.

Erich von Stroheim

❏

I hate to tell you how old I am, but I reached the age of consent 75,000 consents ago.

Shelley Winters

❏

Upon winning a Golden Globe award:
    I'm a little too old to be happy—but just old enough to be grateful!

Jane Wyman

Ambition

The first people who really intrigued me in my life were the killers. I got terribly involved with the adventures of Murder, Inc., as a boy in Brooklyn. And for a long time, I definitely wanted to be a mobster. Not a killer but a big-time hustler, con man or bank robber.

Woody Allen

I could have been a bigger actress if I'd had more ambition. But whenever I think back about it all I end up believing that perhaps the fact that I wasn't too ambitious is the secret of my career longevity. I never burned myself out and never worked so much the public got tired of me. Instead they just got used to me.

Mary Astor

I'm only interested in two kinds of people, those who can entertain me and those who can advance my career.

Ingrid Bergman

When I go to a movie, I am entertained best if it is unabashedly a movie, and not a piece of dull hoke posing as something else. I fell for *Below the Sea*, rubber octopus and all, but I detested *Cavalcade*. I liked *The Champ* but *Cynara* gave me a pain in the neck. I think that is the way most of the customers feel, and I think it shows the way to a proper sphere for moving pictures. In other words, it is better to shoot at a balloon and hit a balloon than to shoot at a star and hit a cornfield.

James M. Cain

My career was not the longest, but I had a high batting average. Now Claudette Colbert lived next door and she'd finish a movie on Saturday—we worked Saturdays in those days—and begin wondering what she was doing Monday. I lacked that terrifying ambition. I drifted into acting and drifted out. Acting is not everything. Living is.

Irene Dunne

❏

What I'd really like to do—and this is my great fantasy—is to remake every movie Irene Dunne ever made.

Joan Hackett

❏

The only thing that would take me to Hollywood would be a chance to play Scarlett O'Hara in *Gone with the Wind*. It's the most dramatic part I've ever read. I'd love to get my teeth into it. It's got everything, lightness and gaiety and great emotional depths. What a woman that Scarlett is! But there isn't any use even thinking about it. They'll give the role to a Hollywood star with an established reputation in American films.

Vivien Leigh

Androgyne

Ty Power was the handsomest man I ever saw! He was very popular. How shall I put it—he appreciated the human foible. I recall an evening in the '50s at the Pump Room in Chicago. It was during my first stage tour, a five-month engagement in *John Brown's Body* with Ty and Raymond Massey, who was also present this evening with his wife. Suddenly Ty said, "I've done everything. I could die tomorrow." I got angry and said, "How *dare* you say that? You've only *begun* to live!" He was still a very young man. Then he got angry with me and snapped, "You don't know anything." Tragically, he died a short time afterward—in his 40s. Beauty is a great curse. It distorts lives, making the wrong things important. Do you *know* what it means to be that adored? These beautiful people may have luxurious lives, but somewhere along the line it becomes very difficult to live with. It was that way with Ty.

Anne Baxter

❏

That is not fair, to think I dress in trousers to get publicity. I have never done anything to start publicity about myself. I would be afraid to do so because who can control publicity once it is started? I wore trousers long before I came to America. In fact, I used to dress up in boy's clothes when I was a little girl. I have always liked the freedom of men's garments.

Marlene Dietrich

Irene Dunne
"Drifted" to the top

Marlene Dietrich
She wore the pants

46

❑

I have a great interest in sexuality, and I don't mean just man-woman sexuality. My interest extends to the behavior of two people of the same sex who are just friends. Fortunately, as an actress there are many ways open for me to explore this in my work.

Faye Dunaway

❑

I have not lived my life as a woman. I have lived it as a man. I've done what I damn well wanted and I've made enough money to support myself.

Katharine Hepburn

❑

You know, I don't differentiate between any of it—it's all love to me. I feel that you can get just as real a love from a guy as you can from a chick. Well, maybe not just 100 per cent. There's something you get from a chick that you can't have with any other being on the planet and that is something super special. I mean, if there were nothing but old whores and nasty old hard women around, I'd be out looking for some young, sweet little 15-year-old boy. But instead, I've got a young, sweet little girl, and that's enough for me right now.

Don Johnson

❑

I once said to Ernst Lubitsch, "Why is it that every time I see Gary Cooper on the screen, he reminds me of Garbo; and every time I see Garbo, she puts me in mind of Cooper?" "Naturally," said Ernst. "They are the same person. Have you ever noticed how you've never seen them in the same picture?"

Garson Kanin

❑

Aldous Huxley's conference with Garbo took place in her dressing room, from which he came straight to me to report, "The Divine One wants me to write her a film on Saint Francis of Assisi," he announced. "What a great idea, Aldous! She'd be heartbreaking as Clare!" "So I told her," Aldous chuckled.

Don Johnson
If young girls vanished

Robert Mitchum
Pretty in pink

"But Greta wants to play Saint Francis! I tried to talk her out of the idea; told her the role posed an insurmountable problem because it is universally known that the Saint wore a beard." "Oh, yes," Greta had agreed, "but the make-up department can easily make me one"!

Anita Loos

❑

I got into an elevator at MGM once and there in one of her famous men's hats was Garbo. I said hello, and when there was no reply, I said, "Oh, sorry, I thought you were a fellow I knew."

Groucho Marx

❑

I was a guest once at Eleanor Roosevelt's place. I saw this pink nightgown, and just for a gag put it on over my clothes. Noel Coward walks in and says, "My dear, you look simply di-vine!" and kisses my hand. Next time I see Eleanor at a party she says loudly, "Why Bob, last time we met you were in a pink nightgown being kissed by Noel Coward!" What could I do but admit it?

Robert Mitchum

❑

I'm mad about Westerns, and no matter what anyone else tells you, this is all I want to do ... I want to play a real frontier woman, not one of those crinolined-covered things you see in most Westerns. I'm with the boys—I want to go where the boys go.

Barbara Stanwyck

Art

You can't do just the things you know will be accepted. When you stop trying to hang yourself in an art form, you're dead.

Charles Laughton

❑

The cinema has given precisely one great artist to the world: Greta Garbo—
unless you also count that damn mouse.

Louis B. Mayer

❏

Modern paintings are like women. You'll never enjoy them if you try to
understand them.

Vincent Price

❏

Modern art? When I look at one of those smeary paints, the Jackson Pollack
kind of thing, my only thought is: "Thank God I didn't step in it!"

Arthur Treacher

❏

Isn't it pieces of yourself, of your life, that you inevitably use making movies?
You suck art out of your finger in a way.

Billy Wilder

Awards

I won the Oscar, but Rhoda, my wife then, started wearing the dark glasses.

Ernest Borgnine

❏

Awards are nice, but I'd much rather have a job.

Jane Darwell

❏

I do feel like the Academy is slacking off in the class quotient—after all, *I* won.

Sally Field

❏

I been an actress, see, since 1915, and damn it, I never got a Tony. What does it mean, I say—but the fact remains I guess I'd like to *have* one. I remember once Armina Marshall called me and asked me to give a Tony to Tyrone Guthrie for directing me in *The Matchmaker* and I said, "*Liss*-en, go screw yourself!" I did that play for 68 weeks and if those damn Tonys are any good at all, *I* shoulda had one!

Ruth Gordon

The reports were true about what (producer) Walter Wanger said when I won the Academy Award. He said, "Thank God, now we can all relax. Susie finally got what she's been chasing for 20 years." I was glad I got the award for *I Want to Live!* because it was Walter's picture. I was devoted to that man.

Susan Hayward

Hollywood—that's where they give Academy Awards to Charlton Heston for acting.

Shirley Knight

I'm not knocking the Academy Awards, I'm just saying that there's no actual cultural value to them—they're no judge of quality. I'm against people like Brando and George C. Scott turning rather loudly against the Oscars and going in for these prima donna scenes. They render themselves ridiculous, in my opinion. It's really absurd. It's like using a mallet to squash a fly!

James Mason

For my second and third pictures I won Academy Awards. Nothing worse could have happened to me.

Luise Rainer

I love actors. That's how my turning down the Oscar for *Patton* came about, you know. I just can't stand our people—I mean actors—being put in a position of sweating in front of those television cameras and hoping and

Barbara Stanwyck
One of the boys

Shelley Winters
Won one, lost one

hoping, with all that contrived suspense focused on them, and the envelope-opening and all of that. It's offensive, it's barbarous and it's innately corrupt. It simply shouldn't be done. Actors are delicate people, and they're ensemble people. We all have such good feelings about each other. There's a wonderful team feeling about any production. It's awful to put all those opposite feelings in for technology and ratings for some damned television show.

George C. Scott

❏

I think I'll play *The Nun's Story* next, one who's a lesbian and who's deaf and gets raped. Then I'll get an Academy Award to go with the Tony.

Alexis Smith

❏

When I got the Academy Award, my father called me up and said, "What'd they give yuh? They give yuh a plaque, or what was it?" "Nooo," I said, "it's sort of a statue." And he said: "Well, you better send it home, and I'll put it in the (hardware) store window." Which I did, and it was there for 20 years.

James Stewart

❏

I'll never forget the night I brought my Oscar home and Tony (Franciosa) took one look at it and I knew my marriage was over.

Shelley Winters

❏

Upon winning the Academy Award for *Johnny Belinda*, in which she portrayed a deaf-mute:

I accept this award gratefully for keeping my mouth shut for once. I think I'll do it again.

Jane Wyman

Billing

I once asked, "Has it ever occurred to you to switch billing once in a while?" He replied, "No." So it was with the team of Tracy and Hepburn. The gentleman came first. Spence's position as a Metro superstar meant that there was nothing to discuss, and, in those days, Kate did not particularly care about billing. It was always Tracy and Hepburn. I chided him once about his insistence on first billing. "Why not?" he asked. "Well, after all," I argued, "she's the lady. You're the man. Ladies first?" He said, "This is a movie, chowderhead, not a lifeboat."

Garson Kanin

❏

Murder in the Music Hall in 1946 was the last time I let the studio bill me as "Vera Hruba Ralston." Americans called it everything from Rhubarb to Rhumba, and when someone actually called it Rumbum, I knew it had to go.

Vera Ralston

Books

Nobody's done anything to my book (*The Postman Always Rings Twice*). It's right up there on the shelf. Hollywood mangles *movies*, not books.

James M. Cain

❏

If my books had been any worse, I should not have been invited to Hollywood, and if they had been any better, I should not have come.

Raymond Chandler

❏

Why am I alone? Why aren't my children flocking around me now? "How are you, Dad?" "What's going on, Dad?" Everybody's writing *Mommie Dearest*. I'm going to write *Son and Daughter Dearest*.

Tony Curtis

Spencer Tracy
Demanded top billing

❏

At one time I thought I might write a book; Harcourt Brace had approached me. I had even begun it. Until one day my husband said to me, "Do you think people really care about your grandmother?" That ended it.

Irene Dunne

❏

I'm never going to write my autobiography as long as I live.

Samuel Goldwyn

❏

Bing Crosby's son Gary wrote a book about his father. Joan Crawford's daughter wrote one about her mother. So did Bette Davis' daughter. It explains to me why certain species eat their young.

Bob Hope

❏

I've given up reading books. I find it takes my mind off myself.

Oscar Levant

❏

When Judy (Garland) died, I was asked—they *begged* me—to write a book about her. Five or six jerks jumped on it right away. I wouldn't do it because the memories are too dear, too personal.

Mickey Rooney

❏

I wouldn't have filmed *The Color Purple* if the Alice Walker book had been a big, fat novel. I know this must sound terrible, but the reason I read it is because it's thin. I hardly read anything at all. It was unusual for me to find the time to read this.

Steven Spielberg

❏

My God, I think there have been more books on Marilyn Monroe than on World War II, and there's a great similarity.

Billy Wilder

Business

Moviemaking today doesn't deal with people, but with enormous structure. Every star, whether it be an actor, a writer or a director, is now his own corporation. Every corporation is like a ship. It has barnacles hanging on it: lawyers, agents, financial advisers, accountants.

Samuel Z. Arkoff

❏

It was George Hamilton who said the immortal line: "Joan, better to be a shrewd businesswoman than a screwed actress."

Joan Collins

❏

A verbal contract isn't worth the paper it's written on.

Samuel Goldwyn

❏

The highest creativity in Hollywood in 1986 is calling off a picture.

Michael Kanin

❏

Hollywood is full of rather sleazy, unscrupulous people. Los Angeles is where they make deals and do business in the classic corporate American way— which is screw everybody and do whatever you can to make the biggest profit.

George Lucas

❏

The businessmen don't care if you mess your life up, as long as you don't die during the film.

Richard Pryor

❏

The town I was born in (in Ontario) is proudest of having the deepest shaft in North America. Whoever believes that has never done business in Hollywood.

Alan Thicke

Candor

I was young and only starting in *To Have and Have Not* when Bogie and I met. Howard Hawks (the producer-director) said he would like to put me in a picture with Cary Grant or Humphrey Bogart. I thought, Cary Grant— terrific. Humphrey Bogart—yuck.

Lauren Bacall

My theory is never to stand when you can sit and never sit when you can lie down.

Joan Collins

I believe in supporting people who may not have as much as you have. I believe in love and peace and rock and roll. I believe it's possible that war is wrong. I believe you have to speak out when you think stuff is not right, and sometimes it's hard, because it's like pissin' in the wind.

Whoopi Goldberg

Movies are one of the bad habits that have corrupted our century. They have slipped into the American mind more misinformation in one evening than the Dark Ages could muster in a decade.

Ben Hecht

Darryl Zanuck kept trying to foist me off onto his producers. They just didn't want me. All the producers said, "Why did they bring this dog out here? Can't even photograph her!" I was never pretty. I used to go to the Powers and Conover model agencies and they thought I looked like an old poached egg on a radiator. When I dressed up I looked *great* for five minutes, then I started to look drunk. Finally, somebody slipped up and gave me a bit in *Winged Victory*.

Judy Holliday

The only film that I ever made that I'm truly ashamed of was a Western called *Sea of Grass*. I was completely intimidated by Spencer Tracy and Katharine Hepburn, and it showed. Every time she went to the toilet she came back in a new gown and he was supposed to be a cowboy born to the saddle, but he took one look at the horse and he hated the horse and the horse hated him, and the whole thing was a disaster.

Elia Kazan

Vivian Leigh
Not like Scarlett

❏

People have addressed me as Scarlett and I think, good heavens, I'm not Scarlett; I'm not as brassy or bright as Scarlett. Actually, Scarlett is not one of my favorite people.

Vivien Leigh

❏

I have directed 50 pictures, and I'm still crapping in my pants on the first day.

Ernst Lubitsch

❏

I was invited to a screening at Paramount of the new epic *Samson and Delilah*, starring Victor Mature and Hedy Lamarr. Afterward, one of the studio brass asked me how I liked it. I replied, "I never like a movie where the hero's tits are bigger than the heroine's."

Groucho Marx

❏

Most of the motion pictures in Hollywood are made for half-wits and certainly not for intelligent people.

James Mason

❏

The big films of the '80s are like cartoon strips, and the dialogue is the kind that you read in their balloons.

Joseph L. Mankiewicz

❏

I remember Tallulah Bankhead telling of going into a public ladies' room and discovering there was no toilet tissue. She looked underneath the booth and said to the lady in the next stall, "I beg your pardon, do you happen to have any toilet tissue in there?" The lady said no. So Tallulah said, "Well, then, dahling, do you have two fives for a ten?"

Ethel Merman

❏

To the unwashed public, that woman (Joan Collins, his ex-wife) is a star. But to those who know her, she's a commodity who would sell her own bowel movement.

Anthony Newley

❏

Kim Novak was so darned serious on *Vertigo*. Early in the shooting, Kim came up to Alfred Hitchcock and said, "Mr. Hitchcock, about the next scene. It's just not clear to me. I'd like to go over it with you because I'm not sure of the reason for the motivation that I have in dealing with the problem that I have with Mr. Stewart." And Hitchcock just looked at her and said, "Kim, it's only a *movie!*"

James Stewart

❏

They say I'm outspoken, but not by many.

Shelley Winters

Censorship

I had a scene in *Invisible Agent* which was a wonder. The invisible man went to his bath, turned on the water and got under the shower. The drops of water sticking to his skin were visible, but the skin wasn't. The censors said the bathroom door was open and there was a woman in the other room. They said you can't have naked men, even invisible naked men, in the same room with females. My scene went out. If we'd only had the door closed, we'd have been all right.

Jon Hall

❏

The trouble with censors is they worry if a girl has cleavage. They ought to worry if she hasn't any.

Marilyn Monroe

❏

The script of *The Moon is Blue* was rejected. Unless I changed six lines the Hays Office would withhold its seal of approval. "I have the right of free expression," I told them. "I will not accept any censorship." The Catholic Legion of Decency added its disapproval. Looking back, it is laughable what all those people found objectionable: the words "virgin," "seduce" and "pregnant." When the film was released it was denounced from pulpits of Catholic churches as evil. In small towns priests stood outside the theaters taking down the names of parishioners who went in. As a result the box office suffered somewhat in small communities, but in cities *The Moon is Blue* was a huge success.

Otto Preminger

❏

We had rules about how far we could go in pictures. Everybody makes a joke of it now, but in those days, when you were in bed—it didn't matter whether you were in bed with your mother or your wife or your sister or a prostitute—you had to keep one foot on the floor. With those restrictions, we left a lot to the imagination of the audience. And I think that was the right thing to do.

James Stewart

Childhood

A couple who owned a mortuary offered us free room and board if Mother would be their receptionist. I was 10 years old. We lived there for three years. We had a living room, dining room and kitchen. I slept on a sofa bed in the living room. That's where the mourners assembled. There were about three funerals a week, and I'd have to wait in the dining room until they left before I could go to sleep. There were doors from ceiling to floor with curtains and right next to that would be the coffin. That's where I would practice my piano.

Ann-Margret

I wasn't a child star. I was a child laborer. In the morning my mother would deliver me (to the MGM studios) like a dog on a leash. I had four rummies to support. I mean my family, you understand. My father jumped off the boat and he just hung around the house singing to Caruso records and wearing a cape. I think he wanted to be Valentino or something. And my mother's sitting in the dressing room out to lunch with the sewing needles, right? She gave her life to Jesus. And so anyway they all had to eat. I was like most child performers. I acted only because I was told to, and you can hardly consider what I did acting. I didn't like it. It was no kind of life. Forcing a kid to become a performer is one of the worst things that can happen to a child. It's turning them into adults when they're still youngsters.

Robert Blake

I wasn't born with a spoon in my mouth. More like a shovel. A number two shovel they use in the mines. There was no love in my home. I was one of

15 children, and the only contact I had with my mother was when she took me between her knees to pull lice out of my head.

Charles Bronson

I was a shy, ugly kid who led a big fantasy life. I thought I was an angel from Heaven, sent to cure polio. When Dr. Salk did it, I was really pissed off.

Cher

Look, if I hadn't had a shitty childhood, I wouldn't have worked my tail off to get where I am. And who I am, Baby, is the only thing that counts.

Joan Crawford

I knew I had dyslexia when I was a kid, eight years old. My mother's dyslexic, all my sisters, too. I had to have special reading courses. But it was something I'd never tell anyone. I didn't want to be held back. But when you don't admit to something, it becomes a lot bigger than it is . . . When I speak with someone, I have a very good memory, but reading something, just getting over the words, became a big deal. My z's were backward, b's are backward, b and d, and you drop letters in writing. But it's less and less.

Tom Cruise

There's no such thing as a tough child—if you parboil them first for seven hours, they always come out tender.

W.C. Fields

During the war years, my mother was very big with the Army, Navy and Marines. I never knew which branch she was going to bring home. If there were 10 men at a table, my mother would pick up the check. She spent all my money.

Peggy Ann Garner

Tom Cruise
Disability no handicap

❏

I started in the business when I was three-and-a-half. There was this training school in Hollywood called Meglin Kiddies. Shirley Temple and a lot of others went there. My father, who was an insurance salesman, dropped by the school one day to try and sell Mrs. Meglin a policy. She said she'd buy one if my father enrolled one of his children. So my father signed me up for 10 lessons. That's how it happened.

Darryl Hickman

❏

When I was a youngster in Cleveland, I sold newspapers on the corner of 105th and Euclid Ave. One of my regular customers was an elderly man who had his limousine halt every night at my corner before he drove to his home in the suburbs. One evening, I didn't have change for the dime he gave me, so I told him he could pay me the next night. To my surprise, the man reproved me, saying, "Never give credit when you can get cash. Now go and get my change." When my customer had driven away, the streetcar checker on the corner asked, "Do you know who that man is? He's John D. Rockefeller, the richest man in the world."

Bob Hope

❏

I was the homeliest kid you ever saw. I was covered with huge freckles, and my hair was straw white and stuck out straight like a scarecrow's thatch. One cheek was raked with a big scar where a boy had pushed me off the dock and my face got torn on a nail, and I had another scar over one eye where I got bopped a few days later with a golf club. I was a mess, and a double-mess compared to my older sister, Marion, who was beautiful and sweet and always behaved like a lady. Looking the way I did, the boys naturally had no interest in romancing me. I was okay for tin-can hockey, or even halfback on the sandlot football team, but when it came to post office they passed by me in a beautiful rush to collect letters from Marion and other pretty girls. I soon discovered the only way to get any attention at all was to be the life of the party. I didn't sing good, but I sure sang loud.

Betty Hutton

❏

When I was young, it was considered bad manners for a child to address an adult stranger in the street, let alone bum sixpence or a dime off him (unless, of course, the child happened to be starving). Bumming an autograph strikes me as being precisely the same thing.

James Mason

❏

Soon after *Champion* was released, I visited a Santa Monica grade school to see a teacher friend. You may recall that the gal I played in *Champion* had champagne tastes, and when she tried to seduce Kirk Douglas she told him something like "I just didn't want you to think you'd get off cheap. I'm expensive, honey—*awful* expensive." It was recess when I left the school and headed toward my car. Some of the kids recognized me so I stopped to visit. But I sure left in a hurry after one of those little twerps called out, "Hey, Marilyn—are you *really* expensive?" Can you imagine any of those little kids remembering something like *that*?!

Marilyn Maxwell

❏

I've been acting since I was three. Because my voice was low and I was taller than the other girls, I always did character parts. I've played men, I've played witches. Even in *The Three Bears*, when I was five, I was the mother bear, not Goldilocks. In *Pinocchio* I was the scrubwoman. I was never the heroine until I hit Hollywood.

Eleanor Parker

❑

I was considered different by the neighbors who saw me making movies on the weekends with 12- and 13-year-old kids dressed up as adults with fake mustaches and beards, Army uniforms and sometimes monster suits. And I think that probably several of my friends were warned about playing with me—that nothing good could come of knowing someone who makes movies in eight millimeters at 12 years old. I had a good time growing up.

Steven Spielberg

❑

I was born in Brooklyn. I was legitimate, I think. At four I was put in a foster home. Foster homes were nothing much in those days. It wasn't cruel and it wasn't even mean. It was just impersonal. An older sister—she was a show girl—paid them for keeping me.

Barbara Stanwyck

❑

I didn't have what you'd call a happy childhood. For one thing, I thought no one liked me. Actually, I'd say I had pretty good evidence. The kids would chase me up into a tree and hit my legs with sticks until they bled. Besides that, I was ugly. With my glasses and permanented hair, I looked like a mini-adult. I had the same face I have today, and let me tell you the effect wasn't cute or endearing.

Meryl Streep

❑

I had a dog named Duke. Every fireman in town knew that hound, because he chased all the firewagons. They knew the dog's name, but not mine, so next thing I was Duke, too. I was named for a damn dog!

John Wayne

❑

Don't go hinting that I had an unhappy childhood. Oh, sure, there were certain things that I missed as a child because of my acting, but don't ever knock private tutors—I was far advanced because of them. Also, I got to travel and saw a lot of things that most kids that age don't see. I don't agree with that sob stuff about child actors. I think it's wonderful for children to work in pictures. They're always play-acting anyway, and what a great release it is for them to do it professionally, in front of a camera! At least it was for me. I lived it, and I loved it, and I don't regret a moment of it.

Natalie Wood

Colleagues

Because of the difficulties with the *Casablanca* script we'd all been a bit on edge and I'd hardly got to know Humphrey Bogart at all. Oh, I'd kissed him, but I didn't know him. He was polite, naturally, but I always felt there was a distance; he was behind a wall. I was intimidated by him. *The Maltese Falcon* was playing in Hollywood at the time and I used to go there and see it quite often during the shooting of *Casablanca*, because I felt I got to know him a little better through that picture.

Ingrid Bergman

❏

Kate Hepburn talks a blue streak. We listened for the first couple of days when she hit Africa (to film *The African Queen*), and then began asking ourselves, "How affected can you be in the middle of Africa?" She used to say that everything was "divine." The goddamn stinking natives were "divine." "Oh, what a *divine* native!" she'd say. "Oh, what a *divine* pile of manure!" You had to ask yourself, "Is this really the dame, or is this something left over from *Woman of the Year?*"

Humphrey Bogart

❏

Judy Garland was, without a doubt, the finest actress I ever worked with. I was her favorite comedian. She could never sing when I was around. She would always laugh uncontrollably. One day when we were making *Summer Stock* she laughed so much she developed pleurisy. And she was out for three weeks. Judy was an absolute joy. When she returned to the studio, I

Ingrid Bergman
Bogie—hardly knew him

wasn't allowed to be around so that she could work. Even if she heard my voice in the next room, she would crack up.

Eddie Bracken

❑

Bob Hope will go to the opening of a phone booth in a gas station in Anaheim, provided they have a camera and three people there. He'll go to the opening of a market and receive an award. Get an award from Thom McAn for wearing their shoes. It's pathetic. It's a bottomless pit. A barrel that has no floor. He must be a man who has an ever-crumbling estimation of himself. He's constantly filling himself up. He's like a junkie—an applause junkie. Christ, instead of growing old gracefully or doing something with his money, be helpful, all he does is have an anniversary with the President looking on. It's sad. He gets on an airplane every two minutes, always going someplace. It didn't bother him at all to work the Vietnam war. Oh, he took that in his stride. He did his World War II and Korean war act. "Our boys" and all that. He's a pathetic guy.

Marlon Brando

❏

Jean Arthur was an enigmatic figure because she doesn't do very well in crowds, and she doesn't do very well with people, and she doesn't do very well with life, but she does very well as an actress. She's afraid. She'd stand in her dressing room and practically vomit every time she had to do a scene. And she'd drum up all kinds of excuses for not being ready. Well, I finally got to know her. All I had to do was push her out in the lights, turn the camera on and she'd blossom out into something wonderful. And when the scene was over, she'd go back into that dressing room and cry. She's quite a study.

Frank Capra

❏

Alfred Lunt is an actor who has his head in the clouds and his feet in the box office.

Noel Coward

❏

Susan Hayward, my co-star in *The Lost Moment*, was an ice queen—very like Grace Kelly that way. Oh, Susan wasn't mean or anything, but when we'd be standing ready to shoot our scenes she was so silent and remote. It was so different from working with an actress like Barbara Stanwyck who, when we were waiting to go into our scenes for *The Bride Wore Boots*, would whisper, "Come on, Bob. You know you'd like to fuck me. Admit it. You'd like to fuck me."

Robert Cummings

❏

Betty Grable? She'd murder you. I remember once I got her angry on the set. She stormed over and said, "You know why I'm doing this picture? I thought they said Dan Duryea!"

Dan Dailey

❏

Paul Muni was a fascinating, exciting, attractive man—Jesus, was he attractive!—and it was sad to see him slowly disappear behind his elaborate make-up, his putty noses, his false lips, his beards. One of the few funny things Jack Warner ever said was, "Why are we paying him so much money when we can't find him?"

Bette Davis

There was a marvelous testimonial for Jack Warner on one of those big, big sound stages. It was a most emotional and fantastic evening marking the end of an era. And all of the Warner stock players were there, *everybody* was there. And naturally the governor was invited. And instead of very simply taking his place, just sitting down like one of the actors that he once was— we all had to *stand up* for little Ronnie Reagan when he walked into the room. Oh! It was agony.

Bette Davis

When I made *The Scapegoat* with Alec Guinness, he cut my part into such shreds that my appearance in the final product made no sense at all. This is an actor who plays by himself, unto himself. In this particular picture he plays a dual role, so at least he was able to play with himself.

Bette Davis

Of all the people I performed with, I got to know Cary Grant least of all. He is a completely private person, totally reserved, and there is no way into him. Our relationship on *A Touch of Mink* was amiable but devoid of give-and-take. For somebody who is as open and right out there as I am, it was hard at first to adjust to Cary's inwardness. Not that he wasn't friendly and polite —he certainly was. But distant. Very distant.

Doris Day

Clark Gable was highly professional. He was a bigger star than we could create today. I was just a mini-star when we did *Gone with the Wind*. I was afraid to talk to him. People can't understand it now, but we were in awe. Clark Gable didn't open supermarkets.

Olivia de Havilland

❏

A day away from Tallulah (Bankhead) is like a month in the country.

Howard Dietz

❏

Six pictures I did with Don Ameche—and not once did he breakdance. Actually, we made the *same* picture six times. All they did was change Don over here and Ty Power over there. My voice was always deeper than the plot.

Alice Faye

❏

When I went to Hollywood to appear with Bette Davis in *Dark Victory*, I was warned about her—she'll upstage you, etc. She couldn't have been more helpful. They also said that she needed composer Max Steiner's music on the soundtrack to embellish her acting. When she was ready to begin climbing the stairs to her death scene, she went to the director and asked him if there would be any background music in the scene. He said he didn't think so, and Bette replied, "Well, you'd better make up your mind. Either Max Steiner is going up those stairs or I am, but we're damn well not going up the stairs together!" Later, the producers betrayed her. Max Steiner and everybody but the Vienna Boys Choir was there helping her to die.

Geraldine Fitzgerald

❏

Welles' influence on *Jane Eyre*? You cannot battle an elephant. Orson was such a *big* man in every way that no one could stand up to him. On the first day, we were all called on the set at one o'clock—no Welles. At four o'clock, he strode in followed by his agent, a dwarf, his valet and a whole entourage. Approaching us, he proclaimed, "All right, everybody turn to page eight." And we did it (though he was not the director). I knew if I underplayed—in front of the camera and off—I wouldn't get hurt.

Joan Fontaine

❏

Clark Gable was the only real he-man I've ever known, of all the actors I've met.

John Huston

❏

Judy Garland: a vibrato in search of a voice.

Oscar Levant

❏

Judy Garland, already a star at 12, was a compulsive weeper. There are some characters who simply cannot endure success. Judy was one of them. She loved to pace the lot, stopping all and sundry to whimper over some imagined affront. "Nobody loves me!" Judy would lament. She was "persecuted" by L.B. Mayer; her family "neglected" her; even the servants overlooked Judy. "When I come home from work exhausted and ask for a cup of tea, the maid forgets all about it and I have to make it myself." Judy was such a good actress that listeners were frequently impressed. Not screenwriter Bob Hopkins. He called Judy's tears "a Hollywood bath."

Anita Loos

❏

When I worked with Audrey Hepburn in *The Children's Hour*, she taught me how to dress and I taught her how to cuss.

Shirley MacLaine

❏

Orson Welles—there but for the grace of God goes God.

Herman J. Mankiewicz

❏

A Steve McQueen performance just naturally lends itself to monotony. Steve doesn't bring much to the party.

Robert Mitchum

❏

Duke Wayne had four-inch lifts in his shoes which pushed him forward—you know that, don't you? I'm serious. He had the overheads on his boat accommodated to fit him. He had a special roof put in his station wagon. "I wanna make 'em WAYNE-conscious," he used to say. The sonofabitch, they probably buried him in his goddamn lifts. It was a business to him. That's okay with me. He was Saturday's hero, wasn't he?

Robert Mitchum

Oscar Levant was bright, wise-cracking, with a touch of vicious humor, but always brilliant. To Joan Crawford, who knitted continuously while rehearsing, eating, arguing, looking at rushes: "Do you knit when you fuck?" There were icebergs on the set of *Humoresque* for days.

Jean Negulesco

A neighbor of ours in Pacific Palisades was a rarity—a Hollywood hermit. Richard Haydn first made his name as "Mr. Carp—the only living fish mimic," and Hollywood commandeered him. He became a sought-after director, as well as character actor, but his joy in life was to be completely alone, tending the most beautiful concentration of flowers and plants in any garden in California. I suspected that he went near the studios only in order to earn money to buy seeds and fertilizer, and it took weeks of patient prodding and the absorption of countless rebuffs on our part before this enchantingly fey creature could be persuaded to visit our house. When he finally became tame enough to do so, he appeared unexpectedly, saying, "Come quickly. I *must* show you my phlox and scabiosa." I had an urge to call the doctor.

David Niven

On *All I Desire*, I don't recall finding the director, Douglas Sirk, very sympathetic, nor did I find *her* sympathetic. Barbara Stanwyck, I mean. She was always so popular and everybody adored her, but I found her a cold person, and she was the only actress in my working experience who ever went home leaving me to do the close-ups with the script girl, which I thought was most unprofessional. I was quite surprised. There, that's the only unkind thing that's *ever* been said about Barbara Stanwyck!

Maureen O'Sullivan

❑

I'll never forget Bette Davis. She sent me a bowl of gardenias on the first day's shooting of *Of Human Bondage*, with a note stating she hoped the role would do as much for my career as it did for hers. Another great lady is Joan Crawford. She was at Warners then, and somehow she got her hands on all the scripts. She put me on to *Caged*. Said she was too old to do it, but that I MUST do it.

Eleanor Parker

❑

Working with Jimmy Stewart in *It's a Wonderful Life* was very demanding. He's so natural, so realistic, that I never knew whether he was talking to me or doing the scene. He's the most demanding of all the actors I've ever worked with.

Donna Reed

❑

Mario Lanza had a little problem about being fat. You had to record his songs when he was fat. Then you had to close down the show while he reduced. You would then make the picture. His ability as an actor was somewhat less than zero. He was the only man who had pubic hair on his head. He used to pee on his leading lady. If he didn't like the scene, or he didn't like Doretta Morrow, he'd be holding her close saying "I love you" and he'd let go.

Leonard Spigelgass

❑

Charlton Heston has a bad memory. He still thinks he's Moses parting the Red Sea.

Barbara Stanwyck

❑

Maureen Stapleton gets the Oscar and I get the congratulations. As long as she's working, thank you very much, I enjoy being mistaken for her. We were down at the Kennedy Center a couple of years ago when they were honoring George Abbott. I was staying at the Ritz and she was at the Watergate. We met at the White House reception and she said, "Well, I've got your candy,

Eleanor Parker
Thanks Bette, Joan

your flowers and now I'm getting your phone calls. And if another damn person asks me if we're sisters, I'm going to say yes." Later, she said somebody just asked her if we were sisters. She said, "I said yes. And Jean's the one who drinks!"

Jean Stapleton

Some of my best leading men have been horses and dogs.

Elizabeth Taylor

When they make a better man than George Raft, I'll make him, too.

Mae West

Audrey Hepburn's like a salmon swimming upstream. She can do it with very small bozooms. Titism has taken over the country. This girl single-handed may make bozooms a thing of the past. The director will not have to invent shots where the girl leans way forward for a glass of Scotch and soda.

Billy Wilder

❏

Greer Garson? Very bright. Fantastically beautiful. Very much the lady. She was a great Irish wit. There are actors who work in movies. And then there are movie stars. She was a *movie star*.

Teresa Wright

❏

I've known Ty Power since we worked together in *Suez*, and I'm happy to say that he is, today, as unspoiled, as sensible and as humorous as he was then. Probably he has kept his balance in spite of his world-wide fame because he is so intelligent. His intellectuality is a delight because it is not obvious and he never parades his knowledge. However, the things he knows he knows perfectly. Men enjoy Ty because they can count on what he says. Women enjoy Ty because what he says counts. When he issues a compliment, you may rely on its sincerity.

Loretta Young

Columnists

Hedda Hopper had been taking potshots at me in her column for years. I finally got fed up and around 1950 I had a live skunk shipped to her house. Later, she wrote that she'd christened it Joan. A columnist always got the last word.

Joan Bennett

❏

During my Metro years both critics and columnists were laughable. If monsters like Hedda and Louella and Jimmy Fidler didn't happen to like *you*, they didn't like your pictures, but if they liked you, or they were beholden in some way to the studio, they'd call a piece of shit a birthday cake. It was all so biased—no, downright dishonest—that you didn't get a swelled head when they praised you and you didn't get hurt when they attacked.

Joan Crawford

Joan Bennett
The scent of power

Loretta Young
In praise of Ty

77

❏

Louella Parsons is stronger than Samson. He needed two columns to bring the house down. Louella can do it with one.

Samuel Goldwyn

❏

I don't care what they print about me, as long as it isn't true.

Katharine Hepburn

❏

I've always thought this description suited us best: Louella Parsons is a reporter trying to be a ham; Hedda Hopper is a ham trying to be a reporter.

Hedda Hopper

❏

The late Hedda Hopper once came up to my table in Chasen's when I was having dinner with my husband, Don Murray, and said, "What the hell are you doing here? I've got a headline in the papers that you've broken up with Don and are in San Francisco with Glenn Ford. How can you ruin my big exclusive?"

Hope Lange

❏

If Louella Parsons ever printed one *fact* in her column, her publishers would have fired her. She asked me to her house once and said, "Where were you born? I don't think that's ever been established." I said, "Before I answer, can I have some champagne?" The next day she reported that I was born in Champaign, Illinois!

Robert Mitchum

❏

When I accepted *A Walk on the Wild Side*, Louella Parsons called excitedly and said, "I heard you're going to play a madam and a lesbian," and I said, "Quite a parlay, eh kid?" And she said, "I'm shocked." And I said, "What do you want them to do? Get a real madam and a real lesbian?"

Barbara Stanwyck

Combat

During *Magnificent Ambersons*, Orson Welles, drunk on Joe Cotten's Machiavellian martinis, secretly sending his chauffeur home and pleading no transport, would I drive him? Gad, what a drive. I prayed for a policeman. Six feet four, 250 pounds, and what seemed like six hands in my shirt. All he kept saying was, "Oh, the beauty of it, Oh, the beauty of it." In tears of rage I finally shoved him out at Sunset Boulevard, threw my tattered bra in the gutter and gunned up the hill to home and Mother. Poor Orson. I always wondered how long it took him to get a cab.

Anne Baxter

❏

Humphrey Bogart always told me movies were like a slot machine. If you played long enough, you'd eventually hit the jackpot, which he did with *Maltese Falcon*. But I was a fool. I stuck to my Irish logic instead of saying yes to everything. I fought Jack Warner for better parts, and I finally lost.

Geraldine Fitzgerald

❏

Men are gluttons for punishment. They fight over women for the chance to fight with them.

Vincent Price

Courtship

You can never tell what a man has in mind when he asks you for a date in this town (Hollywood). He may be thinking of romance or he may just want his name in the papers.

Kathryn Grayson

❏

Men treat women like prostitutes, giving them presents for all the wrong reasons—but I always treat a woman like a lady. Men try to buy the attention and affection of women—but women love to be treated like ladies. Too many men have turned their backs on taste and good manners, yet that's what women crave. Chivalry may not be dead, but it's certainly on the critical list.

George Hamilton

❏

I do not spoil women. I am not what is known as "attentive." I do not send flowers, gifts. I do none of these things because I have found it isn't necessary. I am saving all that for when I am an old man and have to.

George Sanders

Crime

I dropped out of high school at 15. I ran into a guy who showed me how to hot-wire cars. I got so good at stealing cars that I soon set up my own shop in Nogales, Mexico. At 16, I had about 50 men working for me in the 11 Western states. Eventually, I was arrested and put into reformatories in El Reno, Oklahoma, and Springfield, Missouri. I was freed at 21.

Rory Calhoun

❏

If a thing's worth having, it's worth cheating for.

W.C. Fields

❏

If I hadn't become an actor, I might have become Public Enemy Number One.

John Garfield

❏

My advice to young actors? Stay out of jail.

Alfred Hitchcock

❏

When I was a kid, I tried to rip off a sled from a department store. I put it under my coat. Naturally the cops caught me before I left the store. "What do you have there, kid?", they asked—though they could see what I had. "How did you get it?" "Well," I explained, "I went up to see Santa Claus and when he asked me what I wanted for Christmas I pointed to the sled and he told me I could take it right now. It would save me an extra trip. So I took it." I could have ended up in reform school. I can't remember why they didn't pull me in. Maybe because of my answer. But they let me go.

Telly Savalas

I know a lot of those guys (Mafia figures). People have said to me: "Why did you have friends in the mob?" I say, "I was not *friends* with them." They say, "Do you know so-and-so?" I say, "No, but I've met him." When the Copacabana was open, there wasn't one guy in show business who didn't meet them there. Let them buy you a drink. So I've stopped trying to explain that to people. I was having dinner with Rosalind Russell once, and I said, "Why don't they get off my back about this thing?" She said, "Forget it. If they had anything to go on, you'd have been indicted years ago."

Frank Sinatra

Critics

Fuck the critics. They're like eunuchs. They can tell you how to do it, but they can't do it themselves.

Harry Cohn

Oh, fuck Pauline Kael, fuck her—and I don't use that language all the time. I don't care what she has to say. She's a bitch. She's spiteful, and she's wrong. Let's not talk about Pauline Kael.

George Cukor

Anne Baxter
Action with Orson

Frank Sinatra
A mob of acquaintances

It's only the best fruit the birds pick at.

Bette Davis

❑

The critics are looking for something, I think, that I can't give them—and really don't want to give them. They want ART. In caps. And me, I'm strictly commercial. I'm not arty or Bohemian. There are no little theater movements with me. Actually, I believe that 90 per cent of my public won't read reviews. If they want great acting, they go somewhere else. If they want something in spangles with nice tunes and a little hoofing, they make for Grable.

Betty Grable

❑

I think the underlying problem is that the critics have become performers. They see their names in lights ... They are over-quoted and over-rated. The ones on TV do seem to spend more time in the hairdressers and make-up rooms than some actresses. Then they become "experts" on film after being promoted from some dull desk job having nothing to do with entertainment. They just want attention ... They want to be quoted and cloak their insults and ignorance in puns. It disguises, thinly, the fact that they do not do their jobs properly.

Ross Hunter

❑

Critics? You can't accept one individual's opinion, particularly if it's female ... When they get a period, it's really difficult for them to function as human beings.

Jerry Lewis

❑

Percy Hammond reviewed us at the Majestic Theater in Chicago. He said the Marx Brothers and several relatives ran around the stage for about an hour, why he'd never understand. That was one of his *good* reviews. Later, he came to New York and went to work for the *Herald-Tribune*. They had a meeting at the *Trib*, six or eight of the big factotums. Ring Lardner was working there at the time. The editor suggested sending Percy Hammond to Europe to cover the war. "For Christ's sake," Lardner says, "you can't do that! Suppose he doesn't like it?"

Groucho Marx

❏

I exclude from appreciation the so-called critics who try to make a name for themselves by passing off glib wisecracks and create artificial controversy. Rex Reed is an example of that type. He is a special enemy of mine. When he published his list of the 10 Best and 10 Worst films of 1973 he added a note that, to his regret, there had been no Otto Preminger film released that year. Therefore he had none for the Rotten classification. I could only laugh. Reed is a frustrated little man who wanted to become an actor but couldn't make it.

Otto Preminger

❏

Those who can't—teach. And those who can't do either—review.

Burt Reynolds

Death

❏

If I come back in another life, I want to be Warren Beatty's fingertips.

Woody Allen

❏

I'm not afraid to die—I just don't want to be there when it happens.

Woody Allen

❏

The good die young—because they see it's no use living if you've got to be good.

John Barrymore

❏

If I were to be left without her (Elizabeth Taylor), I should surely die. If I didn't dwindle into death from a broken heart, then I would die by my own hands. Yes, life without Elizabeth is a desolate existence, at best. I must have her to continue. I would not be a man if I did not treasure her body and her mind.

Richard Burton

Believe in the hereafter? I don't! I do not believe that heaven—or hell—are places. Nor do I believe in the wishful-thinking of personal survival. What I do believe is that, in death as in life, it is the survival of the fittest. That is to say, if what we do on earth is great enough, we live on in the hearts and memories of others. My grandmother, for instance, will never die while I live. She left me too much of herself: the love of truth, of work well done, of patience, the love of gardens and sunrises and firesides. My mother will never die while I live. When she goes, she will leave me her devotion, her wisdom, her courage. In other words, *what she was, will live*. Shakespeare, Madame Curie, Edison, Marconi, Lister—such mortals as these have a vicarious immortality because what they did was great enough. I, on the other hand, shall probably not survive because of the things I do. My work is not important enough.

Bette Davis

I survived, because I was tougher than everybody else. Joe Mankiewicz always told me, "Bette, when you die, they ought to put only one sentence on your tombstone—'She did it the hard way' "! And he was right. And you know, it was the only way.

Bette Davis

Hearing about Errol Flynn's death was a profound shock. The whole first period of my career was identified with him and the films we made together, and though toward the end of that time I had become impatient to go on to more difficult and complex work, just before Flynn left us so suddenly and tragically I had come to reassess the quality and value of those films and to appreciate them. I had taken my young son to see *The Adventures of Robin Hood* on the Champs Elysées, and was enchanted by the gaiety and charm of the movie and its excellence in its own terms; it was this experience which made me realize that Flynn's adventure movies were really the very best of their kind and probably will never be surpassed. I was moved to write him a letter to say so, but unfortunately had a restraining second thought and instead of mailing the letter destroyed it. Two weeks later the phone rang and a French journalist told me that Errol was dead. You can imagine how much I regret that I had not had enough courage to send him a letter which might have made him happy.

Olivia de Havilland

I'm not afraid of death. I have no feelings about it. But I don't believe in a superior power and that we all end up hovering above. Honestly! That's *meshugenah*.

Marlene Dietrich

I'd sooner be dead in Los Angeles than alive in Philadelphia.

W.C. Fields

Nobody told me the truth about my mother, man. I was 10 years old and I didn't understand. I just knew she was dead and I was all alone. My father won't even talk to me about *today*, so he's not gonna talk about yesterday. There are too many yesterdays for him to get into, baby. I didn't find out how my mother died until I was 15. I was sitting in this barber's chair in Rome and I picked up a magazine and read about her doing herself in in an insane asylum. It blew my mind, man.

Peter Fonda

When I die, I have visions of fags singing "Somewhere over the Rainbow" and the flag at Fire Island being flown at half-mast.

Judy Garland

When I'm dead, I'm not sure if I want to be burnt, buried, put in a mausoleum or eaten.

Elliott Gould

❏

On his deathbed:
  Dying is hard. But not as hard as playing comedy.

Edmund Gwenn

❏

I hope when I die someone has the presence of mind to say, "Ding Dong, the Witch is *really* dead."

Margaret Hamilton

❏

When I die, I want to be cremated and have my ashes sprinkled on Darryl Zanuck's driveway so his car won't skid.

George Jessel

❏

I got back to Hollywood in time for Bogie's funeral. Niven, Romanoff, Leland Hayward, Irving Lazar, looking like the upper third of Yul Brynner, and I were ushers. We did nothing but stand back and let them come in. We were supposed to seat the gentry in certain choice locations and the peasants otherwise, but I couldn't tell the peasants from the gentry, and neither could any of the other ushers. The occasion brought out more oddities than any I've attended since John Barrymore's funeral. We had nothing really as horrifying as John Carradine afflicted with grief or W.C. Fields at 11 o'clock in the morning, an unbelievable sight, but there were a few singularties. One was an Indian wearing a flat hat and his hair in two long braids with three white squaws in their early 20s. I passed them along to Romanoff, whom I put in charge of Indians for the day. Mike steered this Vanishing American up to the balcony, which he described as temporary Indian reservation. We figured him to be Geronimo Bogart, an uncle on Bogie's father's side.

Nunnally Johnson

❏

Funerals are another way of making death seem odious. I think they are barbaric. I don't want people moaning and weeping when I'm gone. I'd rather have them open a bottle of champagne and remember the good times. But society insists on imposing grief when death comes. I can remember how shocked my grandparents were when my mother refused to wear mourning clothes when my father died in 1934. "He never liked me in black," she told them.

Deborah Kerr

❑

Gable? Very ordinary, very cheerful fellow. He'd been passed over for insurance, you know. Had a couple of heart warnings. After he died, Hedda Hopper called me up and said, "Your friend John Huston just killed Clark Gable." "I know," I said, "and he's trying to kill me, too."

Robert Mitchum

❑

I have often thought that my tombstone might well read: "Here lies Paul Newman, who died a failure because his eyes suddenly turned brown."

Paul Newman

❑

Someone once asked me what I want on my epitaph when I pass away. Just two words—I tried. And that's what this game is all about—*trying*. There's the tryers, the criers and the liars. Now I sound like a philosophical sage, but that's because it's true. I *am* a philosophical sage!

Mickey Rooney

❑

I will have had enough of this earth by the time I am 65. After that I shall be having my bottom wiped by nurses and being pushed around in a wheelchair. I won't be able to enjoy a woman anymore, so I shall commit suicide.

George Sanders

❑

I believe in suicide. In classical times, suicide was the honorable way to go. The Judeo-Christian ethic doesn't believe in that, but I'm an atheist. I can name to you 50 actors who have taken their own lives in the past 30 years. I'm not saying that's a good thing or a bad thing, but it's not necessarily anathema to morality. Why hang on until 85 and be incapacitated, deaf and blind and have to be taken care of by somebody that you don't even know? It will happen to all of us. Either you die in a car crash, or you live to be too bloody old.

George C. Scott

❏

Observing the large turnout for the funeral in 1958 of Columbia Pictures President Harry Cohn:

Well, it only proves what they always say—give the public something they want to see, and they'll come out for it.

Red Skelton

❏

Errol Flynn suffered a fatal heart attack in 1959. I saw (lawyer) Jerry Giesler, Duke Wayne, Mike Curtiz, Gary Cooper and other Flynn friends at the funeral, and I said wistfully to Giesler, "I wish you could get him out of this one, Jerry." After the service, I saw director Raoul Walsh, who with Jack Oakie, Mike Romanoff, Mickey Rooney and others, served as a pallbearer. "You seemed to be having an awful struggle with that casket, Raoul," I said. "It was heavy, Jack," he said. "I peeked inside and there were six cases of Scotch."

Jack L. Warner

❏

The trouble with death is that you don't get two weeks' notice that your contract is being cancelled out.

Jack L. Warner

❏

Upon learning that James Dean had died:

How could he *do* this to me after all my work to build him up into a big star?

Jack L. Warner

Directors

We used to have the meanest directors in the world. They all had accents, and they all had laryngitis. "Do it this way, you dumb sonofabitch!" I didn't mind. You know where you are with a screamer. Directors are so polite now. It isn't as good today. With these guys, you don't know where the hell you are. "*You*, idiot!" or "*You*, jerk!" is better than "Miss Adrian."

Iris Adrian

On *Little Women*, as we always did have, we had small dressing rooms on the set for the actors and actresses to go sit in while they made the new camera set-ups. When director George Cukor was ready for us, Kate Hepburn, Jean Parker, Frances Dee and myself, he'd always say, with a great sense of humor, "C'mon, you four little bitches, the set is ready!"

Joan Bennett

The director Edmund Goulding did something that drove actors crazy. He'd get out there and act out everybody's roles for them—even the women! And we were supposed to imitate him. We wanted to give our own interpretations.

Joan Blondell

I read the book *Such Good Friends* and I called my agent and said, "I wanna do this part." She said, "Otto Preminger is directing it in New York." I was warned about him—but could anybody really be *that* bad? Yeah, they could. Elaine May wrote a great screenplay. He took a piece of beauty and screwed it up. It was an incredible part. I was in *every* frame of that film—except for one short scene—and he destroyed it. I have been the victim of some killers in my time. He's one of the biggest. He's a *horrible* man. I was absolutely destroyed by that man. *Phew!* But who ever hears of him anymore? Is he still alive?

Dyan Cannon

Established Hollywood directors don't do very much to help new talent break into directing. The problem here is that unique Hollywood principle: "I want my film to be good and his to be lousy," which is based on the old adage of Le Rochefoucault, "It is not enough that I succeed; my best friend must also fail."

Francis Ford Coppola

❏

When we made *Lifeboat*, it was a very, very vigorous undertaking. Tallulah Bankhead was not entirely a model of modesty. One of the things she didn't believe in was underwear. The lifeboat was on a mechanical rocker. Tallulah getting into that boat had to hike her skirt up to her waist. There was a considerable amount to be seen. It got boring to the cast and crew, but visitors to the set were shocked. Somebody finally went up to the director, Alfred Hitchcock, and said: "Mr. Hitchcock, would you speak to her?" Hitchcock threw up his hands. He said: "This is an interdepartmental matter, and I don't like to get involved. It's a matter for wardrobe, for costume—even hairdressing."

Hume Cronyn

❏

Michael Curtiz was a savage, a real beast. A Hungarian Otto Preminger. He was a tyrant, he was abusive, he was cruel. Oh, he was just a villain but I guess he was pretty good. We didn't believe it then, but he clearly was. He knew what he was doing. He knew how to tell a story very clearly and he knew how to keep things going; you had to transmit vitality. I was astounded by *Robin Hood*'s vitality, its effervescence. That was a revelation (when I saw it years later), and I thought, well, he had something to do with it and he did; I have to admit it.

Olivia de Havilland

❏

The way to make a film is to begin with an earthquake and work up to a climax.

Cecil B. DeMille

❏

There will never be another (John) Ford. He had instinctively a beautiful eye for the camera. He was so egomaniacal. He never would rehearse, didn't want to talk about a part. If an actor started to ask questions, he'd either take those pages and tear them out of the script or insult him in an awful way. He loved getting his shot on the first take, which for him meant it was fresh. He would print the first take even if it wasn't any good.

Henry Fonda

❏

Bill Holden and I had a wonderful director, a dear friend, George Marshall. On *Texas*, Bill and I were supposed to ride up a hill, jump off a bluff, then crawl along and sneak up on some hold-up men. We'd be crawling along and George'd say, "Cut. Listen, you two, you're supposed to be scared. Now look scared!" Well, we'd do it again, hot and miserable, and he still didn't think we looked scared enough. So finally he gets out a rifle, climbs up a big stepladder, tells the camera to roll and starts shooting over our heads. "Hey," says Bill, "those are real bullets!" We crawled, hugging the ground and sweating with fear. George yells, "Now, dammit, that's what I wanted you to do the first time!"

Glenn Ford

❏

We were deep into shooting *Gone with the Wind* and very happy with director George Cukor's sensitive approach. But Gable was growing more and more restless, convinced that Cukor was giving all the attention to the girls. He was aching for Victor Fleming, to whom he could relate: Fleming was a man's man and liked to talk about women, chase them and bed them, and he liked his generous swigs of Scotch, would follow football and baseball and liked to box and work out in a gym, and he boosted Gable's ego by telling him what a stud he was. Cukor was interested in costumes and jewelry and hairstyles and had never been near a racetrack or a diamond or a gym in his life. Finally, one horrible afternoon, Gable suddenly put his hand up and stopped the shooting. He shouted furiously, "Fuck this! I want to be directed by a man!" Everybody froze. You could have heard a pin drop. Vivien Leigh and Olivia de Havilland were deathly pale and walked to a corner. Cukor stood there trembling and finally made a clumsy, shattered exit. It was obvious that Cukor was finished on this picture.

Lee Garmes

❏

They were looking for someone to play God in *Skidoo* and I suggested Groucho (Marx). They leaped. So I called him up and he said, "I don't want to work." I said, "Come on, it's only a couple of days—we'll have some fun." Then, right after he got on the picture, Otto Preminger started in on him, giving him a hard time. And Groucho was old and feeble. Preminger, what a son-of-a-bitch! Preminger also started berating Frankie Avalon, and, Christ, it was just terrible to see. So when that was over, I said, "Otto, come here. If you ever talk to me like that, I will hit you over the head with a fuckin' chair!" From then on, he was as gentle as the rain with me.

                                                            Jackie Gleason

Every director bites the hand that lays the golden egg.

                                                            Samuel Goldwyn

You know why I favor sophisticated blondes in my films? We're after the drawing-room type, the real ladies, who become whores once they're in the bedroom.

                                                            Alfred Hitchcock

Hitch (Alfred Hitchcock) relished scaring me. When we were making *Psycho*, he experimented with the mother's corpse, using me as his gauge. I would return from lunch, open the door to the dressing room and propped in my chair would be this hideous monstrosity. The horror in my scream, registered on his Richter scale, decided which dummy he'd use as the Madame.

                                                            Janet Leigh

Billy Wilder's talent goes beyond just writing and directing. He's a great picture-maker. He can do the entire thing rather than scene by scene. I've had directors who were marvelous at breaking scenes down and handling people. But when you would string all the pearls together, they wouldn't make a beautiful necklace. But Billy is the kind of picture-maker who can make a beautiful string of pearls. He makes the kind of movies that are classics and last forever.

                                                            Jack Lemmon

❑

This dopey *auteur* thing Americans picked up from the French . . . When we shoot, I'm dependent on the weather. I'm dependent on the drunk who won't get out of the shot until we pay him off. What am I really in control of?

Sidney Lumet

❑

Ernst Lubitsch was a great director, worthy of his enormous reputation, but I found working under him in *Design for Living* cramped my style a bit. He left one no leeway at all, telling you when to light a cigarette, when to put your hands in your pockets, regulating every movement and gesture, every expression. I felt like a robot after a few days.

Fredric March

❑

Cecil B. DeMille would have been the greatest general in a Prussian army because his handling of crowds, masses of people, his organization ability was fantastic; but I don't think he knew a damn thing about acting. He couldn't tell you the first word about how to play a scene. Never did. He set it up camera-wise, you see, and there is nothing you can do but repeat the lines and go to the spots he tells you to go. You're on your own from then on. He had drama coaches on the set who would tell him what to tell us.

Ray Milland

❑

John Huston treats me like an idiot—"Honey, this" and "Honey, that."

Marilyn Monroe

❑

The best thing about becoming a director is that you don't have to shave or hold your stomach in anymore.

Dick Powell

❑

Cecil B. DeMille handed me the script of *North West Mounted Police*, and when I'd read it he asked me how I liked it. I said, "It's the same part I played for you last year. I'll change costumes and play it again," and he said, "You ungrateful son-of-a-bitch. If it wasn't for me, you'd still be parking cars at Santa Anita." He was no director. He didn't know what to tell us. Also, he was not a nice person, politically or any other way. I think the only man DeMille ever envied was Hitler.

Robert Preston

❑

Funny Girl was Barbra Streisand's first picture, and she thought she was going to tell William Wyler, who'd made many classic pictures, how to direct. But he fixed her. He'd make her do 41 takes on a single scene—that took some of the wind out of her sails.

Mae Questel

❑

Barbara Stanwyck sent me a letter when I signed to direct *Now, Voyager*: "Dear Irving. You are going to do a picture with Bette Davis. Don't you know there are such things as fresh air and sunshine?"

Irving Rapper

❑

Bill Wellman was a wild man. For instance, in the morning scene in the tent (in *Battleground*), when they're all asleep, James Whitmore comes in to wake them and says, "Grab your socks"—a polite version of what they used to say. Bill told the men, "Look, I wanna hear noise. I want a bunch of guys really sleeping, some of you snoring, some of you coughing, and listen, if you want to break wind, go on and break wind." A couple of the guys did and you could hear it on the soundtrack! I said, "Bill, it's very funny but what's the use of doing it?" But the sounds that came out of the tent were very real. You felt that these guys were tough, and yet we didn't use any four-letter words.

Dore Schary

❑

William Wyler would ruin a lot of takes. He'd smoke and cough. The smoke would get in front of the lens.

Barbra Streisand

❏

I thank God that neither I nor any member of my family will ever be so hard up that we have to work for Otto Preminger!

Lana Turner

❏

It's not necessary for a director to know how to write, but it helps if he knows how to read.

Billy Wilder

❏

I don't care what goes on on the set. I don't care if we all hate each other. I only care what the finished product looks like when that audience goes to the theater.

William Wyler

Divorce

Why do Hollywood divorces cost so much? Because they're worth it.

Johnny Carson

❏

Somebody recently told me that in Hollywood there's a group called Divorce Anonymous. It works like this: If a male member of the group starts to feel the urge to get a divorce, they send over an accountant to talk him out of it.

Sean Connery

❏

In Hollywood, after you get a little success, the next thing you usually get is a divorce. Wouldn't it be a refreshing change if my wife and I didn't?

Dan Dailey

I am a very good housekeeper. Each time I get a divorce I keep the house.

Zsa Zsa Gabor

My last husband charged calls to his girlfriend in Berlin on my phone, so I refused to pay and had to change the number I'd had for 18 years. What I really missed after he left was that phone number.

Viveca Lindfors

If it comes to a divorce with Jane (Wyman), I think I'll name *Johnny Belinda* corespondent.

Ronald Reagan

I read about a wife who plans to divorce her husband as soon as she can find a way to do it without making him happy.

Arnold Schwarzenegger

The first couple of years (after divorcing Robert Taylor) were rough, very rough. Because there were 11 and a half years to throw out along with the garbage. It's a lot rougher when you *don't* want it but the other person does. If it's mutual or if *you* want it, then it's easy. He wanted it, and I'm not the kind of person who wants somebody if he doesn't want me. I just say, "There's the door, you can open it. You've got a good right hand, just turn the knob, that's all you have to do. If you can't open it, I'll do it for you."

Barbara Stanwyck

Viveca Lindfors
Misses phone most

In all my divorces, I never took alimony. I always wanted to start my life again with a clean slate. Just like a baptism, I wanted to enter the water, wash away the old and come out a new person.

                                                                    Ruth Warrick

I thought when my divorce (from Ronald Reagan) was final, the telephone would ring itself right off the table. Well, it has. The vet has called to say we could take the dog home. The dentist has called about the children's teeth. The dressmaker has called, the hairdresser has called, even the radio survey people have called. But after six o'clock things quiet down considerably.

                                                                    Jane Wyman

Egos

The pictures I've turned down were either no good or somebody involved was playing the kind of big shot games I won't go along with. Barbra Streisand called me to come over to read for the part of Billy Rose in *Funny Lady*. She had to do the "star" bit, see. So I went over to have some fun. She said, "Here, read this scene." I said, "No, let's read the whole screenplay." She read it with me and when we finished a couple of hours later she said, "Man, that was great! You've got the part." I told her, "Thank you very much, but I've just done that role." And I left. They gave the part to Jimmy Caan and they paid him at least a half-million.

Robert Blake

My favorite among my films is *Love Affair*. And shortly before he died, my co-star, Charles Boyer, told a reporter that it was his favorite, too. The last time I saw *Love Affair*, I said to him, "You know, Charles, you really were *good*." "Ah," he said, "so you finally looked at *me*."

Irene Dunne

Many people feel that having children gives them an eternal spark. The dynasty bit. We have friends, like Bob and Lola Redford, who are on this ego trip; they think it's wonderful to go ahead and have all the children they can. They'll just grow like flowers and everything will be wonderful. Well, there are *already* plenty of children in this world who desperately need homes. Richard and I are actors and our security is in flux now, but some day we'd like to have lots of *adopted* children. We don't need three-foot images of Joan Hackett and Richard Mulligan walking around.

Joan Hackett

Cary Grant, Douglas Fairbanks, Jr., and Victor McLaglen, with whom I appeared in *Gunga Din*, were wonderful people. My wife, however, called the film *The Big Close-Up* because every time one of the stars would get a close-up, the others would dash to phone their agents to demand close-ups, too.

Sam Jaffe

There is a thin line between genius and insanity. I have erased that line.

Oscar Levant

❏

An actress must never lose her ego. Without it she has no talent and is like a clock without a main spring.

Norma Shearer

❏

Addressing a small lecture audience:
I'm an actor on the stage, screen and radio. I write, and I'm a director. Also I'm a producer. I'm only sorry that there are so many of me, and so few of you.

Orson Welles

❏

I didn't want to do *Broken Lance*. Darryl Zanuck was teed-off because I wouldn't re-sign and said, "I'll show the s.o.b." He threw me into a small part. I told (Spencer) Tracy that I was trying to get out of the movie, but that it had nothing to do with him. "You're the greatest actor, and I've admired you since I was a babe in arms." A few weeks later we were shooting a scene and I had nothing to do—just stand around. It was Spence's scene; he was doing all the talking. I happened to be standing in the wrong place or something, and he looked up and said, "Who the fuck do you think is the star of this picture?" I said, "Oh, Spence, come on." Then he got embarrassed. That's the other side of Tracy. He could be very petty and egomaniacal.

Richard Widmark

❏

The trouble with marrying an actor is they grab you in their arms, hold you close and tell you how wonderful *they* are.

Shelley Winters

Fame

I guess I have a burning resentment of the fact that when people meet you, they're meeting some asshole celebrity movie actor, instead of a person, someone who has another view, or another life, or is concerned about other things. This *idiot* part of life has to go in the forefront of things as if it's of major importance.

Marlon Brando

❏

I am known in parts of the world by people who have never heard of Jesus Christ.

Charles Chaplin

❏

In the final analysis, it's true that fame is unimportant. No matter how great a man is, the size of his funeral usually depends on the weather.

Rosemary Clooney

❏

How does it feel to be a celebrity? It feels fine when it helps to get a good seat for a football game. But it never helped me to make a good film or a good shot in a polo game, or command the obedience of my daughter. It doesn't even seem to keep fleas off our dogs—and if being a celebrity won't give one an advantage over a couple of fleas, then I guess there can't be much in being a celebrity after all.

Walt Disney

❏

If I had my way I'd have every actor in the business sit down once a week for a solid hour and read 10-year-old fan magazines. I've been doing it lately. When you look through them and see who was important 10 years ago and realize what those same people are doing now, you know that fame is fleeting. You know that it's not so vital to get items put in the paper as you thought it was ... Maybe you see that Jim Murgatroyd has the first Duesenburg car in town. No doubt Jim got a thrill out of that item. But now you can't remember who Jim was.

Glenn Ford

❏

The boys of the R.A.F. named their life-saving jackets their "Mae Wests." I wrote and thanked the boys and I told them, I've been in Who's Who, and I know what's what, but it's the first time I've ever made the dictionary.

Mae West

Family

I appreciate the chance to visit my mom on Mother's Day—it's like taking a refresher course in guilt.

Woody Allen

❏

Actresses can't win! Metro wanted me for the mother in a television series to be called *Meet Me in St. Louis*, but ABC insisted on another actress on the grounds that I'm not the motherly type and the public wouldn't accept me as such. Whereupon I discovered I was expecting my seventh child.

Jeanne Crain

❏

Faye Dunaway says she is being haunted by Mother's (Joan Crawford) ghost. After her performance in *Mommie Dearest*, I can understand why.

Christina Crawford

❏

Mother has never let me down. I can remember when I had to have an operation on my teeth, she was right there with me. And when I first went away to school, I'd get so homesick I would call her. And she would drive out to see me. Sometimes at the beginning she would take me home.

Christina Crawford

❏

A pillow is a lousy substitute for somebody who really cares. And when it comes right down to it, aside from Alfred Steele and the twins, I don't think I came across anyone who really cared.

Joan Crawford

❑

My mother was illiterate when she came to this country. I taught her how to write her name—B-R-Y-N-A. She would say proudly, "My boy—the whole world knows him. His name is up in lights." A year later I took her in a limousine to Times Square where, in big lights, a marquee said, "Bryna Presents *Spartacus*." I said, "See, Ma, there's *your* name in lights." She said, "You know, America is such a wonderful land."

Kirk Douglas

❑

I used to believe in Christmas until I was eight years old. While carrying ice in Philadelphia, I'd saved several quarters to buy my mother a present for Christmas. I hid the money in a milk bottle in the basement. One day I caught my father stealing the money. Ever since, I've remembered nobody on Christmas, and I want nobody to remember me.

W.C. Fields

❑

When I signed with Columbia they wanted me to change my name. I said absolutely not. I am the granddaughter of the speaker of the Dutch Parliament and the Governor General of the Dutch East Indies. I said, "I'm not going to change my name for you or anybody." I did, however, change the K to H— for obvious reasons.

Nina Foch

❑

I resent that book (*Mommie Dearest*). I resent the daughter and the publisher and everything about it. I knew Joan (Crawford) during those days. Worked with her and was often at parties at her home; pool parties in the afternoon, when the children were there, and I never saw or heard anything that would give me a clue that the stories were true that the daughter wrote. I think whatever is truth about them has been exaggerated so that it makes her more of a monster than she was.

Henry Fonda

❑

To my knowledge, Mother saw only one film of mine. She acted as my substitute when I was in the hospital—Brian (Aherne) escorted her to the premiere of *Rebecca*. Meeting the powerful columnist Louella Parsons at the postpremiere press party at Ciro's, Mother was fawned over. "This must be a golden moment for you, Mrs. Fontaine ... your daughter catapulted to stardom by this film." Mother looked coolly down her aquiline nose and replied, "Joan has always seemed rather phony to me in real life, but she's quite believable on the screen."

Joan Fontaine

❑

Mother was the real-life Wicked Witch of the West. Mother was no good for anything except to create chaos and fear. She didn't like me because of my talent. She had a crude voice and my sisters had lousy voices, too. And today when I review my financial problems, I have to admit they began with Mother.

Judy Garland

❑

I get my energy from my mother. She was Italian and my father was Irish. I left home when I was 17 and had to learn how to do everything. I became a landlady and learned how to buy caskets for them when they died. I grew up fast, and my mother instilled it all in me. She was incredible. When her father died, she was so melancholy they signed her into Bellevue and she jumped out of the goddamn window and swam the East River. I can't look at the East River to this day without smiling. She was the only one of 14 kids in her family who finished school. She was four feet 11 inches high, wrote and spoke three languages, and when she died she was suing three people and acting as her own lawyer.

Joan Hackett

❑

My mother was a bootlegger during Prohibition, and when I was three I was singing on top of the kitchen table. I sang "Black Bottom" and my mother played the guitar. They'd throw nickels and dimes on the floor. Then we got busted by the police and were told to get out of Lansing, Michigan. We went to Detroit—now this is the Depression—and my mom couldn't find work. Sometimes we had one can of beans for the three of us: my mother, my older sister Marion and me. Then my mother started drinking, because she couldn't bear to see what was happening to us. I'd pick up my mom at bars and sing in the bars for nickels and dimes. I was making a damn good living for that time, but I'd wanted to be a star since I was three, when I'd say to my mother, "I'm gonna be a 'tar!" I couldn't even say "star."

Betty Hutton

I've a perfectly logical excuse for being a ham. Can you imagine what dinner table conversation is like in an acting family? You have to play the second act of *Hamlet* to make anybody know you're there. You don't ask anyone to pass the salt . . . you declaim!

Ida Lupino

Mama (Judy Garland) rarely used profanity, but when she did it was always funny. We were someplace like Lake Tahoe and went into the ladies' room. There was an old lady drunk there, and with very slurred speech she said, "Oh, Judy, you're terrific. You got to always remember the rainbow." When Mama went into one of the stalls, the lady knocked on the door. Mama said, "Yes?", and she said, "Judy, never forget the rainbow." Later on, she went up to Mama and went on and on again about her not forgetting the rainbow. Finally, Mama turned and said, "How can I forget the rainbow? I've got rainbows up my ass!"

Liza Minnelli

Success came to me in a rush. It surprised my employers much more than it did me. Even when I had played only bit parts in a few films, all the movie magazines and newspapers started printing my picture and giving me write-ups. I used to tell lies in my interviews—chiefly about my mother and father. I'd say she was dead and he was somewhere in Europe. I lied because I was ashamed to have the world know my mother was in a mental institution—and that I had been born out of wedlock and never heard my illegal father's voice.

Marilyn Monroe

To me the (Andy) Hardy pictures exemplified what a family should be. For instance, Judge Hardy, played by Lewis Stone, had a maiden aunt living with the family, and she was *part* of the family. That was Aunt Milly, and the part was done beautifully by Sara Haden. Maiden aunts do not live with their families today. Now the relatives probably call them old lesbians and shunt them off to institutions for the retarded or homes for senior citizens.

Ann Rutherford

Fans

My idea of a good time is to take a walk from my house to the office and not for the entire walk have to worry about hearing my name being called from a passing car or being spoken to at all. That would be perfect.

Woody Allen

Fan club? That's a group of people who tell an actor he's not alone in the way he feels about himself.

Jack Carson

Hollywood is a rotten town. When you're not on top, everyone forgets you. The only loyalty you get is not from the industry, it's from the fans. Thank God many of them still write to me. Thank God they remember me.

Broderick Crawford

Dark glasses are silly, and all this nonsense about wanting to be alone is even sillier. The public is my boss, and they're entitled to see the girl they "employ." Besides—it's fun to be recognized.

Rhonda Fleming

I never know how to react (when people stare at me). The right way is the way Bette Davis does it. I saw her in a hotel in Madrid once and went up to her and said: "Miss Davis, I'm Ava Gardner and I'm a great fan of yours." And you know, she behaved exactly as I wanted her to behave. "Of course you are, my dear," she said, "of course you are." And then she swept on.

Ava Gardner

❏

I don't think there are as many fans around now as there used to be; maybe for rock musicians, but not for actors. People today are more sophisticated; they can accept a performer for what he does and not idolize him. I could never understand youngsters putting actors on a pedestal; it should be men and women who really contribute something to humanity. The man who makes a really fine law or does something in medicine—they're the ones who should have fans. Not actors.

Susan Hayward

❏

I could never turn the fans down, because I was one of them. I was a bobbysoxer myself, and I just happened to make it over the gate. I used to sit outside waiting for Joan Crawford to come in. I used to go there an hour early. That's how I got hemorrhoids, sitting on those cold brownstone steps.

Van Johnson

❏

I know darned well that if it weren't for those kids (autograph hunters) I wouldn't be able to own a car. I'm one guy in Hollywood who realizes those kids pay my salary.

Alan Ladd

❏

Bobbysoxers? They are vile, loathsome, wretched barbarians. They are ill-bred, badly mannered and, for the most part, morons.

James Mason

❏

I'm repelled by the aggressiveness of people who ask for autographs or ask me to pose or demand that I take off my glasses so they can see my so-called

Technicolor eyes. I feel like saying, "Show *me* your gums." There's nothing like that to make you feel like a piece of meat.

Paul Newman

❏

I used to love to watch people. I'd go to the railroad station in Chicago to watch them. I can't do that anymore. I can't watch people; they're watching me.

Kim Novak

❏

Actors are fools to complain about the public's attention. They should be glad to have it, not claim they dislike it—and yet go out of their way to seek it.

Gregory Peck

❏

The ones who hang around stage doors and ask for an occasional autograph—they're fans. But the ones who follow me all over the place— they're fiends!

Frank Sinatra

❏

I was a fan of Garbo's and would have done anything to meet her. One time I was working on the stage next to her and I found out that when she left she would go right from the stage door to her limousine, and nobody would see her. But I got to know the sound man on her set. And he told me just how much time it took her to get from her dressing room to the stage door. "So I'll give you a call one of these days when we finish," he told me, "and maybe you'll be able to run out your door and get to see her before she gets into the limousine." A couple of days later he called: "Hurry. Go out your door because she's just leaving." I had to go on the dead run to get to the end of the stage. And as I went around the corner to the door, I ran smack into somebody. But I wasn't going to let that stop me. I just kept running, right out to the door, and as I was about to open it, I stopped and looked back. And there was Greta Garbo all right—flat on her ass.

James Stewart

❏

James Mason
Found teenagers morons

James Stewart
When stars collide

Nowadays when a fan runs up to me, it isn't to get an autograph, but a closer look at the wrinkles.

Elizabeth Taylor

Fashion

When Joan Crawford came to Warners for *Mildred Pierce* she was a monster. Whatever you suggested, she fought tooth and nail. She hated the house-dresses and waitress uniforms at the beginning of the picture. We had many expensive-looking clothes for the latter part, but she didn't like those either, because they weren't gaudy like the clothes she'd had at MGM. I knew she was terrified that her career might be over, and she had no faith in the project. I did everything I could to accommodate her, but I knew that the director, Michael Curtiz, wanted the clothes simple and, above all, no shoulder pads! One day, as a special favor, we went to Joan's house for a fitting. When she discovered we hadn't brought any pads, she kicked us out! She sent me the most touching letter of apology, but a couple days later it was the same old thing again. She always wanted everything made so loose. She'd grab a suit jacket by the cuffs and pull and pull until the seams popped, then say, "You see, I told you. It's too tight."

Milo Anderson

You could toss a bolt of fabric at Carole Lombard, and however it would land on her she would look smart.

Travis Banton

Often when Hedy Lamarr would come into my salon for fittings on *Samson and Delilah*, she'd float past my secretary, one hand dramatically placed on her forehead, and immediately plop down on the floor, complaining that her back gave her constant pain, that she had never been the same since she had had children. She'd get up to fit a dress but in between pinnings she'd plop down on the floor again, which gave me the impression that her back wasn't really aching; she was just lazy. We fitted a multitude of rather bare bras and skirts for her role as Delilah, but the real work came from helping her get up off the floor.

Edith Head

❑

Susan Hayward was terribly ill with an inoperable brain tumor, so I was surprised when she told me she needed a wonderful dress because she was going to be a presenter at the Academy Awards. We were great friends, and I knew she was struggling tremendously. "You have to make me look beautiful," she said, "because it will be the last time the public will ever see me." I told her, "Don't worry, my love, we're going to make you gorgeous." I later did some sketches and took them over to her house. She chose the one she wanted: dark bottle-green chiffon covered with green paillettes—very simple—with long sleeves and a deep V neck. She liked the way she looked so much, she had a clause put in her will that she wanted to be buried in the dress.

Nolan Miller

❑

On *Gone with the Wind*, I worked very closely with the descriptions that Margaret Mitchell put down in the book. But I did notice that she seemed to have Scarlett dressed almost exclusively in green. We had already shot the first scene, the one where she stands on the steps of Tara, and, following Miss Mitchell's directions, I had made a pale green muslin dress for Vivien Leigh. She was also to appear in this same costume for the barbecue scene. I told David Selznick, the producer, that Vivien would be going through the entire picture in just this one color. And he said, "Oh, God, we'll have to change that!" Fortunately, in the color-processing lab all the colors of that first scene came out so strong that Vivien looked like Lucille Ball—bright red hair and all—so it had to be re-shot and I was able to design a new dress. It was the white one with the red velvet ribbons at the waist. Today, 37 years later, that is the one dress everyone seems to remember.

Walter Plunkett

❑

By 1962 L.B. Mayer was no longer around and the stars were beginning to edit the scripts, cast the films and, in some instances, design the wardrobe. A newcomer to MGM, Jane Fonda was cast in *Period of Adjustment* as a small-town girl. The clothes could have been bought in a budget shop rather than specially designed, but Jane insisted that everything be made especially for her. I was told to send the sketches of the wardrobe to her in New York for her approval. A few days later she called to ask if she could wear a "Mongolian Goat" coat in one sequence instead of the one I designed. No one had ever heard of Mongolian Goat, so Jane brought back something resembling a very tired, very shaggy, unkempt sheep dog. By the time we got through with the fittings, she had changed every outfit. When the wardrobe was finished she loved every piece of that disheveled mess, which looked as though it had come from some third-rate thrift store on the wrong side of town. Jane requested a new set of sketches to match the re-designed wardrobe. To keep her happy I had them made, but refused to sign them. I told her that she should sign them herself. I then did something I had never done before or since—I had my name omitted from the film credits.

Helen Rose

Feuds

A director is a ring master, a psychiatrist and referee. Crawford and Davis were perfect pros on the set (of *What Ever Happened to Baby Jane?*) until six p.m. Then I'd get a call from Joan asking, "Did you see what that (bleep) did to me today?" A couple of minutes later Bette would call and ask, "What did that (bleep) call you about?" First one and then the other. I could count on it every night.

Robert Aldrich

Bette Davis and Joan Crawford didn't fight at all on *What Ever Happened to Baby Jane?* I think it's proper to say that they really detested each other, but they behaved absolutely perfectly. There was never an abrasive word in public, and not once did they try to upstage each other. Nor did Miss Davis allow her enmity with Miss Crawford to color her playing of the scenes in which she was supposed to torment her. People who loved the violence of it read that into it and thought it was inherent, but it wasn't. They both behaved in a wonderfully professional manner.

Robert Aldrich

Ginger Rogers and I got along very well. We've laughed about the (feud) rumors. We didn't have problems; we never had *time* to fight. We did discuss things. We said to each other, "I don't like this ...", but we didn't fight.

Fred Astaire

Fred Astaire
No time for feud

FRED ASTAIRE. Metro Goldwyn-Mayer

❏

I refuse to be brutalized any longer. And by the most incredible people! I read a quote from Raquel Welch that "Carroll Baker wouldn't be sexy if she was spread-eagled naked on the cover of *Life* magazine"! What does she want from me? I don't even know this girl, I've never done anything to her. But it upset me because it didn't sound like a statement from a real woman at all. It would never occur to *me* to think of another woman spread-eagled naked. It was cruel, but it was also very perverted.

Carroll Baker

❏

After seeing 1950's *All About Eve*, in which she was rumored to have been the inspiration for star Bette Davis' character:

Don't think I don't know who's been spreading gossip about me and my temperament out there in Hollywood, where that film was made: *All About Me*. And after all the nice things I've said about that hag. When I get hold of her I'll tear out every hair of her mustache!

Tallulah Bankhead

❏

Imagine Katharine Hepburn playing *Mary of Scotland*. Kate, with her station-wagon Connecticut voice, playing the Queen! Mary of Scots, let us remember, was six-foot-three, with a bosom like a Holstein cow. But day after day Kate kept saying she really wanted to play *both* Mary and Queen Elizabeth (played by Florence Eldridge). We all got tired of hearing it. So one day I told Kate, "If you played both parts, how would you know which queen to upstage?" She walked off the set and didn't speak to me for 20 years.

John Carradine

❏

Director Robert Aldrich's publicity people thought that the best way to promote *What Ever Happened to Baby Jane?* was to make a big thing about a feud between me and Bette Davis. They were half right, because before filming began, Bette, in an interview, referred to me as a "movie star" and to herself as an "actress." I still wonder what the hell she meant. So I had no great beginnings in legitimate theater, but what the hell did she become if not a movie star? With all her little gestures with the cigarette, the clipped speech, the big eyes, the deadpan? I was just as much an actress as she was, even though I wasn't trained for the stage, but we were competing in the same medium, so weren't we both actresses? Film stars? Former film stars, whatever? That kind of snobbery is beside the point. She has almost as many failed marriages and troubled children and financial problems as I have. I don't really find her all that superior.

Joan Crawford

❏

I don't hate Bette Davis even though the press wants me to. I resent her—I don't see how she built a career out of a set of mannerisms instead of real acting ability. Take away the pop-eyes, the cigarette and those funny clipped words and what have you got? She's phony, but I guess the public likes that.

Joan Crawford

❏

Look at Sterling Hayden. How dare he write a book attacking Hollywood! It was this industry that gave him the money and the fame which allowed him to buy that boat of his and raise his children. Now he attacks it, and I think it's shameful.

Joan Crawford

❏

On *Johnny Guitar* we had an actress (Mercedes McCambridge) who hadn't worked in 10 years, an excellent actress but a rabble-rouser. She was perfectly cast in the picture, but she played her part offstage as well. Her delight was to create friction. "Did you hear what *he* said about *you?*" she'd tell me. "And in front of a group of people!" I couldn't believe it. I thought I'd known that actor so well. The picture became a nightmare. She would finish a scene, walk to the phone on the set and call one of the columnists to report my "incivilities." I was as civil as I knew how to be.

Joan Crawford

❏

Working with Bette Davis was one of the greatest challenges I've ever had. I meant that kindly. Bette is of a different temperament than I. She has to yell every morning. I just sat and knitted. I knitted a scarf from Hollywood to Malibu.

Joan Crawford

❏

I truly felt sorry for Miriam Hopkins. She was such a capable actress. It could have been a pleasure to work with her. She made it an ordeal by her tricks and mistrust of everybody. It was sad to see her ruining her career. Finally no one would work with her.

Bette Davis

❏

Joan Crawford—I wouldn't sit on her toilet!

Bette Davis

❏

Miriam Hopkins and I acted together in *The Old Maid* and *Old Acquaintance*. We were always old something-or-others—everything except old friends.

Bette Davis

❏

Miriam Hopkins? She was a swine!

Bette Davis

Miriam Hopkins was an impossible woman, completely self-destructive. It was sad, really, because she was talented. On the set of *Old Acquaintance*, when she tried to upstage me by wandering around the set not listening to my character's big speech of reproval, I stopped the action and said to her: "By God, Miriam, if I have to get on top of the piano, you're going to look me in the eye!" The rafters were filled with spectators from all over the lot. They were hoping to see me slap her. It was in the script and I must admit I was pleased by the prospect.

Bette Davis

Tallulah wasn't madly in love with me. We met at a Warners party where she said, "You've played all the parts I've played on the stage, and I was so much better." And I said, "Miss Bankhead, I agree with you." She did a radio show for years on which she used to take me to the cleaners all the time, but, well, she wasn't terribly good on the screen, which I think was a big disappointment to her.

Bette Davis

The best time I ever had with Joan Crawford was when I pushed her down the stairs in *What Ever Happened to Baby Jane?*

Bette Davis

The bitch (Joan Crawford) is loaded half the time (on *What Ever Happened to Baby Jane?*)! How dare she pull this crap on a picture with me? I'll kill her! . . . And those falsies! Christ! You never know what size boobs that broad has strapped on! She must have a different set for each day of the week! I keep running into them like the Hollywood Hills! What does she think she's doing, for Christ's sake? She's supposed to be shriveling away while Baby Jane starves her to death, but her tits keep growing!

Bette Davis

Bette Davis
Falsies' growth galled

❏

The first day we began shooting *The Old Maid*, Miriam Hopkins swept in wearing *an exact replica* of the gown I had worn in my award-winning picture *Jezebel*, in the same role she had played on the stage. It was a grand entrance to end all grand entrances—weeks of planning had obviously gone into it —and it undoubtedly was calculated to make me blow my top. As fate would have it, the entire sequence was cut out of the film. After that, nearly everything she did seemed to be designed to throw me off stride. If I had a long, difficult speech, she'd break in with, "Oh, I'm so sorry. One of my buttons came unbuttoned." In one instance this tactic forced me to make 20 takes of a single scene.

Bette Davis

❏

What annoys me most? Unused fireplaces, pink sweet peas, badly made beds—and Miriam Hopkins.

Bette Davis

❏

119

A feud between June Allyson and me? Of course, although not as far as I was concerned, really. We're very good friends now. Our difficulties started in 1943 when we did the movie version of *Best Foot Forward*. This was the show that brought June to Hollywood, along with all the other young people who had been in the original cast, with one exception. Victoria Schools, who had a featured role and whom everybody in the cast adored, killed herself just before they came West. Naturally, they *all* arrived with a hate for whoever took over her role. Enter Gloria De Haven. I was from Hollywood, too, which didn't help matters. Then they took out June's big number with Kenny Bowers, "What Do You Think I Am, Just a Baby?", and replaced it with the new "Wish I May, Wish I Might," which June and I sang. The following year they gave *me* "What Do You Think I Am?" to sing in *Broadway Rhythm*—with Kenny Bowers, yet! That did it. She was out to get me. Dick Powell, whom she was going with at the time, finally smoothed it over between us.

Gloria De Haven

The year of *Hold Back the Dawn* I was up against my sister Joan Fontaine for the Oscar—she for *Suspicion*, a part much more difficult than mine. Joan deserved to win and did. But Joan is 15 months younger than I and I knew I would lose prestige with her if I lost—I had always been a heroine in her eyes—and I did!—I lost. The goddess had feet of clay—and she let me know it, too!

Olivia de Havilland

Loretta Young was and is the only actress I really dislike. She was sickeningly sweet, a pure phony. Her two faces sent me home angry and crying several times.

Virginia Field

Everyone wants to know about the feud between my sister, Olivia de Havilland, and myself, and why shouldn't I admit that I haven't been able to forgive her for not inviting me to our mother's memorial service . . . and for other cruelties. I married first, won the Oscar before Olivia did and if I die first she'll undoubtedly be livid because I beat her to it.

Joan Fontaine

Olivia de Havilland
Lost face with sister

Joan Fontaine
Won't forgive sibling

121

❏

Olivia (de Havilland) was up for the Oscar for *Hold Back the Dawn*, and I was up for *Suspicion*. When my name was called, I thought she was going to pull out my hair.

Joan Fontaine

❏

Was our sisterly rivalry a beauty competition? Not at the age of four when all girls are beautiful. I wish I *had* a sister. I've just always been the intruder in her life, the interloper. As my older sibling (by 15 months) Olivia (de Havilland) could have looked after me. *Au contraire*, her desire my whole life has been to get me off-balance. We've not spoken since Mother's death in 1974, and that's it, kid. Never again.

Joan Fontaine

❏

Producer Milton Bren took me to a sound stage where Miss Bennett was holding court. "Connie," he said, "I want you to meet Sheilah Graham." Miss Bennett measured me with a slow, insolent glance, then drawled in a voice that carried to every corner of the huge set, "It's hard to believe that a girl as pretty as you can be the biggest bitch in Hollywood." There was a hush. I heard myself say clearly, "Not the biggest, Connie. The second biggest."

Sheilah Graham

❏

There is not enough money in Hollywood to lure me into making another picture with Joan Crawford. And I like money.

Sterling Hayden

❏

My "feud" with Bette Davis? It wasn't a real feud. The studio thought it would be good publicity. They even sent out pictures of us in boxing gloves. But it was Bette's studio and I think I fared badly. It made me look downright rude and intolerable. Finally I was keyed up, there was real tension on the set and everybody pointed at me as the villain.

Miriam Hopkins

I was on the set the day Mae West and Alison Skipworth were ready to play a scene. Skippy was edgy. She knew beforehand that Mae was going to steal it. When she could stand it no longer she turned to Mae haughtily and said, "I'll have you know I'm an actress!" "It's all right," Mae said. "I'll keep your secret."

Hedda Hopper

I tell you the truth. I wouldn't even stand next to her (Susan Saint James) at a cocktail party!

Rock Hudson

So Proudly We Hail was an interesting film to make for many reasons. One had to do with the pre-production theories many people held about how Paulette Goddard, Claudette Colbert and I would function together. I got along famously with Paulette and Claudette. But they didn't get along with each other. There was one incident about which I always laugh. It concerned an interview with Paulette Goddard. She was asked whom she liked best—Claudette or Veronica. "Veronica, I think. After all, we are closer in age," she said. Claudette read the interview and flipped. She was at Paulette's eyes every minute, and Paulette fought back with equal vengeance. I smiled.

Veronica Lake

Ray Milland didn't want to make *Golden Earrings*. He didn't like Marlene Dietrich; he thought he was too young to do it, so he was a real bastard at first. He calmed down a little by the end, but he and Marlene fought the whole time. When we were shooting the scene where he first meets "Gypsy" Marlene as she's eating the stew, over and over she would stick a fish head into her mouth, suck the eye out and then pull out the rest of the head. Then, after I yelled cut, she would stick her finger down her throat to make herself throw it up. This whole performance made Ray violently ill.

Mitchell Leisen

Miriam Hopkins
Called film's villain

Veronica Lake
Fun for one

124

Joan Crawford had wanted Claire Trevor for my part in *Johnny Guitar*. Everything was all right until an exterior scene shot on location in Arizona. I had a four-page monologue, and, because of my (stage and radio) background, I knew all the lines. We shot it in one take and the crew, realizing they'd get home early, applauded. Joan was in her trailer and heard the applause—and that started it. Wow! It sounds as though I'd done something great. I hadn't—any girl in my speech class at college could have done it. But it made Joan mad—and *she* was the star of the picture. I guess if I were Joan Crawford I'd be mad if some Mamie Glutz horned in on my territory that way.

Mercedes McCambridge

Poor old rotten egg Joan (Crawford). I kept my mouth shut about her for nearly a quarter of a century, but she was a mean, tipsy, powerful, rotten-egg lady. I'm still not going to tell what she did to me. Other people have written some of it, but they don't know it all, and they never will because I am a very nice person and I don't like to talk about the dead even if they were rotten eggs.

Mercedes McCambridge

There seems to be a fable that *Naughty Marietta* started out as mostly Jeanette MacDonald, that it picked up more and more Nelson Eddy as it went along, and that his becoming famous in it was something I didn't anticipate or want. And that there has been "bad blood" between us ever since. A nice, preposterous little tale! From the beginning, Nelson had a very fine part. It was the male lead in a romantic story. As the picture whipped into shape and really began to look like something, they decided to retake Nelson's whole first sequence. They wanted to put in another song and impress audiences immediately with his fine voice. They had wanted me to sing "Neath the Southern Moon" in my balcony sequence. I liked the song, but I didn't think it was suited to my voice. I did think it was suited to Nelson's. I said so. They were looking frantically for a song for him. They took my suggestion about "Southern Moon." And it was one of the best things he sang in the picture. We got along very smoothly—immediately. On the third day Nelson came to me with a sort of sheepish grin and said, "I was all prepared not to like you. I heard you were pretty tough to work with—you'd try to crowd me out of every scene. I want to apologize. I know you've been throwing scenes my way."

Jeanette MacDonald

Jeanette MacDonald
"Bad blood" denied

❏

Debra Winger and I got along (on *Terms of Endearment*). We just had different approaches to working. This is the only picture I've done with her, but she apparently *becomes* her character—every time. Before the set call and after. It was difficult, but we got along. Look, Debra is 21 years younger than I am. She has very different interests and different ways of looking at life. Just because you work intimately with someone for three or four months on a film doesn't mean there's any breeding ground for friendship. I don't think there was much of one. She loved to sit in her trailer in her combat boots and miniskirt, listening to real loud rock 'n' roll. Right there, I mean, what am I going to do that for?

Shirley MacLaine

❏

A tabloid printed an article quoting me saying I keep in shape but the other old MGM stars like Esther Williams and Kathryn Grayson were falling apart. Katie Grayson is my best friend, so I called her in tears, saying I never gave any such interview. They just made it all up. She said she understood, but Esther wrote me the most vitriolic letter I have ever received from any human being, threatening to pull every hair out of my head and using words no truck driver ever heard of!

Ann Miller

❏

Ginger (Rogers) drove Fred (Astaire) crazy with her dresses. There was the molting one with all the feathers in *Top Hat*. And for the "Let's Face the Music and Dance" number in *Follow the Fleet*, she wore a beaded gown that must've weighed 50 pounds! And when she turned around one time, her long beaded sleeve knocked Fred clear across the room!

Hermes Pan

❏

It happened on *The Big Country* in 1958 when I wanted to do a scene over because I had delivered my lines badly. Director William Wyler refused to have a retake, so I walked off the set. When I returned he wanted me to apologize in front of the crew, but I wouldn't. We finished the film without saying a single word to each other. We kept the feud going even though our wives tried to patch it up. Finally the opportunity came for a reconciliation when he won the Oscar in 1960 for *Ben-Hur* and I was Academy president. As Wyler walked off stage with his Oscar, I stuck out my hand and said, "Congratulations, you really deserved it." He replied, "Thanks, but I still won't re-shoot that scene."

Gregory Peck

❏

Liz Taylor should be grateful to me—my jokes are one of the reasons she went on a diet. It was embarrassing. When I took her to Sea World and Shamu the Whale jumped out of the water, she asked if it came with vegetables.

Joan Rivers

❏

Did Fred Astaire and I ever quarrel? Even married people have differences of opinion, I'm told. Studio publicity men were always trying to make it look like we fought, just to keep our names in the papers. There actually were a few disagreements—like the time I insisted on wearing a feather-trimmed gown when we did "Cheek to Cheek" in *Top Hat*. He complained that the feathers kept getting in his mouth and up his nose, but it was the most beautiful dress I'd ever worn and I knew it was right. It proved to be a trademark for us. Years later he even gave me a gold feather for my charm bracelet.

Ginger Rogers

❏

I didn't direct *Old Acquaintance*, I refereed. Edmund Goulding, who had directed Bette Davis and Miriam Hopkins in *The Old Maid*, was originally supposed to do it, but he had a heart attack—perhaps at the thought of working with Davis and Hopkins again. As we got into the shooting, Hopkins began to do little things that drove Davis up the wall. Me, too. For instance, she decided to use a long cigarette holder and took to holding it in front of Davis' face. Another thing: as Davis got older in the story, Hopkins got younger. Davis complained that she'd done the same thing in *Old Maid*. Hopkins complained that we were all showing Davis favoritism because Warners was her home lot. When it came time for the scene in which Davis was to shake Hopkins, Hopkins just let her head go limp, and it wobbled unnaturally. Davis was furious. I told Hopkins that it looked funny, and we did it again. This time we got it.

Vincent Sherman

❏

That horrible blonde woman (Joan Rivers)? I couldn't be bothered paying any attention to anything she says about me.

Elizabeth Taylor

❏

I can't deny that Shirley MacLaine and I fought on *Terms of Endearment*. We're not having lunch today. We challenged ourselves, and when we got tired of challenging ourselves, we challenged each other. But I think there was always a respect between the two of us.

Debra Winger

Friendship

Susan (Hayward) is not easy to know or make friends with because of her shyness and reserve in meeting people. Unlike most actors and actresses who call people by their first names on first meeting and "Darling" on the next, she is slow to establish a chum-chum basis and even more cautious in friendship. But after she has accepted someone as a friend, he or she is a friend for life. Her caution has sometimes been misinterpreted as aloofness, but people have found her friendship is worth working for.

Jess Barker

❏

Bob Hope was a loner ... in a crowd. He was a gregarious man. He had a million acquaintances, but I doubt if he had one real friend.

Eddie Bracken

❏

There was never much of a camaraderie among the women stars at MGM. I imagine that was because of envies real or imagined. There were often petty little scenes which I could not understand. I remember when I was in *East Side, West Side* the star was Barbara Stanwyck. I had only one scene with her, but I'll never forget it. Barbara never even looked at me through the scene. Even when we were off camera, she ignored me. I am convinced her aim was to make things as difficult for me as she could. She succeeded. I was shy and inexperienced, so that was quite a blow.

Cyd Charisse

❏

The bad thing about being with an actor is that the role he's in stays with him all the time. The good thing about being with an actor—well, I can't think of any good thing.

Sally Field

❏

Actress-friends? Do Merrill and Lynch lunch with Shearson and Hamill? I once told Celeste Holm, "You're so lucky not to be a big Hollywood star, bound to a contract." Celeste is cool to me to this day.

Joan Fontaine

❏

I once said to Spencer Tracy, who was a great friend, "I wish I'd made just one film like *Inherit the Wind*." And you know what he said? "Jim (Granger's real first name), I'd love to have done *Scaramouche*."

Stewart Granger

❏

The picture's the most important thing. Someone once said to me, "Isn't friendship more important?" and I said, "No. The friendship is gravy. We didn't go in here to improve our friendship. We didn't both sign the contract to work on our relationship. We signed the contract to make as good a movie as we could."

Dustin Hoffman

❏

Bing Crosby and I weren't the types to go around kissing each other. We always had a light jab for each other; the public expected that. One of our stock lines used to be: "There's nothing I wouldn't do for Bing, and there's nothing he wouldn't do for me. And that's the way we go through life—doing nothing for each other."

Bob Hope

❏

I'm a controversial figure. My friends either dislike me or hate me.

Oscar Levant

❏

Bogie and I were good friends, and he gave me some good advice. He said, "Whatever it is, be against it." I told him, "I've got a lot of scars already from being an againster." He said, "You've got a lot of scars, but you're still alive."

Robert Mitchum

❏

Sometimes I think the only people who stay with me and really listen are people I hire. Why can't I have friends who want nothing from me?

Marilyn Monroe

Doing a picture with Garbo does not constitute an introduction.

Robert Montgomery

We (MGM) actors then were a warm brotherhood. At the end of a day we'd gather in Clark Gable's dressing room, or Lionel Barrymore's or Bob Taylor's and have a drink or two or three and discuss the pleasures or pains of whatever we were filming. Remembering those times makes me feel that Hollywood now is somewhat lonely—and a little sad. The camaraderie is gone—and, I think, missed.

Walter Pidgeon

It's difficult to live with people in this business. You never know what they'll be next. Say you have a swashbuckling type of friend, who overnight is cast in a grave, pensive role. Chances are, the next time you meet him he'll be grave and pensive, too.

Tyrone Power

When we co-starred in *Becket*, I wanted Larry (Olivier) to be my buddy. I wanted to include him in everything. I wanted us to be a team. But he didn't want to know. He just wasn't interested. I tell you I felt like a schoolboy with a crush on his teacher. I loved and was not loved. I was terribly hurt.

Anthony Quinn

Every film is like an ocean voyage, a trans-Atlantic crossing. You swear you will meet each other again, but you never do.

George Sanders

An actor's life ... No place to put down roots, always traveling, no end in sight. I travel with two bags. I need only a dark suit and a light suit. When I need a shirt, I buy one. I read paperback books, then throw them away. I can rent a phonograph for two dollars a week, borrow records from friends. The only thing I like to take with me is friends. Friends cannot be rented or bought.

Maximilian Schell

I'm going to play this little Indian kid in Rudyard Kipling's *Kim* and Errol Flynn is going to play the other guy. I come onto the sound stage with my mother and the studio teacher, the perfect Norman Rockwell portrait of middle America—63 years old, sweet, giving, a long-suffering spinster. Flynn came up to me and somebody said, "This is Dean Stockwell." He stuck out his hand and said, "Hi. Have you had your first fuck yet?" I'm just looking at this guy, thinking, I finally found a friend, a father.

Dean Stockwell

Fun

It's the good girls who keep diaries. The bad girls never have the time.

Tallulah Bankhead

Most conversation in Hollywood has a boring sameness. It's all shoptalk. Nobody talks about anything but the movie business. After working in it all day, it bores me still to go to a dinner party and hear nothing but talk about the recent movies.

Anne Baxter

I don't have a very active social life, because most of the parties (in Hollywood) are so boring. I remember when I came here in the 1950s they were wonderful. Everybody was dressed up, having fun and cracking jokes. There were roomfuls of stars. Gary Cooper, William Holden, Cary Grant, Susan Hayward. Now they can't even get stars to go to the Oscars and the Emmies.

Joan Collins

❏

I travel light—and I travel alone! And I will not take a trans-Atlantic phone call! Romance gets rusty on long distance. The only thing I like to hear a man say on the telephone is—"I'll be there in five minutes"!

Paulette Goddard

❏

My life has been backwards. When I was in my 20s—I call those the dark ages—I didn't go out. I didn't have any fun, I studied my tail off trying to learn what this thing is they call acting. Now, past 50, I'm out to have fun.

Rock Hudson

❏

The Jean Negulescos had everybody dress up and come to their house. It was a cross section of Hollywood society, and I could hardly bear it. I never saw so many people I destested in one room. I had hardly sat down behind the woodbox before Virginia Zanuck (wife of Darryl), whom I don't dislike, came over and complained that someone had poured a martini on her foot. For one of those mysterious reasons that nobody will ever be able to understand, other things got poured on her all evening. Just seemed to be hexed. The minute somebody got really tight they either threw their drinks on her or put out their cigarettes on her back. She began to look like an old spittoon.

Nunnally Johnson

❏

I've never been very good at being a member of any group—more than a group of two, that is.

Marilyn Monroe

❏

Tyrone Power
Never knew what next

Rock Hudson
Out for good time

134

I know a doctor in Los Angeles who's a better dancer than Fred Astaire ever was. There are many men who never danced professionally who are superb ballroom dancers. Fred was never much better than an average dancer at parties. He always felt a little awkward at parties when we danced together. I'm not taking anything away from him, though. He's a great dancer. He was able to do what so many professional dancers cannot do—be perfect in front of a camera time after time after time.

Ginger Rogers

❑

At the completion party for *The Women* at the Trocadero, I was dancing with George Cukor when Ernst Lubitsch fox-trotted by and said to me, "If you want more close-ups in the picture, never mind dancing with your director, you'd better dance with Norma Shearer!" (She was recently widowed from Irving Thalberg, MGM's production head.) So then Norma and I did a turn on the floor.

Rosalind Russell

❑

No Hollywood house was ever worth visiting unless you made a point of leaving your hat and coat at home. Then, one quick look around the room told you precisely how boring the party was likely to be; if you had a hat and coat you had to stay to the end to collect them, but I soon learned that without them you could make your way swiftly upstairs and escape through the bathroom window in no time at all. I got to know a lot of bathrooms like that; the best was undoubtedly Greer Garson's. It was all done in pink marble, and had a huge glass wall which opened onto a private garden. It was the biggest production for the smallest audience that Hollywood ever achieved.

George Sanders

❑

If you stay away from parties, you're called a snob. If you go, you're an exhibitionist. If you don't talk, you're dumb. If you do talk, you're quarrelsome. Pardon me while I change my nail polish.

Lana Turner

❑

Ginger Rogers
Rates famed partner

Rosalind Russell
And the merry widow

Visiting his first Hollywood sound stage:
This is the biggest electric train set any boy ever had.

Orson Welles

❑

I don't do the Hollywood party scene anymore. You *can't* come home and say to the kid, "Hi, here's a little switch: Daddy's going to throw up on *you!*"

Robin Williams

Gaffes

Career and parties were great, but my husband Dick Powell and I wanted a baby ... The name of the picture was *Royal Wedding*. I had just started to rehearse with my idol, Fred Astaire, and it felt so good gliding over the floor with his masterful touch guiding me. And suddenly I didn't know what was happening—I felt faint. I went directly to my doctor. And from his office I called Fred Astaire excitedly and said, "Fred, I want you to be the first to know—I'm pregnant." There was a stunned silence. Then a horrified voice said, "Who *is* this?"

June Allyson

❑

My most embarrassing moment? I tried to get a job in summer stock and had only one minor play to my credit. The stage director who interviewed me asked me what I'd done. I rattled off the titles of a dozen Broadway plays, including *They Shall Not Die*. He seemed interested and asked me what role I played in it. I mentioned a part and he grew even more interested. "It's funny," he said, "that I never met you. I played that part myself."

Dane Clark

❑

Apparently Joan Crawford can't forget an innocent remark I made at my first Hollywood party. Back in 1947 I was a teenager looking forward to meeting movie stars, and Joan Crawford was my favorite. Like all young kids will, I put my foot in my mouth. At the party I said, "I'm glad to meet you, Miss Crawford. You've always been a great favorite of mine—and my mother's, too." I didn't mean to say she was older than Methuselah, but there was such an embarrassing silence I wanted to die. Since then she's been needling me in print and at parties.

                                                            Arlene Dahl

It was funny, before we started shooting *Police Woman* someone said, "Have you ever played sleuths before?" And I said, "Oh, many times." What I thought he meant was sluts!

                                                        Angie Dickinson

I always felt sorry for poor Herbert Marshall because of his wooden leg. Of course we never mentioned it. One day during the ship scene in *Ivy* he tripped, and I could see that he was uncomfortable. Afterwards, we sat chatting when I spied the columnist Sheilah Graham heading our way. I said, "Oh, Bart, watch out for her. She'll talk your leg off."

                                                          Joan Fontaine

I sat in on the screen test Alan Ladd made for *This Gun for Hire*. Sue Carol, who was Ladd's agent (she later married him), was there, too, of course. I came out of the rushes and, not knowing Sue was romantically involved with Ladd, announced, "He *stinks!*" Sue Carol didn't care—she was too big a person—and later I came to appreciate Ladd; he was an "acquired taste."

                                                         Susanna Foster

Garbo doesn't like me. I don't much blame her. I pulled an awful corny gag when we were introduced. I said, "Pardon me, I didn't catch the name."

                                                          Oscar Levant

I once got an invitation from the American Film Institute when they voted on the best films of all time. My *All About Eve* was in the top 10. And I got a mimeographed letter inviting me to buy a ticket for $350 and come and mingle with the men who had made those films. I had *made* one of them!

Joseph L. Mankiewicz

❏

As grim headlines daily forewarned World War II, the following item appeared in a Hollywood column on April 7, 1939:

The deadly dullness of the last week was lifted today when Darryl Zanuck announced he had bought all rights to Maurice Maeterlinck's *The Blue Bird* for Shirley Temple.

Louella Parsons

❏

I remember a dirty stunt Humphrey Bogart pulled one day. He told me the studio had bought a new property and that I was a natural for the lead and that I should go to Jack Warner if necessary to get the part. I began spreading the word that I was perfect for the lead and wanted the part until somebody explained to me just who Fanny Hill was.

Ann Sheridan

❏

Director Gregory Ratoff's thick Transylvanian-Gypsy accent added to the delirium on *Footlight Serenade*. And Betty Grable, a real scamp, helped him along. Ratoff explained: "You arrr chorruss girrl and he (Victor Mature) ees big star from price (prize) fighting, but now in show. You want to make heem think he's terrific. You want to play up to heem. You want to suck heem." (I guess he meant suck up to him.) The set rattled with belly laughs, work suspended for five minutes. Ratoff, bewildered: "What did I sayed?" In subsequent scenes, before the camera rolled, Betty leaned toward Mature's belt and asked: "I do it now?"

Phil Silvers

❏

I was doing those sailor-suit movies at MGM. Then our boss, Louis B. Mayer, fell off his horse and was put in a cast up to his chin. On the set one morning I wise-cracked, "I heard Mayer fell off Ginny Simms (the singer he was then dating)." Someone reported this to Mayer, who hollered and screamed at

me, and before long I was fired. In a while I was doing important dramatic
movies and won an Academy Award. But if it wasn't for that wisecrack on the
set one day I might still be wearing a sailor suit.

Frank Sinatra

Glamour

They thought of us glamour girls as they used to think of color photography.
When the story was weak, they shot it in color as a cover-up. If the feminine
lead was a weak role, they cast a glamour girl in it. But if you tried to find
the girl's part on paper, it wasn't there. Actresses rise or fall with the parts
they play, so no glamour girl could ever be an actress. Think. Did you ever
hear of an Oscar being given to an actress in a bad role?

Marlene Dietrich

❏

Anyone will tell you that I'm the easiest person to get along with on the set.
What my fellow players and members of the unit don't know is that I've
thrashed it all out beforehand. Mine is the calm *after* the storm. Two weeks
before I'm scheduled to begin a picture I go into conference with my producer and director—and a terrific battle invariably ensues. However, by the
time shooting commences, it's all over. Everything is nice and peaceful—
and that's why people say: "That nice Irene Dunne. She isn't glamorous—
but she's so pleasant."

Irene Dunne

❏

Can't figure why I'm still around. I've never been glamorous. I remember
my publicity man at Paramount would run up to me every morning and say,
"What did you do last night?" And I'd tell him, "Well, you know, in back of
the sink, the plaster came out. And I had to fix it." He'd look at me and say,
"That's all you did?" The poor guy. All the lucky publicity guys had actors
who went to the Mocambo, got drunk and got into fights.

Fred MacMurray

❏

While I was at MGM they were doing *The Wizard of Oz*, and Mervyn LeRoy (the producer) had a sudden thought that there I was, and we began to test to make a glamorous witch instead of an ugly witch. We actually did the costumes—a high, pointed hat, but of sequins, a very glamorous sequined gown. She was to be the most glamorous but wicked sort of witch. And we got into testing for it, and it was absolutely gorgeous. And then, I suppose Mervyn got to remembering that this was a classic by now, and the children who read it, and grown-ups, too, were going to say, "That isn't the way it was written!" And everybody agreed that you could not do that to *The Wizard of Oz*. And Mervyn said to me, "I don't want you to be an ugly witch." So we dropped the whole thing, and of course Margaret Hamilton played the role, and it's a classic.

Gale Sondergaard

❏

Making movies is like ditch-digging. It's going to work at General Motors. There's no glamour. You must get up at five, six o'clock in the morning, stumble over the set, slap a little make-up on, try to wake up, and then you're digging a ditch all day long. You might sit around, waiting to do a shot that takes only a minute, but that minute shot can entail crackling nerves for six or eight hours. It's a very physical job.

Richard Widmark

Gossip

There's money in gossip. It's a multi-million-dollar industrial complex, and in Hollywood (New York, too) if you don't kowtow, if you don't call up every time you get an attack of gas and say, "This is what I feel and this how I feel about it," and when you don't describe the most intimate details of your life, and when you presume to keep some vestige of self-respect and independence, you are considered an enemy of the people by Hollywood columnists and people like Dorothy Kilgallen.

Marlon Brando

❏

It isn't what they say about you—it's what they whisper about you.

Errol Flynn

Fred MacMurray
Plastered in Tinsel Town

Marlon Brando
Enemy of columnists

Richard Widmark
Movies like ditch-digging

It's amazing, really, how small-town Hollywood is. If you live in a big city, you have a private life. In fact, you rarely know who your neighbors are, much less anything about them. In Hollywood, as in Denison, Iowa, things are different. Everyone knows everyone else's business. We knew it by word-of-mouth back home, we know it through the gossip columns here. Almost before a girl leaves her doctor's office, you know she's going to have a baby—and when. You know how much your co-workers earn. And greatest similarity of all, let a man be seen with the same girl twice, and tongues start wagging. Immediately speculation starts as to whether they're engaged.

Donna Reed

If I had as many affairs as they say, I would now be speaking to you from inside a jar at the Harvard Medical School.

Frank Sinatra

They have called me a scarlet woman for so long I'm almost purple.

Elizabeth Taylor

Happiness

My recipe for happiness? Good health and a bad memory.

Ingrid Bergman

❑

The only really happy people are married women and single men.

Marlene Dietrich

❑

Happiness, what is it? I have never known it.

Greta Garbo

❑

When you become a star, people are no longer honest with you; they're not themselves with you. Nobody criticizes you to your face, but you know they do it behind your back. Even the people you knew before the change. That's the process when you go from unknown to known. You can tell a kid till doomsday, "Listen, you won't find happiness through stardom," and he won't believe you.

Evelyn Keyes

Hate

I'm one of life's great self-haters. I figure you've got to hate yourself if you've got any integrity at all.

Woody Allen

❑

I exist on hate. I hate everything that is wrong with the world. I eat six meals a day and never worry about my weight. Hate burns off calories.

Robert Blake

❏

I loathe every picture with a special effect in it, including *E.T.* Plant-eating pictures! I write pictures where *people* eat plants.

Julius J. Epstein

❏

I was never happier than when I lived in a hall bedroom and spent 50 cents a day for my food. That was when I was a barker at the Old Mill at Coney Island. I learned a lot in those days, much of which has served me since. There is only one thing it spoiled me for—hot dogs. I ate so many that I avoid them now as if they had rabies.

Cary Grant

❏

If I hear one more chorus of "Singin' in the Rain," I'll scream. We did that number on the MGM lot and I've had a head cold ever since.

Gene Kelly

❏

At a Masquers dinner for W.C. Fields:
    Gentlemen, I claim that any man who hates babies and dogs can't be all bad.

Leo Rosten

Health

A girl I was seeing and I were dress extras in one of Carole Lombard's pictures at Paramount in the late '30s. On this one day the girl had a bad cold. Carole said, "I can get rid of it for you. Do you drink?" The girl said no. Carole said, "You'll drink tonight. Pick up a pint of whiskey on your way home, get in a hot tub, then drink your whiskey, get into bed and cover yourself with a hot Jew. Your cold will be gone in the morning."

Larry Carr

❏

During my teenage years I fell victim to bulimia—eating binges followed by self-enforced vomiting—and also became dependent on Dexedrine and diaretics to help keep my weight down.

Jane Fonda

❏

I'm moody, non-verbal and shy. Socially, I'm gauche. I can't remember names. And I don't take care of myself, in terms of health. I smoke too much, two packs a day; don't get enough sleep and have bad eating habits.

Jessica Lange

❏

I went on an MGM junket to Africa once and Jeanette MacDonald had her own bottled water sent from Montana, and her own sheets, and she even slept in a certain direction facing the moon every night. I said right then and there I never wanted to be like that, but I do take care of myself. Vitamins, exercise, no booze or cigarettes, everything in moderation. I live a healthy life.

Jane Powell

Hollywood

I thought my new picture was pretty good until I got a wire from someone in Hollywood saying it was excellent. That's a very weak word for Hollywood where everything is spoken of in superlatives. Since it is only called "wonderful," I'm worried.

Fred Allen

❏

Hollywood—that flatulent cave of the winds.

John Barrymore

❏

There is one word which best describes Hollywood. It is "nervous."

Frank Capra

❏

In 1940, I had my choice between Hitler and Hollywood, and I preferred Hollywood. Just a little.

René Clair

❏

I took my road test in Los Angeles, and I almost crashed into a parked car. But I still passed with a high enough score to be an instructor. That tells you something about Hollywood.

Jon Cryer

❏

Hollywood was fabulous. One thousand and one nights, and then some. Everything you ever believed glamour was. People used to go to my movies to watch what I wore, not what I took off.

Arlene Dahl

❏

I drove in there (the Universal Pictures lot) not long ago and a policeman shouted, "By what right are you driving around back here?" "By helping to pay for half these sound stages, sir," I roared back.

Yvonne De Carlo

❏

I may have to fall back on this jumbo violin (cello). Nothing's certain in Hollywood, nothing except brawls at the nightclubs and tourists.

William Demarest

❑

It's tough out there. I used a phrase once and it got coined to my credit and it's true. It's very simple: "They've taken no prisoners here in Hollywood." They take no fucking prisoners, let me tell you. And that's what it's all about. That's the business. They don't give a shit. Everybody has had "no" said to them 100 times and it'll be said 100 times again. You're not attractive enough, you're not this, you're not that.

Bruce Dern

❑

In Hollywood, I moved into an apartment owned by Errol Flynn. It was close to the studio, but the furniture was padlocked to the walls. "Strange place," I thought. I was told it was necessary. Hungry actors had been known to eat furniture, sell or hock it.

Jeff Donnell

❑

It's hard to tell where Hollywood ends and the DTs begin.

W.C. Fields

❑

I was in a rut in Hollywood. I get addicted very easily to things I like, and I got addicted to the lazy lifestyle, and I wasn't doing anything. I wouldn't have died if I had stayed out there, but I might as well have been dead.

Eddie Fisher

❑

Hollywood is my biggest regret. I let money, fame and greed ruin my life. Hollywood is where I wasted the best years of my life.

Greta Garbo

❑

Hollywood is a strange place when you're in trouble. Everyone is afraid it's contagious.

Judy Garland

There is a world out here in Hollywood that is beyond my comprehension. I come from a place and time where your word is your bond. Now I find these people would rather lie than tell the truth.

James Garner

When I first went to Hollywood I made $250 a week and I had more fun than I did in my entire life. It's a whole different climate now. Segregated as hell. There are $500-a-week actors, and they hang out together. Then there are the $1,000 ones, the $2,000, the $5,000. And they all hang out with their own. It's so boring. It stinks.

Jackie Gleason

In Hollywood you have to take the bitter with the sour.

Samuel Goldwyn

Hollywood? It's always up Gower and down Fountain.

Edmund Goulding

I go back to Hollywood to pick up a dollar, but that's all. Everything is wrong with that city. It epitomizes all that's wrong with life.

Sterling Hayden

I made a lot of money for Paramount, and $9.5 million for myself, and ended up without a quarter. But the minute I got into trouble here, no one was around. In Hollywood, nobody wants to be around a loser. I never understood the way the town works, and I got on drugs and booze and was a mess. Thank God, I got all that straightened out. I now live in a condo in Newport, Rhode Island; I live very well, I've got friends and support and life is good. But I

Greta Garbo
Her biggest regret

Betty Hutton
Back from depths

150

start shaking when I come to Hollywood. It's not a place I should ever be around for very long. I can't wait to get out.

Betty Hutton

❑

Hollywood has a willful blindness to what makes movies good: a creative imagination that is let loose. Hollywood is full of people putting their fingers in the pie. They say, "Here's a wonderful script. Let's see how we can change it."

Richard Jordan

❑

Through the profession of acting I was catapulted to Hollywood, where I thought the war was over and everybody loved everybody. I found out nobody loves anybody, and the resentment against the Germans was so tremendous it made me absolutely speechless. I was put on ice and dragged out every time they needed a glamorous spy in a Darryl Zanuck movie. I went from a dictatorship to a dictatorship operetta.

Hildegard Knef

❑

Hollywood is a mimic. If you tell Hollywood that some hysterectomy kits are the rage, you'll have five films out within three months pertaining to that rage. It's not immoral, it's amoral.

Jerry Lewis

❑

If the scripts were as great as the sets, what a town Hollywood would be.

W. Somerset Maugham

❑

Hollywood is much more comfortable these days. The fascism is gone. In the old days, if you insulted someone, it would be Siberia. I disliked Hollywood enormously then, a terrible place to live, a snobbish society, rigidity at every studio. I felt like a kind of mongrel in that group. It was a very difficult place to be.

Burgess Meredith

❏

Hollywood—that's a place where the bride tossing the bouquet is just as likely to be the next one to get married as the girl who catches it.

Geraldine Page

❏

It's an actor's haven, Hollywood. It gives him security.

Claude Rains

❏

Hollywood is two things. It's a state of mind, and it's a particular location in Los Angeles. Hollywood as a location is pretty grim. I mean, there is really nothing there. And it's certainly nothing to write home about. Probably hasn't been since the early '20s. But as a state of mind it certainly does exist, even more strongly than as an actual location. It's the movie business, but the movie business is where you go. If you're making a Western in Colorado, then Colorado is Hollywood for that period of time. If you're in New York making *Mean Streets*, that's where it is. It's definitely a state of mind. As far as being decadent—there is a Babylon quality about it, but that's what it's supposed to be. It's the end of the rainbow, the melting pot, the edge of the continent.

Robert Redford

❏

What do they know about glamour in Hollywood? The whole town is run by get-rich-quick artists who have short memories. They've burned or lost so many old films they're now calling me for prints from my personal collection. I gave everything to Texas Christian University. I have the only complete, uncut version of *Roberta* in existence. Don't tell me about Hollywood!

Ginger Rogers

❏

Hollywood is the coldest town in the world. There is no "Southern hospitality" in Hollywood for the beginner, least of all for the contest winner, of all things! I'd be introduced to people and the next time they saw me they wouldn't recognize me and we'd have to be introduced all over again ... The people in Hollywood would rather not be friendly unless they can be friendly with people who can be of some advantage to them ... Even the young set, kids who, you would think, would care only for a good time and good-time people, even the kids look down their noses at you unless they think you can do something for them. They'd rather NOT have good times than have them with nonentities.

Ann Sheridan

When Clark Gable left MGM, the only one who said goodbye was the old guy at the gate. Gary Cooper, Cary Grant and Katharine Hepburn were all box office poison at different times. So it's not what you are in Hollywood —it's what people *think* you are.

Robert Stack

Ann Sheridan
Cold to Hollywood

In Hollywood, you judge people by the level at which they compromise.

Lionel Stander

❏

In Hollywood, the executives have Picassos and Chagalls on their walls and would kill to have lunch with Chuck Norris. That's why you have movies like *Howard the Duck*.

David Steinberg

❏

Secrets have always been harder to keep in Hollywood than youth and marriage.

Gloria Swanson

❏

When Kipling said, "Treat failure and success the same, they are both imposters," he couldn't have been living in Hollywood.

Lily Tomlin

❏

When I first went to Hollywood, my heart was seldom in my work. I was bewitched by the legitimate stage and regarded Hollywood as a bad joke. But perhaps my indifference to Hollywood wasn't *all* my fault. More than 30 low-budget "B" pictures in five years!

Claire Trevor

❏

I don't spend too much time in Hollywood. I'm afraid I might wind up as one of Hugh Hefner's bunnies.

Liv Ullmann

❏

In Hollywood, it doesn't really matter what they say about you. The only thing that matters is what you say about a guy's picture. You can seduce a man's wife here, attack his daughter and wipe your hands on his canary bird, but if you don't like his movie, you're dead.

Josef von Sternberg

Hollywood is the only place in the world where you can freeze to death under a rose bush.

Clifton Webb

I've been in Hollywood over 50 years. I have watched Tinsel Town vacillate between despair and fear.

Billy Wilder

Hollywood is a place where they shoot too many pictures and not enough actors.

Walter Winchell

I came to Hollywood when I was 19. In those days it wasn't so dangerous. Now it is. I was chased around the desk by a lot of agents, but dope didn't exist. So the worst that could happen was that someone would throw you down and have a go at you. I see some of these old, old men creaking around town, and I say to myself, "I wonder if he remembers chasing me down some stairs. . . ?"

Marie Windsor

In Hollywood, where careers depend on that sort of thing, I remember everybody told me I couldn't have a suntan because it meant you weren't working.

Michael York

Michael York
Suntans are out

Doris Day
Pickin's are slim

156

Homosexuality

I suffered a lot of guilt because I was gay. I nearly married because of it. (The 1940s–50s) was a time when people believed that if you wanted to change you could. It was like living under a microscope. There was gossip about everyone. I dated starlets—I'm sure they were confused by my attitude—and lived in fear of gossip-mongers like *Confidential* magazine. I was a very lonely actor.

Robert Arthur

❑

I got a job as assistant stage manager with a small English repertory company out in the sticks. All the men were gay. For ages, I never met an actor in the provinces who wasn't. Each rep company was a little gay society. Here I was—this big, tough, 20-year-old guy, six-feet-two and 180 pounds, just back from Korea and hard as nails—and I didn't know what gays did. I knew gays were strange in an amusing sort of feminine way. Even when someone finally told me what they did, I didn't believe it. When I talk about gays in the British theater at that time, I mean real "whoops, dearie" types. Looking back, it's very funny—when you think of doing *The Corn is Green*, with all those supposedly tough coal miners coming off stage with black faces and going, "Hello, dearie."

Michael Caine

❑

There aren't many men on the loose out here. You know what they say about Hollywood—they're either married, going through divorce or want to do your hair.

Doris Day

❑

A miserable newspaperwoman wrote something implying that Rock Hudson, Julie (Andrews) and I were a sexual threesome. She also implied that Rock and I had spent a lot of time together in San Francisco leather bars ... I walked up to Rock and repeated the story to him, and I loved his response: "How in the hell did she find out so quick?"

Blake Edwards

❏

Do gentlemen really prefer blondes? These days, gentlemen seem to prefer gentlemen!

Paulette Goddard

❏

They all repeat the rumors that I'm a tightwad and that I'm homosexual. Now I don't feel that either of those is an insult, but it's all nonsense. And it's only half-true. I am not gay, but I am tight with a dollar. And what's wrong with that? When I was married to Barbara Hutton, my valet gave an interview saying I was so cheap I kept the buttons when I threw away my shirts. Well, I did, but it seemed a sensible thing to do.

Cary Grant

❏

There's no way this story (that Marsha Mason left husband Neil Simon for her) could be true—and I have to believe that anyone who knows the three of us knows that. But I'm fearful about what others will think: the strangers, the college students I could be addressing next month. I can understand why someone might spread a vicious rumor like this about me. I'm divorced, and though I do have a boyfriend, I live alone, am outspoken politically and have been very involved with the equal rights movement. But Marsha? She's the most patriarchal woman in the world. We aren't even particularly close friends. The last time I saw her was at a public event last Christmas.

Joan Hackett

❏

They sent Oscar Wilde, that poor man, to Reading Jail for doing what all other actors today get knighted for.

Wilfrid Hyde-White

❏

I really have no desire to go into a discourse on why heterosexual people should buddy around with homosexual people. I simply do and enjoy every gay minute of it. My "Nellie" friends have crowned me unofficial champion of the pool table, a little skill I learned in Texas. I'm really not very proficient with a cue stick, but they've been kind enough to honor me with this title. There was a time long ago when a homosexual revolted me. So did a lot of other types of human beings. I've changed. Don't hurt me, allow me a mis-cue now and then and I'll accept you. Who the hell am I not to accept anybody?

Veronica Lake

It was only after we'd been married about two years that I learned of (Charles Laughton's) homosexuality. One night the police came around and said they were holding a boy who claimed Charles owed him some money. It was then that he broke down and confessed his homosexuality. He cried and admitted he picked up boys from time to time. I told him it was perfectly all right, that I understood, that it didn't matter. But of course it did—particularly his deception. If he had only told me *before* our marriage.

Elsa Lanchester

Meeting a man in Hollywood is like looking for a needle in a haystack. But who wants to go out on their own? I don't and so, whenever I can't get a date, I go out with a gay instead. There's no pressure to have sex and gay men are good company—talkative and fun.

Virginia Mayo

We lived in fear of an exposé, or even one small remark, a veiled suggestion that someone was homosexual. Such a remark would have caused an earth-quake at the studio. Every month, when *Confidential* came out, our stomachs began to turn. Which of us would be in it? The amazing thing is that Rock (Hudson), as big as he became, was never nailed. It made one speculate that Rock had an angel on his shoulder, or that he'd made a pact with the devil, because he seemed under supernatural protection.

George Nader

Cheetah, that bastard (chimp in the Tarzan films), bit me whenever he could. The apes were all homosexuals, eager to wrap their paws around Johnny Weissmuller's thighs. They were jealous of me, and I loathed them.

Maureen O'Sullivan

❏

I've heard the rumors that Eddie Fisher says I'm anti-Semitic and gay. I was married for seven years to a Jew, Harry Karl. As for being gay, I have never been gay nor have I ever had a gay relationship. Regarding rumors linking me with the late Agnes Moorehead . . . For seven years I never made love to Harry Karl. I didn't know he had girlfriends in the afternoon. So when he came home he was too tired for Debbie. When the kids would go to sleep, I had nothing to do in the 10,000-square-foot mansion we occupied in Beverly Hills, so I would go over and visit my friend Agnes Moorehead. It was *purely* visiting and she was *purely* a wonderful friend and wouldn't know what the word gay means.

Debbie Reynolds

❏

Kay Francis was shown falling in love with an officer (in *Four Jills in a Jeep*). This was a tribute to her acting skill, because she had very little interest in men.

Phil Silvers

❏

Hollywood parties? If you didn't take the young lady on your right upstairs between the soup and the entrée, you were considered a homosexual.

Walter Wanger

❏

I dropped out for a while because all they offered me were ax-murderers and lesbians. I won't play lesbians, honey, not *this* kid.

Jane Wyman

Illness

When I was about eight I was almost killed in a freak accident while I was riding my bike. There had been a storm and the wind and heavy rains had loosened a dead branch on a huge tree near our house. Neighbors had been complaining about this rotten tree but the city had conveniently ignored their

Debbie Reynolds
Gay? No way

Paulette Goddard
On what gentlemen prefer

161

protests. Then the thing fell on me, totaling the bike, killing my dog and breaking half the bones in my body. I had to learn to walk all over again.

June Allyson

I'd cracked. Some people can face the rough spots in their lives and get through them, but I was in pieces. At Menninger's, they took all responsibility away from me and gave me things to do like chopping wood. You don't know the satisfaction you can get just chopping wood—you stand back and look at it and say, "I did that." I did some sculpting, too, and they even had me take some college courses, even though I'd never gotten beyond the seventh grade in school.

Dan Dailey

For eight years I was an inmate in a state asylum for the insane. I passed through such unbearable terror that I deteriorated into a wild, frightened creature intent only on survival. I was raped by orderlies, gnawed on by rats and poisoned by tainted food. I was chained in padded cells, strapped into straitjackets and half drowned in ice baths. And I survived.

Frances Farmer

I was 15. My crush, a 17-year-old high school boy who delivered our daily newspaper, had deigned to attend the party. He liked my dress. It was black—my first black dress, and almost off the shoulder. Suddenly he looked at me so strangely. "Why are you making such a funny face?", he asked. "Oh, I always look this way," I quipped. I walked to a mirror and screamed! My left eye was bloodshot and watering. My mouth, slack-jawed, gaped open. The left side of my face was distorted in a Frankenstein grin. I cried myself to sleep that night. I woke up the next morning with one side of my face completely paralyzed. It was Bell's palsy. I rented a heat lamp, had it on and off a few minutes at a time for a month. I held a hot water bottle to my face all day and night. I tried to feel, to see. One side of my face felt numb, but I kept moving it. It took me months, just trying to make it go up to match the other side. Then one day it went up an eighth of an inch—just a flicker, but the doctor knew that the muscle wasn't completely dead. And I knew I could do it. For hours at a time I'd say "ah" and study my jaws. They had to be exactly even. And finally they were. Then I went to work on my left eye.

Dan Dailey
Fell to pieces

I had to open and close it with my finger tips. Eventually, I was cured. I'd always wanted to be an actress, and suddenly I knew that learning to control my facial muscles was one of the best assets I could have.

Jane Greer

❏

Mental hospitals? I was thrown out of one. I depressed the patients.

Oscar Levant

❏

My late wife Vivien Leigh was too much affected by the parts she played. And if she got ill, which she certainly did, dreadfully, it had a great deal to do with her playing Blanche DuBois in *A Streetcar Named Desire*, being ill in the same way.

Laurence Olivier

❏

Even if Rock Hudson had been healthy when he did *Dynasty*, the scripts would have done him in.

Barbara Stanwyck

❏

During the making of *Son of Fury* I had my first close-up exposure to mental illness—someone else's. Frances Farmer fell ill. I heard the crew buzzing and gossiping about her. She had thrown a brush at one of the hairdressers, had a tantrum on the set and literally snarled at people. I was puzzled by her behavior and by the crew's lack of sympathy for her. I did not know how to react. I never dreamed, of course, that I would someday share her status —the role of casualty.

Gene Tierney

Image

Oh, I know about my Mr. Nice Guy reputation. I read the papers. It's like having a large growth. You learn to get into a cab without breaking it off.

Alan Alda

❏

I had just given birth to Benjamin and I really thought of it as some sort of miraculous event—my motherhood—as if it were a kind of virgin birth and I had just brought forth the messiah. And along came the script for the movie of *A Streetcar Named Desire*. And I thought, "I wouldn't think of playing a prostitute, a defiled woman." Well, the months went by and I thought about work again—"What am I going to do to support 'the messiah'?" By that time it was too late. The role had gone to Vivien Leigh, who was absolutely brilliant in it. I think it was even better than her Scarlett.

Olivia de Havilland

❏

Just before I shot John Wayne in *The Cowboys* he told me, "Kid, oh how they're gonna hate you for this!" He was right. Now we go to a town on location, I still get that—"You killed the Duke!"

Bruce Dern

❑

I was in Hollywood but not of it, I suppose. They used to call me a lady and I resented that title for years. Then I thought, "Well, there are worse things you can be called," so I gave up the fight. People who know me say I'm much more like Theodora (in *Theodora Goes Wild*).

                                                                    Irene Dunne

❑

I first played a gangster's moll on Broadway in *On the Spot*, which led to *Little Caesar* in Hollywood. And then all those wise-cracking, heart-of-gold blondes. I played so many bad girls that when I went to London in 1937, the headline read, "Tough Baby Arrives."

                                                                 Glenda Farrell

❑

Like many a talented man who feels Nature has shortchanged him, Alan Ladd had a hang–up about his height. When he did a scene with a big guy, we laid down planks three inches high for Alan to stand on. Those planks were the equalizer. When *Wild Harvest* wound, we tossed a big bash. One giant of a crasher with a beat-up puss leaned on the bar and started to belt 'em. With each fresh drink he demanded more elbow room. Alan strode up to the surly monster. The behemoth turned and said, "Hi, Shorty." Alan said, "You weren't invited to this party." Gargantua sneered, "And you intend to do something about it, huh?" Alan nodded emphatically, then turned toward the crew and yelled, "GET MY PLANKS!"

                                                                  Tay Garnett

❑

Guys who go to see my pictures are truck drivers and soldiers, so they put me in whorey-looking parts.

                                                                 Betty Grable

❑

My biggest mistake? Allowing myself to be cast and publicized too often as the romantic type of guy. I seem doomed to be remembered as the "great lover" who lit two cigarettes at a time as a gesture of supreme romance (in *Now, Voyager*). I am very interested in politics, art, current events, but invariably I am asked to discuss perfect behavior in the boudoir. I wish someone would give *me* a few good tips!

Paul Henreid

❏

It is not true I was born a monster. Hollywood made me one.

Boris Karloff

❏

I was a product of the '30s and '40s. I was raised in the Depression. My idol was FDR. The Astaires came up from another milieu. Dancing in New York in the '20s, they were friends of the Whitneys and the Vanderbilts. You always danced in white tie and tails. All the dancers looked rich on the screen because they were a product of that. I didn't want this. I wanted to dance in sailor suits and blue jeans, but there was no dancing like this, so I had to make it up. That was my social outlook.

Gene Kelly

❏

Both Harry Cohn and I seemed bent on the destruction of my career. He in his way, I in mine. After he put me in a picture in which I played a deaf social worker (*Mr. Soft Touch*) he followed it with one in which I had smallpox (*The Killer That Stalked New York*). Was it a subtle scheme to set up a defective image to turn off my following? My own tactic was to drop everything and follow where the man in my life led.

Evelyn Keyes

❏

Sex zombie—that really names me properly. I was laughing at everybody in all of my portraits. I never took that stuff seriously. I will have one of the cleanest obits of any actress. I never did cheesecake like Ann Sheridan or Betty Grable. I just used my hair.

Veronica Lake

❏

I never did become the next Ronald Colman. Most often, producers used to say, "Your time is going to come when you're 30." I kept waiting for that magic moment to arrive when I would be Queen for a Day. Then, when I was 34, Joe Pasternak, one of those producers who used to tell me to wait, turned me down for a role I really wanted because I was too old. I asked him, "What happened to that moment when I'd be perfect?" He said, "I guess it just went by."

Peter Lawford

Don't you remember the guy in the movies who rushes into the phone booth, pushes his hat to the back of his head while the tails of his trenchcoat are still flying, drops a nickel in the box, dials a few numbers and then says: "Gimme the city desk. I've got a story that'll split this town wide open!"? That was me!

Ronald Reagan

Each of us—Doris Day, Debbie Reynolds, Shirley Jones—had the girl-next-door look. So we were cast as the girl next door. We had charming roles, good roles. I don't think the audience will ever view you any differently. I think no matter how old I get, I'll be the oldest living Tammy.

Debbie Reynolds

They labeled me "the oomph girl." To me, oomph is the sound that a fat man makes when he bends over to tie his shoelaces in a phone booth.

Ann Sheridan

Why did it take so long for Cagney to die at the end of *Roaring Twenties*? Well, it's pretty hard to kill an actor. And because, you see, in those days Cagney and Bogart were the only two stars you could kill in a picture. You couldn't kill Flynn, you couldn't kill Gable, you couldn't kill Cooper or any of those fellows. The exhibitor wouldn't even play the picture. But with Cagney they accepted it, and with Bogart. So, I thought as long as they accepted it, we'd give them a good load of it.

Raoul Walsh

I remember a lot of people saying to me—as a matter of fact, it came with a sense of *shock*—"You play all those homosexual parts in films," and I thought "Just wait a minute! These were *roles* to me!" And suddenly one saw the power of this whole sort of image business—you talk about hanging labels!

Michael York

I never met a single person who really lived the way the public believed we lived.

Blanche Yurka

Kissing

When I was 13 at school in France, I fell in love with my teacher. It was a deep love, and desperate. For all of one winter I wrote her poems she never saw and many letters I never sent and made plans to be alone with her, so that I might declare my love. At last, late one afternoon in the spring, I contrived to stay after school, and we were alone. Summoning all my courage, I walked up to her desk, embraced her, kissed her on the mouth. She threw back her head—*and laughed.* Since that time I have never kissed a woman, on screen or off, that I do not expect she will laugh at me.

Charles Boyer

One day Hal Wallis approached me with a $5,000 bonus if I could make Joe Cotten have an erection during a scene. Wallis said, "Joe is such a gentleman. He's made no approach to his leading ladies ... Some of us have been wondering. Maybe he's a homosexual." During the shooting of our love scene, I leaned against him, but I could not feel any swelling of his organ. I took a desperate initiative, and my tongue intensely searched Joe's mouth. I could see him react with shock. When I separated from our embrace, Joe had a line in the script. "You think that ..." Suddenly teeth flew out of his mouth in my direction. In my ardor I had dislodged his partial bridge!

Corinne Calvet

Charles Boyer
Waited for laugh

As long as I'm on the screen, I will never hold or kiss a white woman. Hey, our black women have nothing to look forward to in films, nothing to identify with ... Tell me, how often do you see a black man falling in love with and making love with a black woman? So as it is, I want to be seen only with our women—not Chinese or Filipino women, not yellow, green, pink or white. Just our women, black ones.

Bill Cosby

❏

I don't handle a girl well physically on the screen. I don't kiss the way you should. I keep my mouth closed. People tell me, "Shit, Fonda, you can't even kiss good." Not a girl, mind you. No girl ever told me that. Maybe a director. You wanna know something? When I see two people on the screen kiss with their mouths open, I don't like to watch. It seems too personal for me.

Henry Fonda

❏

If people making a movie didn't keep kissing, they'd be at each other's throats.

Ava Gardner

❏

The love scenes I did years ago were sensitive and romantic, but in today's lovemaking couples are trying to swallow each other's tonsils.

Lillian Gish

❏

I remember seeing the movie *Fallen Angel* as a kid. Dana Andrews picks up Linda Darnell and takes her to the beach under a pier and kisses her. The way it was lit, when they separated you could see a string of saliva between them, then it snapped. I thought, "Oh, boy!" That's more than I could take. It's the most erotic thing I've ever seen.

Rock Hudson

❏

So many things were said about Clark Gable being "Ze Great Lover," when he was just tremendously graceful. No director ever had to give him directions in a love scene. There was never any toe-to-toe for a screen kiss. He was a very graceful person with his body, and there wasn't all this enormous clinching and awkwardness. Much like a ballet dancer in a sense, he had rhythm and timing—he knew where to put his feet. He was beautiful to play a love scene with.

Rosalind Russell

❏

Clark Gable and I again co-starred in *Homecoming*. In any love story made then, the challenge was to suggest the passion that the censors kept off the screen. So Mervyn LeRoy (the director) shot close-ups of several fervent kisses. To keep my mouth fresh for those clinches I chewed gum, and during takes I would poke the wad up next to my teeth. But once Clark kissed me too forcefully. When he drew back we were attached by a ribbon of sticky gum! I shrieked with laughter as Clark glumly picked the gum from his (false) teeth. From then on I gargled.

Lana Turner

Life

I don't want to achieve immortality through my work. I want to achieve it through not dying.

Woody Allen

❏

The only reason I'm not still doing *Daughter of Gorilla at Large* is that my personal life had become a shambles. There was a lot of drinking in Hollywood. When I would be driving and get home and wake up in the morning and not know how I got there, I was scared to death. It really began one night in '57. For five years I had been telling myself lies about the kind of life I was living. In reality, every picture I did was worse than the last one, and every man I was in love with was worse than the last one. I was terribly immature ... Someone must have hollered at me too loud because I just went home, packed my bag and asked someone to phone my mother and say I was returning to New York. That was the first time in my life I made a decision entirely on my own. And that was when I was ready to be an *actress!*

Anne Bancroft

❏

The one thing I regret about my past is the length of it. If I had my life to live over again, I'd make all the same mistakes—only sooner.

Tallulah Bankhead

❏

See into life—don't just look at it.

Anne Baxter

❏

What's bad for you can be good for you. When we're touched by pain and loss and don't know why, if we keep going and keep truthful, the reason will appear.

Eileen Brennan

❏

Anne Bancroft
Escaped to New York

Susan Hayward
The game was survival

172

Start every day off with a smile and get it over with.

W.C. Fields

❏

I never "faced facts" in life, so I survived. If I'd faced facts, I would have realized that I was a plain little girl with bow legs from Quincy, Massachusetts, and never gone on the stage. You must never face facts.

Ruth Gordon

❏

I learned at a very early age that life is a battle. My father was first a barker at Coney Island, then a guard on the subway. My family was poor; the neighborhood was poor. I knew that if I got my dress dirty, there was no money to have it cleaned. I had an older sister and brother, and when the soles of our shoes wore out, we stuffed paper in them. It didn't take me long to realize that competition with other kids was impossible to avoid, and that I had to be prepared for it. It's like when you know that one of them is going to swing at you, so you swing first. Survival, that's it.

Susan Hayward

❏

Is life, even a blemished life, worth living? I say decidedly yes, because any ugly life is still better than a beautiful funeral.

Katharine Hepburn

❏

Three things have helped me successfully go through the ordeals of life— an understanding husband, a good analyst and millions of dollars.

Mary Tyler Moore

❏

There's no door in life that opens for you that another door doesn't close.

Cybill Shepherd

❏

You gotta get up early in the morning to catch a fox and stay up late at night to get a mink.

Mae West

Loneliness

If I'm such a legend, then why do I sit at home for hours staring at the damned telephone, hoping it's out of order, even calling the operator asking her if she's *sure* it's not out of order. Let me tell you, legends are all very well if you've got somebody who loves you, some man who's not afraid to be in love with Judy Garland.

Judy Garland

❏

Judy Garland
Lonely at the top

You know what they say. It's lonely at the top, but it's lonely at the bottom and in the middle, too.

Don Johnson

Looks

Claudette Colbert was pretty rather than beautiful; she had some difficult angles to her face—not as difficult as she thought—but every close-up had to be shot showing only the left three-quarters angle of her face. The right side of her face was called "the other side of the moon" because nobody ever saw it.

Mary Astor

❏

When I started shooting *Anastasia* I met Yul Brynner and realized at once that he was shorter. I suggested putting a little block under him. He turned around and said to me: "You think I want to play it standing on a box? I will show the world what a big horse you are." Maybe some actresses would have walked out, but I just laughed and I never had a complex about my height after that.

Ingrid Bergman

❏

I hate myself for choosing a profession that gets me up at dawn. I hate myself all the way to the studio and into the make-up room—"Boys Town," I call it. There we sit, the glamour boys waiting to be made beautiful and feeling like a snail's grandmother.

Humphrey Bogart

❏

I have eyes like a bullfrog, a neck like an ostrich and long, limp hair. You just *have* to be good to survive with that equipment.

Bette Davis

❏

The reason the all-American boy prefers beauty to brains is that he can see better than he can think.

Farrah Fawcett

❑

I was at Warner Brothers at a time when you had to look like Joan Crawford or Garbo or you may as well have stayed home. Warners was the cheapest studio—they wouldn't pay for us to wear eyelashes or have our teeth capped—but they gave us good scripts, and now I think it has paid off. The old Warner movies look better on *The Late Show* than the others because we were allowed to be ourselves.

Geraldine Fitzgerald

❑

As for my looks, they're from being sick so much. I nearly died last week in England. Toxoplasmosis and a temperature of 102. I almost had a tracheotomy. For beauty, just rest and do crossword puzzles. And no booze. I learned in marriage that I could never keep up with my husbands' drinking. They were not drunks, mind you, but I always had my head in the basin.

Joan Fontaine

❑

Louis B. Mayer once looked at me and said, "You will never get the girl at the end." So I worked on my acting.

Van Heflin

❑

I liked to look as if I didn't give a damn. I think you should pretend you don't care ... but it's the most *outrageous* pretense. I said to Garbo once, "I bet it takes us longer to look as if we hadn't made any effort than it does someone else to come in beautifully dressed."

Katharine Hepburn

❑

All Burt Reynolds has to do is wink at the camera and he's a star. I'm short and ugly and really have to act.

Dustin Hoffman

❏

I have a face that would stop a sun-dial.

Charles Laughton

❏

Everything you see I owe to spaghetti.

Sophia Loren

❏

I don't like to get a suntan because I like to feel blonde all over.

Marilyn Monroe

❏

Each time I look in the mirror, I vant to scream; I am so beautiful.

Maria Montez

❏

Orson Welles always carries with him a little suitcase with his make-up. He never appears in a film with his real nose. He's ashamed of his small nose. He has to stick something on his nose, some putty.

Jeanne Moreau

❏

I worked with Loretta Young in *The Lady from Cheyenne*. She worked with a full-length mirror beside the camera. I didn't know which Loretta to play to—the one in the mirror or the one that was with me.

Robert Preston

❏

Five days after we started *Deception*, Bette Davis said, "Have you seen the rushes? What do you think?" I said, "Bette, you're giving me a marvelous performance." And she replied, "I'm not talking about my acting. How do I look?" I told her, "Bette, you sound like Paulette Goddard." She stormed into the projection room, and I came in and there was a big argument going on between her and Ernie Haller. And she said to him, "Ernie, you photographed me in *Jezebel*, didn't you?" And he said, "Yes, what about it?" "Can't you photograph me like that?" And he replied, "Bette, I was seven years younger then."

Irving Rapper

❏

Actresses. When I was preparing to direct *Scaramouche*, I asked our leading lady, Eleanor Parker, who was to play a fiery actress, to dye her hair red for the role. But she said, "I'm a blonde and I'm going to stay that way." So we had these elaborate, costly red wigs made for her, and they gave us plenty of problems during the shooting. A couple of weeks after we wrapped the picture, I ran into Eleanor in a restaurant—and she was now a redhead! I said, "What happened to your hair?" And she replied, "Oh, I thought I looked so good in the red wigs that I decided to become a redhead"!

George Sidney

❏

I don't think I have the kind of face that makes an audience love you. And in the movies with all of those close-ups, that's very important. I think I look like Dame Edith Sitwell. I think the actors and actresses who are loved generally have more cuddly features.

Meryl Streep

❏

Long-haired young people? They don't bother me. If a guy wants to wear his hair down to his ass, I'm not revolted by it. But I don't look at him and say, "Now there's a fella I'd like to spend next winter with."

John Wayne

❏

Alice Faye had a wonderful talent. She was warm, she was real, she sang beautifully and was beautiful to look at, and she *loathed* working in movies. One day I went into wardrobe for a fitting, and David Levy, who ran the wardrobe, came out and said, "Would you mind waiting a minute? Alice Faye is in here and she's upset, so we'll be a little late for your fitting." And after another minute or two he came out again and said, "Loretta, would you mind going in to see Alice? She's crying. She's always upset at fittings because her breasts are so large." Well, little flat-chested me. I looked up at him and said, "She's *crying*? Why? Here I am stuffing Kleenex inside my ... and this girl with the big ..." I couldn't believe it. He said, "She's very sensitive." So I went in and after a few minutes I said something about envying her. And she burst out crying all over again.

Loretta Young

Love

Love between two people is wonderful—if you can get between the right two people.

Woody Allen

❏

Warren Beatty has an interesting psychology. He has always fallen in love with girls who have just won or been nominated for an Academy Award.

Leslie Caron

❏

Love is like anything else worthwhile; it carries a price tag. One cannot live in love without pain.

Diahann Carroll

❏

In my whole life I never had a woman so much in love with me as Ingrid Bergman was. The day after the picture (*Saratoga Trunk*) ended, I couldn't get her on the phone.

Gary Cooper

❏

Love is a fire. But whether it is going to warm your hearth or burn down your house, you can never tell.

Joan Crawford

❏

I fell deeply in love with Rita (Hayworth) and she cared for me, so what we did in *Gilda* was play the truth. Of course I did several films with her after that and she remains my friend today. In fact, Yasmin (her daughter) and I are very instrumental in trying to raise as much money as we can for Alzheimer's Disease. Yassie asked me if I'd like to see Rita, but I told her, "No, I'd like to remember her as Gilda." She was so beautiful and so shy. She had been hurt many times—but I never hurt her.

                                                                    Glenn Ford

❏

By the time we made *The Charge of the Light Brigade* I was sure I was in love with her. Olivia (de Havilland) was only 21 then. I was married, of course, unhappily. Olivia was lovely—and distant. She must have actively disliked me for the teasing I did, for I sprang some very obstreperous gags. There was the time she found a dead snake in her panties as she went to put them on. She was terrified and she wept. She knew very well who was responsible and it couldn't have endeared me to her. It slowly penetrated my obtuse mind that such juvenile pranks weren't the way to any girl's heart. But it was too late. I couldn't soften her.

                                                                    Errol Flynn

❏

Love is a worn-out word. People love their cat, they love their house. I've never been in love with anyone but myself.

                                                                 Hermione Gingold

❏

Bogart fell in love with the character Bacall played in *To Have and Have Not*, so she had to keep playing it for the rest of his life.

                                                                   Howard Hawks

❏

Men fall in love with Gilda and wake up with me.

                                                                  Rita Hayworth

Errol Flynn
In love with Livvy

Rita Hayworth
Not-so rude awakening

181

❏

My wife Dolores has faith in me as a comedian and a lover, but I wish she would remember when to stop laughing.

Bob Hope

❏

As long as it was passionate. Either negative or positive. Then I knew it was love. As long as it was extreme. That was its validity. As soon as anything became too settled, too regular, too placid, I'd have to get in there with the Mixmaster and make sure things were still cooking.

Jessica Lange

❏

Eddie Fisher loves Elizabeth Taylor. How high can you stoop?

Oscar Levant

❏

I love him (Dean Martin). I never have stopped. I'm not necessarily crazy about some of the things he's done and I'm sure I've done some things he's not thrilled with, either. But I don't believe in love being dialed in or out. I'm not ashamed of that. How do I *not* love him? He took me out of a toilet and put me in a castle. What would I have, no gratitude?

Jerry Lewis

❏

White lies are like red roses: both are very important to romance.

Sophia Loren

❏

I have never loved anyone like Gary Cooper, and I never will again. He was the most gorgeous, attractive man I've ever known. When Gary and I were finished, I was heart-broken.

Patricia Neal

❑

From an open letter to Jane Wyman in 1947:

Recently, when I was in the drugstore across the street from the studio, I picked up a magazine and took it to the counter. You were on the cover. I just sat there admiring it. On my right sat an old gal who didn't know me from Wally Beery. "That Jane Wyman sure has got everything," she volunteered. I started beaming. "She sure has," I replied. "And I've got the key to her front door!" "Fresh," she snorted. "Jane Wyman just happens to be happily married to Ronald Reagan. And he's *very* much in love with her." "Lady," I answered—and I've never been more serious. "You said a mouthful!"

Ronald Reagan

❑

Absence is to love like wind to a fire. It blows out the little ones but kindles the big ones.

Donna Reed

❑

Tyrone Power and I knew nothing but loveliness in the year-and-a-half that we went together. Yes, it was one of my happiest times. But after you're that high up with happiness, when you crash you really don't come out of it the next day. No, it took me a long time, because I loved him so much. You see, Tyrone was still married to Annabella, and she lived in Europe, and she was not about to give him a divorce. God, I don't know her side of it, and maybe I don't really know all of his side of it, you know? But by golly, when Linda Christian got hold of him, he got a divorce.

Lana Turner

Marilyn Monroe

Marilyn Monroe was frightened, insecure—trusted only her coach and was always late. During our scenes (in *How to Marry a Millionaire*) she'd look at my forehead instead of my eyes; at the end of a take, look to her coach standing behind director Jean Negulesco for approval. If the headshake was no, she'd insist on another take. A scene often went to 15 or more takes,

Patricia Neal
Getting over Gary

Constance Bennett
Behind a star's appeal

184

which meant I'd have to be good in all of them as no one knew which one would be used. And yet I couldn't dislike Marilyn. She had no meanness in her—no bitchery. She just had to concentrate on herself and the people who were there only for her.

Lauren Bacall

On *Don't Bother to Knock* I worked with another newcomer, Marilyn Monroe. It was a remarkable experience! Because it was one of those very rare times in Hollywood when I felt that give-and-take that can only happen when you are working with good actors. Marilyn played a baby sitter who has done some very destructive things to this child, and everyone in this hotel had become aware of it. It was the scene where they were bringing her down to the lobby to be held for the police. I was just somebody in the lobby; and I was to walk over to her and react, that's all; and there was to be a close-up of her and a close-up of me—you know, to show my reaction. Well, I moved toward her, and I saw that girl—of course, she wasn't the big sex symbol she later became, so there was nothing I had to forget or shake off. There was just this scene of one woman seeing another who was helpless and in pain, and she *was* helpless and in pain. It was so real, I responded; I really reacted to her. She moved me so much that tears came into my eyes. Believe me, such moments happened rarely, if ever again, in the early things I was doing out there.

Anne Bancroft

The final straw for me at 20th Century-Fox came when they would not let me test for *How to Marry a Millionaire*. I'd watched Marilyn Monroe come up from extra and now she seemed to represent the wave of the future. I knew her first as a grubby sort of thing, very frightened, and now she was going to replace (Betty) Grable and all I knew was I wanted out.

Anne Baxter

Marilyn Monroe! There's a broad with a big future behind her.

Constance Bennett

I began taking the young Marilyn Monroe to the big night spots. It was like taking a hungry kid into a bakery ... She wanted very much to be a star. Somehow, she thought that would fill in that "empty feeling"—as she described it—she had had as a kid, when she was going from one foster home to the next. We didn't pretend that our affair was a big thing. It was just part of something nice between us ... The last time I saw Marilyn was in late 1959, when I appeared with her and Yves Montand in *Let's Make Love* at Fox ... The wide-eyed, naive Marilyn I had first known was gone. This Marilyn was more beautiful than ever, but she seemed like someone lost in her own thoughts most of the time ... I think she actually could not remember that she and I had been together for a while 11 years before.

Milton Berle

Marilyn Monroe was a very vague girl. I had lunch with her at 20th Century-Fox four or five times during the filming of *We're Not Married*. And a year later, she was having lunch with Eli Wallach at Jim Downey's in New York. I stopped by to chat with them, and she leaned over to Wallach and whispered, "Who was that?" Part of her problem was that she was too involved in too many things. She was a much better actress than people gave her credit for. Unfortunately, she met the wrong people.

Eddie Bracken

A masseur, Claes Adler, who specialized in walking on your back in his bare feet, insisted I meet one of his clients—an unknown actress he said had great possibilities. I agreed, thinking he was paying off a promise to some girlfriend. I met her. She was plenty curvaceous. But in black floppy hat, cheap brown suit and an almost complete inability to communicate, I paid little attention to her. Her name was Marilyn Monroe. Breasts she had. And a wiggly figure. But to me sex is class, something more than a wiggly behind. If it weren't, I know 200 whores who would be stars. But how could I have passed up Marilyn Monroe? I've been worried about that ever since.

Frank Capra

I met Marilyn Monroe briefly when, as an unknown, she came to my studio, Columbia, to do *Ladies of the Chorus*. Helen Hunt, the hair stylist there, was presenting a new hair fashions show, and Marilyn and I were in it. I was playing leads and Helen said to me, "Be extra nice to Marilyn, because she's shy and feels out of it." Eight years later, she was starring in *The Seven-Year Itch* at Fox, and I was playing a cameo in it. Marilyn was having marital problems at the time with Joe DiMaggio. I had done my role when I received a "cover call" one evening to be at the studio in the morning. Marilyn was not expected to show, and the director, Billy Wilder, was going to improvise some business to enlarge my role. I'd had a restless night, knowing I was to shoot the next day, and was tense and tired in the morning. I was under the Fox dryer when the assistant director came to me and said, "You can go home now. She's coming in." Some make-up and wardrobe friends and I went down to the prop department, got a big baseball bat, put a big blue ribbon on it and had an assistant deliver it to Mr. Wilder who was working in a remote corner of the sound stage. He looked back at us over his spectacles, expressionless.

Marguerite Chapman

Marilyn Monroe gave so much of herself as an actress; working with her was like going up and down an elevator. No, Hollywood didn't kill her—she had many deep-seated problems.

Montgomery Clift

Marilyn Monroe was a very realistic girl who *knew* that she didn't have any technique, that she was just a terribly pretty girl whom all this had happened to, and all of a sudden she was a star, she was going to have to go out and do it and everybody was going to look at her. And she was just terrified! She knew that she was not equal. What made her not show up at the studio was that she couldn't sleep, she had a great deal of problems with that. She'd come to the studio with the line that she was sick, because the one thing she counted on was the way she looked. If she had a line in her face, she would not be photographed. But she'd get into make-up and always comb her hair "just one more time," because she was frightened of coming out; and she was such a little girl that she didn't know how to apologize. If it was Clark Gable who was waiting, she would be beside herself with fear and remorse.

Jack Cole

Marilyn Monroe and Liz Taylor are of an age to be women, but unfortunately for them, and the people around them, they're children. I don't think Marilyn has a friend. She hasn't taken time to make a friend in this industry. And many people have tried to befriend her. And the same with Liz; she's a taker, not a giver. I was raised by the same studio, MGM, and pampered as much as she was. But I didn't take it for granted, *ever*.

Joan Crawford

❏

I think Marilyn Monroe was quite mad. The mother was mad, and poor Marilyn was mad. I know people who say, "Hollywood broke her heart," and all that, but I don't believe it. She was very observant and tough-minded and appealing, but she had this bad judgment about things. She adored and trusted the wrong people. She was very courageous—you know the book, *Twelve Against the Gods*? Marilyn was like that, she had to challenge the gods at every turn, and eventually she lost. A beautiful friend of mine killed herself years ago and Zoe Akins said, "It was the only ending for her." I think it was the only ending for Marilyn, and I think she knew it.

George Cukor

❏

Kissing Marilyn Monroe was like kissing Hitler.

Tony Curtis

❏

Marilyn Monroe was frustrated on *There's No Business Like Show Business*. Why not? There was Merman. And Donald O'Connor. And Mitzi Gaynor and me and Johnnie Ray. Marilyn couldn't sing or dance and there she was plopped into this picture. Her inexperience showed. She was hard to get along with. She was basically a nice, quiet girl who got bad advice from the hangers-on she thought were her friends.

Dan Dailey

❏

After Marilyn Monroe died, a number of guys came out of the woodwork claiming all sorts of things about her. We all know she found a basic enjoyment and inner security when she made love. But she was no whore. Of course, she was unhappy and often insecure. But I never once thought of her as tragic. She was an extremely caring and sensitive person who was easily bruised . . . There was a lovely story of the William Morris agent who happened to be very small. When they slept together, Marilyn puffed up his ego to the point of madness by whispering, "You're hurting me," in his ear. This was all a put-on, of course, but it was typical of MM's feeling for other people.

Sammy Davis, Jr.

❏

During the shooting of *Bus Stop* we went over to visit Josh Logan who was directing. We watched him shoot a scene with Marilyn Monroe. When the take was over she came over and said, "I keep dreaming I'm getting an Oscar. Those stupid bastards never gave me a part like this before, and they never will again." A studio cop approached us and told Marilyn that one of the top studio executives wanted to see her right away. Marilyn turned to us and said, "Don't go away; he's only a five-minute job." Everyone knew that Marilyn was available to three other studio executives, and was having an affair with a New York director, and the word around was that she had fallen in love.

Henry Ephron

❏

When my wife Phoebe and I were writing the screenplay for *There's No Business Like Show Business*, we met with MM one afternoon. She was spending her days in one of the musician's bungalows which were popularly known around the studio as "the little motels." They were furnished with a piano and a couch. When we came in, Marilyn was sipping wine from a glass. So was Mickey, the piano player. The place looked like a cubicle in a whorehouse. Marilyn's sweater was pinned, a few buttons were missing. Her shirt could have stood a trip to the cleaners, her hair a trip to the beauty parlor. She didn't even bother with "Hello." She just said, "Don't make me Donald O'Connor's girl. I could eat him for breakfast."

Henry Ephron

❏

I've made five transcontinental tours in the past five years, 90 cities. And you know, they still want to know about Marilyn Monroe. They still can't understand how a girl so beautiful, so successful, so rich and very, very popular could be so terribly unhappy. It's like the great American dream blew up in their faces when she died. I only worked with her in *Seven-Year Itch*, but we had lunch together every day. Sometimes she wanted to talk; sometimes she didn't. I found her delightful. And I remember when we first met she stood up and a book fell on the floor. An Italian-American cookbook. She was still married to Joe DiMaggio. I liked her, because I knew she was trying.

Tom Ewell

❏

Working with Marilyn Monroe in *The Misfits* nearly gave me a heart attack. I have never been happier when a film ended.

Clark Gable

❏

It was because of me that Marilyn Monroe gained a speaking part in *A Ticket to Tomahawk*. She wasn't given any lines, but in the dance scene with three other girls she counted off her steps—1, 2, 3, 4—loud enough to be picked up on the soundtrack. I asked the director to leave it in because none of the girls was supposed to be a professional dancer. He agreed.

Connie Gilchrist

❏

It may sound peculiar to say so, because she's no longer with us, but Marilyn Monroe and I were very close. Once, when we were doing *How to Marry a Millionaire*, I got a call on the set. My younger daughter had had a fall. I ran home. And the one person to call was Marilyn. She did an awful lot to boost things up for movies when everything was at a low state. There'll never be anyone like her for looks, for attitude, for all of it.

Betty Grable

❏

At dinner I was presented to a beautiful young lady whom host John Carroll had befriended. The girl was unemployed and needed a place to live until she got a break. At John's suggestion she moved into his home, and with chaperone lived there for several weeks. The lady was my dinner partner. My lady guest told me about herself. It wasn't a pretty story. I promised the girl I would be on the lookout for something that would give her a start in pictures. At MGM the next morning there was a very important script on my desk that needed immediate casting: *The Asphalt Jungle*. After reading it, I realized that my promise of help to my dinner partner could be fulfilled. I would cast her as the blonde secretary. Arthur Hornblow was the producer, John Huston the director. I told them about my protégée. Her name was

Marilyn Monroe and she had no experience. Both Hornblow and Huston hit
the roof. How dare I submit an inexperienced girl for such an important
role? Johnny Hyde, a William Morris partner, brought Miss Monroe out to
(L.B.) Mayer the next day. She came—Mayer saw—she conquered. Result?
If Miss Marilyn Monroe hadn't played the secretary, MGM would not have
made the picture.

Billy Grady

I had no idea Marilyn Monroe would become a star. If she had something
different, it wasn't apparent at the time we did *Monkey Business*. She seemed
very shy, and I remember that when the studio workers would whistle at
her, it seemed to embarrass her.

Cary Grant

I think Marilyn Monroe's whole life might have changed if Darryl Zanuck
would have let us do *Of Human Bondage*, with Marilyn and Jimmy Dean,
because after I did *Niagara* with her I found her marvelous to work with
and terrifically ambitious to do better. And bright. She may not have had an
education, but she was just naturally bright. But always being trampled on.
You talk of Rita (Hayworth) being trampled on by men. This little thing was
trampled on by bums! To most men she was, I won't say a bum, but something
they were a little bit ashamed of. If she had been allowed to do this picture,
it would have put her in another category. But Darryl said: "Jesus Christ, how
can you think of it! How can I say I'm putting Marilyn in a very sensitive Bette
Davis-style play? We'd get lampooned before we started. And I'd lose three
to four million dollars on the films I could be making with her being Marilyn
Monroe."

Henry Hathaway

I remember one scene in *Love Nest* where Marilyn Monroe was supposed to
be sunning in the backyard of this apartment house. Well, when she walked
onto the set in her bathing suit and over to the beach chair, the whole crew
gasped and seemed to turn to stone. She was always nervous and shy, but
with the warmth of the crew's reaction she suddenly seemed to be another
person. She became completely uninhibited in her movements—graceful
and seductive at the same time. Mind you, movie crews are quite used to

seeing starlets in brief costumes. In all my years at the studio, though, I'd never seen that happen before. She had that electric something.

June Haver

❑

Marilyn Monroe? Zanuck called me and said, "Howard, we ought to have a great big star here and we're losing money on her films. What the hell is happening?" I said, "Darryl, you're making realism with a very unreal girl. She's a completely storybook character. You've got a great story, *Gentlemen Prefer Blondes*." "She couldn't do that." "The hell she can't." "She can't sing." She used to come to parties down in Palm Springs and she'd come over and say, "Mr. Hawks, would you take me home?" And she's so goddamn dumb that one time I said to her, "Look, if you can't talk . . . the radio's playing . . . *sing*." And she sang. So I said to Zanuck, "She sings good."

Howard Hawks

❑

June Haver
She remembers Marilyn

Marilyn Monroe arrived on the set of *The Asphalt Jungle* scared half to death and dressed as a cheap tart. As soon as we saw her we knew she was the one, but we had to strip that all the way down to get to the basic girl, the real quality, the true Lolita quality.

Arthur Hornblow, Jr.

I always thought Marilyn (Monroe) was a joke. But she's turned it around and now the public's eating her up ... Somebody must have told Marilyn her upper lip is alive or something. Damnedest thing I've ever seen. She moves it around like a snake.

Howard Hughes

Marilyn Monroe continued heavily into the drugs (while shooting *The Misfits*), and finally the young doctor on location refused to give her any more, even though he feared he might lose his job. She got drugs elsewhere, however, and eventually she broke down completely and had to be sent to a hospital. After Marilyn's return we were all sure it would be different. In a few days we knew better. One Sunday afternoon I visited her in her suite to get some idea of what to expect in the weeks ahead. She greeted me euphorically— then went into a kind of trance. She was the worst I'd ever seen her. Her hair was a tangle; her hands and feet were grubby; she was wearing only a short nightgown which wasn't any cleaner than the rest of her. We all knew that something awful was going to happen to her.

John Huston

Marilyn Monroe is generally something of a zombie. Talking to her is like talking to somebody underwater. She's very honest and ambitious and is either studying her lines or her face during all of her working hours, and there is nothing whatever to be said against her, but she's not material for warm friendship.

Nunnally Johnson

It was interesting to see Marilyn Monroe again (on *The Seven-Year Itch*), after all the success. I had often met her at Sam Spiegel's house and around on the arm of Johnny Hyde, the William Morris agent responsible for getting her started. I had never seen what Johnny saw or the camera picked up. I had only seen one more little blonde with the preferred size tits and a funny walk. Success had given her a nice patina, a certain glow.

Evelyn Keyes

It was not easy to work with Marilyn Monroe (in *Clash by Night*). She was a very peculiar mixture of shyness and uncertainty and—I wouldn't say "star allure"—but, let me say, she knew exactly her impact on men. And that's all. Now, just at that time, the famous nude calendar story came up. I didn't mind—what a woman does with herself is nobody's business—but the thing was, because of her shyness, she was scared as hell to come to the studio—she was always late. I don't know why she couldn't remember her lines, but I can very well understand all the directors who worked with her getting angry, because she was certainly responsible for slowing down the work. It was especially hard on Barbara Stanwyck because naturally newspapermen came during lunch hours and, since Barbara was the star, everyone tried to make sure she was interviewed. But the reporters said, "We don't wanna talk to Barbara, we wanna talk to the girl with the big tits."

Fritz Lang

Marilyn Monroe didn't seem to fit in with that group (in *There's No Business Like Show Business*). She was worried about herself all the time. It just didn't work out as far as we were concerned. I guess her limited ability worried her, for one thing, because these were all professionals, and also good. She never seemed to be able to work by the clock; if you wanted her at nine o'clock, you might get her at 10:30. She did that without any regard for the cost. It became worse and worse until she finally didn't make it at all.

Walter Lang

We were very good friends, but I never got close to Marilyn Monroe. Very few people ever did. She was obviously very unhappy, and she'd let you get just so near and then withdraw because she didn't want to be hurt anymore. She'd been hurt an awful lot ... In *Some Like It Hot* we once did 35 or 36 takes in which she had seven words in a particular scene. She had to come into the room and say, "Where's the bourbon ... Oh, there it is." She wouldn't complete the two lines until they were right *for her*. Billy Wilder (director) was going crazy. At about take 33 or 35 they had tried 18 different ways to get it out of her. About take 35, when it was just about to be done again, Billy said, "We can't possibly—" and Marilyn said, "Ssh, don't talk to me or I'll forget how I want to play it." I fell over. But, good for her, she knew what she wanted, and she was damned if she was going to let Billy have that film until it was right. Then she'd turn around and do three pages in one take! Scare the hell out of you.

Jack Lemmon

The night Marilyn Monroe's death was announced, I was performing *Brecht on Brecht* at the Theatre De Lys. Sitting on my stool with Brecht's oversize face behind me, I was filled with Marilyn. She was in me and around me and I wanted to share it with the audience. "In memory of Marilyn Monroe," I announced before the section "Hollywood Elegies," Brecht's brilliant poems: "I fled from the tigers. I fled the fleas. What got me at last, mediocrities." It was deadly quiet in the house. Truth happened that instant.

Viveca Lindfors

I remember an incident that showed Marilyn Monroe's excitement about learning. She had studied with Lee Strasberg, the great acting teacher, and learned about Stanislavsky and Freud, and now she was beginning to apply it. Every time she discovered something she tried to tell poor Don Murray about her discovery. He'd nod and say, "I know, I know, I *know*." He just wanted to be left alone to study his lines. So now comes the scene in *Bus Stop* where Marilyn is in bed and Don comes rushing in and says, "Wake up, Cherry! The sun's out. No wonder you're so pale and white." But Don says, "Wake up, Cherry! The sun's out. No wonder you're so pale and scaly." "Don," she said, "do you realize what you did? You made a Freudian slip. Unconsciously you were playing the scene correctly because it is a sexual scene." He looked at Marilyn with exasperation. "I don't know what the *hell* you're talking about." "Don't you see," she answered, "you said 'scaly' instead of 'white,' which means subconsciously you were thinking of a snake—a phallic symbol. Do you know what a phallic symbol *is*, Don?" "Know what it is?", he said to her, throwing back his hands. "I've *got* one!"

Joshua Logan

With Marilyn Monroe I was very careful. I treated her with respect. I found the poor thing had been treated like a tramp all her life. People yelling at her, "Come on, Blondie, lean over, wiggle your rear." Yet she knew everything there was to know about a camera.

Joshua Logan

Marilyn Monroe gave an adorable performance as Lorelei Lee. I knew her here in New York later. She was always a poor, pathetic creature. There are no two ways about it—she was incapable of handling anything. And she was so naive, *really* naive. That's why she always wanted to get married. She would leave in the morning, put her bicycle on a cab and go over to Brooklyn. I think Arthur Miller was living in Brooklyn Heights at the time, and she was trying to snare him. She would ride her bicycle up and down in front of his house just like a 15-year-old girl. Marilyn was a victim of her own insecurity.

Anita Loos

(Marilyn Monroe) auditioned a great deal, late afternoons, in executive offices. She also functioned agreeably as a companion for corporate elder statesmen visiting from the East, and on hostess committees for sales conventions. Occasionally, she was squeezed into old Betty Grable costumes and used as a dress extra for unimportant bits in some films . . . She was not a loner. She was just plain *alone*.

Joseph L. Mankiewicz

I traveled with Marilyn Monroe, sometimes doing her make-up in the lavatories of airplanes. You know how small those things are? I had to sit on her knees to put on her eyeliner. I've made up so many stars while they were on the john. For me, glamour is working in toilets. And yes, Marilyn was an insecure egomaniac. But she wasn't so different from the rest. Actresses are the most insecure people in the world—that's why they spend so much time on their looks.

George Masters

During the making of *River of No Return*, Marilyn (Monroe) was reading a dictionary of Freudian terms. I asked her why and she said, "I feel one should know how to discuss oneself." I said, "What chapter are you up to?" She said, "Anal eroticism." I said, "That's charming and do you think that will come up in a discussion?" She went back to reading and looked up after a while and said, "What's eroticism?" I explained. A minute or two later she looked up from the book again and said, "What's anal?" My stand-in, Tim, who was working on a scratch sheet nearby, couldn't stand it any longer and butted in: "That's the keester."

Robert Mitchum

❏

Marilyn Monroe was always filled with sly humor. On *River of No Return*, she'd jokingly say, "What a set! A girl doesn't get much action around here!" Once when she'd said something of the kind, my stand-in piped up. "What about a round robin?" Marilyn didn't know what that was. "You and me and Mitch," he said. "OOOOOH, that would kill me!" Marilyn replied. "Nobody's died from it yet," he told her. "I bet they have," she said. "But in the papers it says the girl died from natural causes."

Robert Mitchum

❏

There was a part for a foil for Groucho Marx in *Love Happy* (which I directed). My agent, Johnny Hyde, came in with his client, 23-year-old Marilyn Monroe, with dirty fingernails, a look of bewilderment. But she fairly oozed sex. Hyde never married her, but he was very much in love.

David Miller

❏

I was alone in Hollywood for five months and I'm no saint, and who could resist Marilyn Monroe?

Yves Montand

❏

Marilyn Monroe had a childlike quality, and this was good and also bad. Director Joshua Logan wanted a two-head close-up for *Bus Stop*, one of the first in CinemaScope. She broke me up when, in one of the frames, the top of my head was missing. "The audience won't miss the top of your head, Don," she said. "They know it's there because it's already been established." But, like children, she thought the world revolved around her and her thoughts. She was oblivious to the needs of people near her, and her thoughtlessnesses, such as being late frequently, were the bad side of it.

Don Murray

One afternoon we were doing a silent shot (for *How to Marry a Millionaire*) of Marilyn Monroe asleep, dreaming. She was covered with a rich, shiny silk sheet. Her eyes were closed. I couldn't miss the opportunity to lean over the bed and fix the folds a little closer to her body. After all, I was the director. As my knowledgeable painter's hands were doing the required job, gently folding and pushing the silk under her sheet, I realized that she was completely nude. "Marilyn, are you nude?" I whispered. "What if there is a fire and you have to run out of bed?" She opened her eyes. "The script says *nude*. So I am nude." By the camera, two young priests, visitors on the set, their eyes bulging out of their heads, were leaning forward out of their shoes toward Marilyn. And certainly thinking, this is better than *Heaven*!

Jean Negulesco

If I had the chance to talk to Marilyn (Monroe) or others when they were in the depths of despair, I would have let them know that it all could be OK, that Hollywood is just a place, a job; that whatever happens there, well, there are other jobs, other lives, other people. I wish someone close to Marilyn would have let her know that. But the people close to her wouldn't have known either, I guess. The people around me didn't. I did it alone. You come into this world alone, you have to do it alone.

Kim Novak

I refused to treat Marilyn Monroe as a special case (on *The Prince and the Showgirl*)—I had too much pride in my trade—and would at all times treat her as a grown-up artist of merit, which in a sense she was. Her manner to me got steadily ruder and more insolent. Whenever I patiently labored to make her understand an indication of some reading, business or timing, she would listen with an ill-disguised impatience, and when I had finished would turn to Paula Strasberg (her coach) and petulently demand, "Wasseee mean?"

Kim Novak
Other places, jobs

A very short way into the filming, my humiliation had reached depths I would not have believed possible ... Two years ago a couple of my Hollywood friends, as a sort of joke after a dinner party, ran this now 25-year-old picture. At the finish everyone was clamorous in their praises; how such enchantment could have been poorly received defied imagination. I was as good as could be and Marilyn! Marilyn was quite wonderful, the best of all.

Laurence Olivier

❏

I said to Marilyn Monroe, "Why can't you get here on time, for fuck's sake?" And she replied, "Oh! Do you have that word in England, too?"

Laurence Olivier

❏

In *Love Nest* I played opposite a starlet named Marilyn Monroe, then as obscure as I was. I found her pretty dull. Marilyn spoke in a breathless way which denoted either passion or asthma. She wore dresses with the necklines cut so low it looked as though she had jumped into her dress and caught her feet on the shoulder straps. Marilyn was interested in culture. At the time she had not yet discovered Dostoyevski's *Brothers Karamazov* and, in fact, had only late discovered Hollywood's Brothers Warner. However, she used to carry around the books of Marcel Proust, with their titles facing out, although I never saw her read any of them. She was always holding up shooting because she was talking with someone on the phone. Judging from what's happened, I guess she had the right number.

Jack Paar

Directing Marilyn Monroe is like directing Lassie—you need 14 takes to get the bark right!

Otto Preminger

Monroe! I never could understand what it was all about. She was absolutely talentless. To work with her was agony. In the first place, she never was there. You'd wait; five o'clock at night she'd show up on the set.

Tony Randall

I adored that girl (Marilyn Monroe) from the moment we met. Could I go to see *Marilyn*, the compilation of shots from her films? I'd be too broken up. I loved her too much.

Thelma Ritter

Marilyn Monroe was a very kind, gentle girl, but she was—figure-wise—no designer's dream, nor was she a "fashion plate." Somehow she always looked like she had come in from a windstorm or as Ann Straus, who handled fashion publicity, would say, "like an unmade bed." After *The Asphalt Jungle* at MGM, Johnny Hyde (her agent and boyfriend) came to me with the request that I try to make her look more chic. Lana Turner, who was exactly the same size as Marilyn and was also a beautiful blonde, had just finished a film in which she wore a black silk cocktail suit. In it, Lana looked crisp and stunning, Marilyn only looked untidy and cheap. Marilyn looked much better in a skimpy towel than in expensive, high fashion clothes.

Helen Rose

❏

Marilyn Monroe and I got along great. Marilyn was very shy and very sweet and far more intelligent than people gave her credit for ... I had a ball on *Gentlemen Prefer Blondes*, but I don't think Marilyn did altogether, because she was torn between the front office, who was calling her a cheap, dumb blonde, and Natasha Lytess, her drama coach. It started going wrong when Natasha began directing her on the set. Marilyn's eyes would turn immediately to her when a scene was finished. Howard Hawks, who was trying to direct the picture, wasn't pleased at all. He was a director that even producers didn't interfere with. He was lord on the set. Finally, Hawks threw Natasha off the set.

Jane Russell

❏

While photographing the screen test which led to Marilyn Monroe's first studio contract, I got a cold chill. This girl had something I hadn't seen since silent pictures. She had a kind of fantastic beauty like Gloria Swanson, and she radiated sex like Jean Harlow. She didn't need a soundtrack to tell her story.

Leon Shamroy

❏

Marilyn Monroe was so beautiful and her skin was so perfect that you could hardly believe it. On *Some Like It Hot*, Billy Wilder and Arthur Miller were each giving her so many directions that she was constantly confused. Most of the time Marilyn didn't arrive on the set until two in the afternoon. I remember that one scene had to be shot 58 times. Most of the time Marilyn would have brandy in her coffee, then take a few pills and start to work. But whatever she did off-camera didn't matter once that camera started to roll. The camera was in love with her. It was during the shooting of this film that Marilyn had a miscarriage.

Joan Shawlee

❏

Marilyn Monroe was awkward. She couldn't get out of her own way in *Clash by Night*. She wasn't disciplined, and she was often late, and she drove Bob Ryan, Paul Douglas and myself out of our minds ... but she didn't do it viciously, and there was a sort of magic about her which we all recognized at once. Her phobias, or whatever they were, came later; she seemed just a carefree kid, and she owned the world.

Barbara Stanwyck

❏

During preparations for *Gentlemen Prefer Blondes*, I looked at Marilyn Monroe and had a feeling of doom. She was beautiful, but there was something in her eyes that spelled disaster. We became friendly, and I began to recognize that awful insecurity that some people talked about. Later on, at a big party in New York, I could feel that insecurity, physically feel it. Marilyn came over and whispered, "Ask me to sing." So I did. She came over and sat down on the piano bench beside me and sang "Bye, Bye, Baby." She was digging her fingernails into my upper arm with almost every word. Inside, she was like a drawn bowstring.

Jule Styne

❏

Marilyn Monroe's delivery seemed so very strange and I couldn't hear what she was saying. It seemed dreadful and I thought, "Well, if this is the American idea of acting and glamour I'll just have to put up with it for the rest of the film (*The Prince and the Showgirl*)." Then Larry (Olivier) let me see the rushes, and Marilyn's manner and timing were delicious … She didn't wear any underthings, and you could see everything. She had a delightful way of sticking out her backside … After the filming Larry asked me how he did. I said, "You did just fine, but with Marilyn there nobody will be watching you."

Sybil Thorndike

❏

I remember Marilyn's late-night phone calls. The telephone became her lifeline. Sometimes I was able to talk to her for a while and calm her down, but there were other nights when she needed to see me, to have someone with her. When I did go over to her house, it was like babysitting. I'd mostly just hold her hand and tell her everything would be all right. It was like helping Shirley Temple get through a Mae West nightmare—a little girl with all this adult pain. Eventually she would quiet down, and after she'd fallen asleep I would leave.

William Travilla

❏

Marilyn (Monroe) and I used to lunch often at the Café de Paris commissary at 20th Century-Fox. She'd sometimes accompany me there wearing only a jersey wrapper during a fitting break. I can still see us walking in there, and here's Bette Davis, Tyrone Power, Susan Hayward with their forks frozen halfway to their mouths as they gaped at her. All these stars with their press people and agents and all the background of a studio going on and it all just stopped dead when Marilyn appeared. It was awesome—and she wasn't even trying.

William Travilla

❏

Marilyn Monroe is the greatest *farceuse* in the business, a female Chaplin. In the right kind of picture she is superb and the public will go to see her. It is only when she plays a serious role that she has trouble. The audience doesn't believe her.

Jerry Wald

❏

Marilyn Monroe had great impact. People were mad to see her. But the poor thing didn't know her business. She wouldn't survive today. In some scenes she had to be pushed bodily into what we called the key light. She'd been spoiled, of course. The word came down from the top even before she was a star that she could come to work whenever she wanted. We had a plane scene in *How to Marry a Millionaire*. It went 28 takes. Marilyn blew 27. As the day went on I went downhill and she got better. She came off great and I was washed out. But the business today can't afford 28 takes.

David Wayne

❏

I liked Marilyn Monroe. She was around, under contract, and we all thought she was a bit too much. We thought: Marilyn is not going to make it. That's why I became a hell of a producer! She was a vulnerable kid. Murder to work with, because she was scared to death of acting—even when she had become big. We had a hell of a time getting her out of the dressing room. When it was five o'clock, it got irritating: "C'mon, Marilyn, we want to go home!" She was a movie animal. Something happened between the lens and the film. Nobody knew what the hell it was. On the set you'd think: "Oh, this is impossible; you can't print this." You'd see it and she's got everyone backed off the screen.

Richard Widmark

❏

Here you have the poor girl (Marilyn Monroe) and all of a sudden she becomes a famous star. So now these people tell her she had to be a great actress. It is like a man writes a stupid jingle, "Doggie in the Window," and it becomes a hit, and he's forced to write symphonies for Toscanini to play. They're trying to elevate Marilyn to a level where she can't exist. She will lose her audience. She is a calendar girl with warmth, charm—great charm—and she's being compared to Duse. Duse! I don't know who's to blame. Kazan? Strasberg? Milton Greene? She is being taught acting by the kind of people who don't believe in under-arm deodorants. They believe in sitting on the floor even if there are six comfortable chairs in the room. They'll make her into another Julie Harris! She'll lose everything of her own. She'll make herself ugly. The crowd in the bleachers will hate her.

Billy Wilder

Hollywood didn't kill Marilyn Monroe. But it's the Marilyn Monroes who are killing Hollywood.

Billy Wilder

Making a picture with Marilyn Monroe was like going to the dentist. It was hell at the time, but after it was all over it was wonderful.

Billy Wilder

Marilyn? Surely you are referring to Hollywood's Joan of Arc, aren't you? The Myth? The Legend? Our Ultimate Sacrificial Lamb? She was the meanest woman I have ever met around this town. I am appalled by this cult. It's getting to be an act of courage to say anything but saintly things about her. Well, let me be courageous. I have never met anyone as utterly mean as Marilyn Monroe. Nor as utterly fabulous on the screen, and that includes Garbo.

Billy Wilder

The greatest thing about Marilyn Monroe is not her chest. It is her ear. She is a master of delivery. She can read comedy better than anyone else in the world. I must say I haven't noticed any improvement, however, since she took those elaborate acting lessons. I have always said she should have gone

Claudette Colbert
Of bras and men

to a train engineer's school instead to learn something about arriving on schedule.

Billy Wilder

❏

The question is whether Marilyn (Monroe) is a person at all, or one of the greatest DuPont products ever invented. She has breasts like granite, and a brain like Swiss cheese, full of holes ... The charm of her is her two left feet ... Would I direct a third film with her? I am too old and too rich to go through this again.

Billy Wilder

❏

The thing I remember most about Marilyn Monroe is working with this beautiful lady from early in the morning until late at night. Then as my folks were getting me dressed to go home she came out of her dressing room without any make-up. If I hadn't recognized her voice I'd never have believed she was the same person.

George "Foghorn" Winslow

❏

Whenever there's an election and it looks like the Democrats have a good candidate, they rake out all the crap about the Kennedys and Marilyn (Monroe), and it's just that: crap. She (Monroe) had tried to commit suicide a couple of times. She couldn't believe that she had the comedy technique she did, and the intelligence to go on and play mature roles ... She didn't have a family (and) they had her posing nude when she was 36 years old.

Shelley Winters

❏

Marilyn Monroe's temperamental and not very fit. Wave a script in front of her face and she comes down with a cold.

Darryl F. Zanuck

Marriage

A wife lasts only for the length of the marriage, but an ex-wife is there for the rest of your life.

Woody Allen

❏

Each of us is so finely tuned that to have two people meet and then intermesh is a matter of luck. I've had friends who when they marry say, "I know we're going to have to work at it." I always think they're wrong. The things that are really pleasurable in life, whether it's playing softball or working on your stamp collection, really require no effort.

Woody Allen

❏

My first marriage? She was a philosophy student and we had these long philosophical discussions and she always proved I didn't exist.

Woody Allen

I've always been different. Now, when people all live together, I want to get married.

Brigitte Bardot

It's a grand idea to marry three or four times, have lots of children and remain friendly all around. It's a vitalizing, typically American plan. I endorse it without a quibble or qualm. My wives are lovely, my children adorable. I count myself a very lucky man.

John Barrymore

Marriage requires a special talent, like acting, like writing. I haven't got that talent, so I don't marry. And monogamy requires *genius*.

Warren Beatty

Maybe I might decide to share my life with someone again. But I hope not. There are enormous benefits to be had from solitude. A married woman is like the moon reflecting the light of the sun instead of being a source itself.

Ellen Burstyn

Funny, this marryin' bus'ness. One day me and Bud (Abbott) separated a coupla burlesque girls who were havin' a fight, an' now we're tangled up with 'em for life. Yeah, they married us.

Lou Costello

Would I consider remarriage? If I found a man who had $15,000,000, would sign over half of it to me before the marriage and guarantee he'd be dead within a year.

Bette Davis

❑

Adam may have had his troubles, but he never had to listen to Eve talk about the other men she could have married.

Dom DeLuise

❑

I have been married twice. Both times to men associated with me at the studio. Never again will I marry a man who works with me. I haven't the sort of temperament than can take being with any human being under the sun 24 hours out of 24. Many wives say, "No husband should be around the house during the daytime." Well, I am the wife who says, "No husband should be around the studio during working hours."

Deanna Durbin

❑

If you marry an actress under 30, she'll cook you one meal a week; if she's over 30, she'll cook you two meals a week.

Robert Duvall

❑

They say marriages are made in Heaven. So are thunder and lightning.

Clint Eastwood

❑

Marry an outdoor woman. Then if you throw her out in the yard for the night, she can still survive.

W.C. Fields

❑

In an agent's office, I overheard an actor say Margaret Sullavan was having an affair with the producer Jed Harris ... I'd lean against the fence and I'd stare up at our apartment with the lighted windows on the second floor. I knew Harris was inside with her and I'd wait for him to leave. But instead the lights would go out. More nights than I care to remember I'd stand there and cry ... I couldn't believe my wife and that son-of-a-bitch were in bed together. But I knew they were. And that just destroyed me.

Henry Fonda

In 1946, when my sister, Olivia de Havilland, married writer Marcus (*Delilah*) Goodrich, her agent called to ask what I knew about the groom. Searching my mind for wisps of information, I volunteered, "All I know about him is that he has had four wives and written one book. Too bad it's not the other way around." The agent couldn't resist spreading the remark around town until it finally reached the indignant novelist.

Joan Fontaine

Marriage is great for the young who want to produce offspring. And it's good in the golden years of life when one needs companionship. But for the in-between times it's a very big institution—and that makes me think of steel bars.

Joan Fontaine

Marriage is too interesting an experience to be tried only once or twice.

Eva Gabor

Dahling, this time I married a lawyer so he can handle the divorce!

Zsa Zsa Gabor

And Mia Farrow? Hah! I always knew Frank (Sinatra) would end up in bed with a boy.

Ava Gardner

Ava Gardner
Knew Frank's fate

I've been married to Jack Bean for 32 years. Liz Taylor likes *getting* married. I like *being* married. There's a difference.

Mitzi Gaynor

❏

Why didn't I marry? A good wife has a 24-hour a day job, while acting has required me to work up to 12 or 14 hours a day. I didn't ruin any dear man's life, and I'm grateful for that.

Lillian Gish

❏

I wanted to sleep with him and I didn't know how to do it without getting married. I talked to everybody, my priest, my doctor, and they all said, "Do it. Get married." Now I could punch them in the nose. Richard (Mulligan) was terrific, but I'm not really comfortable with another person in my living area. I hated being married. Every part of marriage outside of sex was un-natural to me.

Joan Hackett

I believe in marriage. I'd be married today if I could find the right somebody, but marriage has always been rather expensive for me, though I must say (director) Anatole Litvak was a very generous man. All the men I was married to were so much more charming than the men I see now that if they came along today I'd marry the same ones again.

Miriam Hopkins

I proposed to Piper Laurie while we were doing retakes on *The Golden Blade*. I said, "Piper, after this picture is over let's go to Mexico. Of course, we'll have to be married." I guess that wasn't the way to frame a proposal properly. She said, "Thank you. And now let's get back to work."

Rock Hudson

My great grandparents were married 65 years, and my grandparents are celebrating their 60th wedding anniversary next week. When I marry, I want to pass both records.

Rock Hudson

Some women have affairs but unfortunately I marry my men. It's funny that a woman can have 25 affairs and nobody says anything, but if she has four husbands she's terrible. I guess I'm just a homebody.

Hedy Lamarr

Marriage is a triumph over hate.

Oscar Levant

In Hollywood, brides keep the bouquets and throw away the groom.

Groucho Marx

❏

I married a Kraut. Every night I get dressed up like Poland and he invades me.

Bette Midler

❏

Husbands are chiefly good lovers when they are betraying their wives.

Marilyn Monroe

❏

Actresses should never marry actors. It's like two streetcar conductors on different lines marrying. They never meet.

Julie Newmar

❏

I was a bridesmaid at Liz Taylor's first wedding, and she was a bridesmaid at mine. It's a good thing we stopped there or it would have turned into a full-time job!

Jane Powell

❏

A bachelor is a man who has the right idea about marriage. He knows it's a device of society designed to make trouble between two people who would otherwise get along very well.

Anthony Quinn

❏

Eddie Fisher was once married to Elizabeth Taylor—that's like trying to wash down the Statute of Liberty with one bar of soap.

Don Rickles

❏

Jane Powell
Always a bride

My mother gave me this advice: Trust your husband, adore your husband and get as much as you can in your own name.

Joan Rivers

I'm a firm believer in getting married early in the morning. That way if it doesn't work out you haven't wasted a whole day.

Mickey Rooney

My marriage license reads, "To whom it may concern."

Mickey Rooney

All I knew when I came to Hollywood is that which a 17-year-old girl learns in a small Southern town—what to do till the minister comes.

Ann Sheridan

❏

Chains don't hold a marriage together. It's threads, hundreds of tiny threads which sew people together through the years. That's what makes a marriage last—more than passion, or even sex.

Simone Signoret

❏

All men make mistakes, but those who are married find out about them sooner.

Red Skelton

❏

To me marriage is an adventure—it's like going to war.

Rod Steiger

❏

My Miami Beach wedding to (comedian) Joe E. Lewis was a sign of what was to follow. A cocktail lounge was converted for the occasion. The bar was disguised by draped rayon and flowers. A floral arbor at one end served as the altar. To me, it was life's big moment and I trembled, just like any bride. The place was packed with Joey's friends—Swifty Morgan, Toots Shor, Harry Richman and others. When Joey and his best man appeared, everybody applauded. He laughed and called greetings to them. The ceremony lasted about 30 seconds. We kissed. Everybody applauded again. The decorations were taken off the bar, and the reception began. I tossed away my bouquet. It was caught by Sophie Tucker.

Martha Stewart

❏

Fighting is one of the greatest exercises in marital togetherness.

Elizabeth Taylor

❏

I think I ended up being the scarlet woman partly because of my rather puritanical upbringing and beliefs. I always chose to think I was in love and that love was synonymous with marriage.

Elizabeth Taylor

I planned on having one husband and seven children, but it turned out the other way around.

Lana Turner

I've married a few people I shouldn't have, but haven't we all?

Mamie Van Doren

Marriage is like a book. The whole story takes place between covers.

Mae West

When Fernando (Lamas) proposed to me, he said, "Let me take you away from all this." And I said, "Away from all what? I'm a movie star!"

Esther Williams

I don't think I'm cut out for marriage. For instance, when I got back from my third honeymoon I just couldn't understand why my husband wanted to come in the house with me. I was just about to say, "Thanks for a nice time."

Shelley Winters

Polygamy would never work in this country. Think of four wives in a kitchenette.

Jane Wyman

❏

I would love to get married again, provided two conditions are met: that I am in love and that I am backed by the Ford Foundation.

Gig Young

Men

I was a bitch in *Humoresque*, and I love playing bitches. There's a lot of bitch in every woman. There's a lot of bitch in every man, too.

Joan Crawford

❏

There aren't any hard women—just soft men.

Bette Davis

❏

I see my films as first aid to the modern male psyche. Masculinity is becoming obsolete. Most jobs today can be held by women. Many men have become defensive and enjoy being taken to another time, another period, where masculinity was important to survival.

Clint Eastwood

❏

I vant a man who only has to be kind and understanding. Is zat too much to ask of a multi-millionaire?

Zsa Zsa Gabor

❏

All men are alike. If you ask any American man, "How are you?", he'll answer "Fine," even if his mother just had a heart attack.

Joan Hackett

Men like me because I don't wear a brassiere. Women like me because I don't look like a girl who would steal a husband. At least not for long.

Jean Harlow

Men are less manly today, but a woman of my age is not in a position to know exactly how manly they are.

Katharine Hepburn

Men are those creatures with two legs and eight hands.

Jayne Mansfield

It's all a bunch of CRAP, that idea about being manly. Because we all know that there are so many kinds of courage. It takes a whole lot more courage, say, to stick by a friend when everybody else turns his back than it does to shoot a deer with a bow and arrow and then let the animal bleed to death and have an arrow scrunch up inside him for a hundred yards until he dies. Or to go down a mountain stream talking about how much you love nature and be throwing cigars and beer cans into the river.

Burt Reynolds

It is possible that blondes also prefer gentlemen.

Mamie Van Doren

Give a man a free hand and he'll try to put it all over you.

Mae West

Minorities

The movie stars are friendly to Negroes. When we finished *High Society*, Bing (Crosby) gave me a golden money clip which I use, inscribed, "To Louis from Bing." And when he had a baby girl, I sent him a telegram, "Now you have jazz." He has a whole wall of my records, and every record he makes, I buy. But we aren't social. In fact, I've never been invited to the home of a movie star—not even Bing's.

Louis Armstrong

❑

Many white chicks feel they'll get soul if they go to bed with a black man they don't even care about, and the black goes to the white because of the white's status in this society. The black person is supposed to gain from making love to a white, and the white is giving up status ... If a white chick is with a black guy, she's saying, "Look at me, look at what I'm giving up, look how I'm going against society. Man, am I brave." Now I'm not talking about love. I'm talking about whites who simply have a desire to make love to a black.

Bill Cosby

❑

What was I? That outdated "tragic mulatto" of earlier fiction? I wasn't fully accepted in either world, black or white. I was too light to satisfy Negroes, not light enough to secure the screen work, the roles, the marriage status available to a white woman.

Dorothy Dandridge

❑

I became the first Negro entertainer to become a millionaire. All the things that Bill Cosby and Sidney Poitier have done wouldn't be possible if I hadn't broken that law. I set up thrones for them to come and sit on.

Stepin Fetchit

❑

I am free of all prejudice. I hate everybody equally.

W.C. Fields

❏

What's the subliminal message in a John Wayne Western? That white people are the civilizers and Indians are violent-prone savages you can't kill fast enough. And what do the women usually do when the burning arrows come flying through the door? Hide or run shrieking into the woods. There's an image that comes across. I am superconscious about how it affected me. Movies are an important means of communication and I don't want to use it irresponsibly.

Jane Fonda

❏

I had all the proper prejudices, too. You see a white girl hanging around with a Negro man, you immediately think she's a tramp. That's the nub of all prejudice, I suppose, and the irony is that it is always the woman for whom you feel contempt, not the man.

Lena Horne

❏

They didn't make me into a maid, but they didn't make me into anything else, either. I became a butterfly pinned to a column singing away in movieland.

Lena Horne

❏

Why should I complain about making $7,000 a week playing a maid? If I didn't, I'd be making seven dollars a week actually being one!

Hattie McDaniel

❏

I didn't mind playing a maid the first time, because I thought that was how you got into the business. But after I did the same thing over and over I resented it. I didn't mind being funny but I didn't like being stupid.

Butterfly McQueen

Lena Horne
Pinned to column

❑

I was not in the least anti-Semitic before I came here (Hollywood). I am now.
It is intolerable to see them enjoying themselves.

Evelyn Waugh

❑

I don't feel we did wrong in taking this great country away from the Indians.
Our so-called stealing of this country from them was just a matter of survival.
There were great numbers of people who needed new land, and the Indians
were selfishly trying to keep it for themselves.

John Wayne

Moguls

(In the '30s), everyone was under a wonderful umbrella—the studio system.
When you were under contract, you had papas—Papa Goldwyn, Papa Mayer,

Papa Zanuck, if you could call Zanuck a papa! You were taken in charge and trained . . . They have none of that today. *Anyplace* . . . I regret the passing of the studio system. I was very appreciative of it because I had no talent. Believe me. What could I do? I couldn't dance. I couldn't sing. I could *talk*. I could barely walk. I had no flair. I wasn't a beauty, that's for sure.

Lucille Ball

Jack Warner is a man who would rather tell a bad joke than make a good movie. He'd give anything to be a comedian, and he doesn't realize that he is.

Jack Benny

Announcing to his staff the casting of Frank Sinatra, Kim Novak and Rita Hayworth:
We've just signed the wop, the Polack and the cunt for *Pal Joey*.

Harry Cohn

I don't get ulcers. I give 'em!

Harry Cohn

Over at Columbia and Fox if you were not sexually operational, forget your career. (Harry) Cohn and (Darryl) Zanuck loved to sample the goodies. I've got to tell you a funny story about Zanuck—I went over to Fox, one of my late films, and when I was ushered into his office he promptly opened a desk drawer and took out a genuine gold casting of his genitals. I must admit he was admirably hung, but I couldn't help wondering what sort of so-called "obligations" had hung over the ladies at 20th over the years.

Joan Crawford

To me, Louis B. Mayer's arm around your shoulder meant his hand was closer to your throat.

Jules Dassin

Once I walked out on suspension for nine months and I remember in the last conversation I had with Jack Warner he said, "Please don't go, Bette, we've got this new book for you called *Gone with the Wind*," and I turned around, leaned across his desk and said, "Yeah, and I'll just bet it's a pip!"

Bette Davis

Warner Brothers was like a model prison farm and Jack Warner was the warden. He never trusted actors.

Olivia de Havilland

Louis B. Mayer offered me a seven-year contract. It had an option for seven more years, and he was willing to pay me $2,000 a week. The trouble started when he said to me, "Of course, we can't do all this for you unless we own you." I said, "You can't own me. I won't be a piece of goods on your counter," and I walked out.

Buddy Ebsen

Harry Cohn, in case you don't know, happened to be one hell of a son-of-a-bitch. He took one look at me and very discreetly tried to bring up the subject of my glass eye. I lost my right eye at three, y'know. Anyway, Cohn called it my "deficiency." I didn't know what he was talkin' about so I said, "*What* deficiency?", thinkin' he mighta meant vitamins or somethin'. Harry replied, "Your eye. You're a little off-center in your vision. It will show on screen." Well, I finally agreed to a stupid screen test to see if my "deficiency" would show up on the screen. Harry called me back to his office. He said, "Thank you, Mr. Falk. But for the same money I can get an actor with two eyes."

Peter Falk

I had fallen in love with a movie called *Laura*, and begged the studio (20th Century-Fox) to find me a drama. So they got Otto Preminger, who directed *Laura*, and Dana Andrews, who starred in it, and found us a property called

Fallen Angel. I had some wonderful scenes in it, but (Darryl) Zanuck cut them all out and behind my back built up a new girl in it named Linda Darnell. I thought Zanuck played a dirty trick. I drove right through the gate and left the key to my dressing room with the guard, along with a note to Mr. Zanuck. I never went back. Zanuck begged me to do *The Dolly Sisters* with Betty Grable, but I never answered his calls. I didn't want any part of the place again. I don't want to say anything bad about anybody, but the only thing I hope is that I live to see Darryl F. Zanuck washed up in this business.

Alice Faye

❏

After about three weeks of filming *Little Lord Fauntleroy*, I was told to report to Mr. (David O.) Selznick's office. I put on my best dress and was ushered in. I thought, "Well, at last I'm going to hear some comments on the rushes. Maybe I've become a star or something." He was on the phone. When he got off, he rose without a word, walked around to the front of the desk, grabbed the front of my dress and ripped it down. I grabbed a decanter from

Alice Faye
A cutting experience

his desk, hit him on the head with it and ran out. I never had any more direct dealings with him.

Virginia Field

❑

This atom bomb is dynamite!

Samuel Goldwyn

❑

I told Louis B. Mayer after I had been at the studio about a year that I didn't want a film career. I didn't feel I was very good in films, and that the films I was in weren't any good for me. Besides, I wanted to leave so I could train for the operatic stage. He said, "Here we are making you a big star and you tell me you don't want to be one. You ungrateful little bitch!" Well, I was only 16 and at home we never even said damn! So I said, "It's you who's the son-of-a-bitch and a pants-presser, too!" I think I had heard that he started off in the clothing business and that seemed to me the worst thing I could call him. Then he had one of his famous attacks. This upset me! Later on I found out that he had them with everybody when he couldn't get his own way.

Kathryn Grayson

❑

The Sam Goldwyns, Louis B. Mayers, Harry Cohns and that bunch were all romantics. They were tough men, but they were pushovers for this business. They wanted to make money, too, but they had a romantic attitude toward the people who made movies and the movies themselves. Now, for the most part, it's a money-making business. The money behind the business today is *cold* money. Theirs (the early moguls) was *hot* money.

Katharine Hepburn

❑

When I came to America 25 years ago to direct *Rebecca*, (producer) David O. Selznick sent me a memorandum. I've just finished reading it. I think I may make it into a motion picture. I plan to call it *The Longest Story Ever Told*.

Alfred Hitchcock

❏

Darryl Zanuck became obsessed with Bella Darvi when she taught him that he could do it in bed, not only on a desk.

Nunnally Johnson

❏

The only time we ever met Jack Warner he said to "Friz" Freleng, "The only thing I know about our cartoon unit is that we do Mickey Mouse." Jack and Harry Warner believed we did Mickey Mouse until 1962, and when they found out we didn't they shut it down.

Chuck Jones

❏

I speak of most of the men (in my life) with affection. There are a few exceptions—notably the bosses of the studios. Hollywood in the '30s was a totally chauvinistic place. Young girls were just so much stock that the bosses felt they could do with what they wanted. It's not so much better today.

Evelyn Keyes

❏

For years Marlene Dietrich used to play a game. Her friends had to name the one person in the world each would not go to bed with even if their children's lives depended on it. Most named Hitler, but Marlene invariably named David O. Selznick.

Gavin Lambert

❏

I went to see L.B. Mayer—whom I didn't "see" because he was stretched out on a barber's chair in his suite with someone giving him a pedicure, another one giving him a manicure and another one shaving him. His face was covered with lather. There was this corpse being worked on by three people and an entourage standing around, and he said, "I heard some of your radio shows. They're damn good. You want to come to Hollywood?"

Joseph Losey

❏

I had one date with Howard Hughes. And that was enough. One night I was awakened from a sound sleep by the ringing of the telephone. It was two o'clock in the morning. "Hi, Annie. This is Howard Hughes . . . When can I see you?" Tomorrow night, I said. I got all dressed up in a pretty cocktail dress and waited. Nine o'clock came. Then 10. Finally about a quarter of 12 the doorbell rang. He was wearing a dirty old coat with grease spots all over it and patches on the elbows, a beat-up shirt, wrinkled trousers and old tennis shoes. We got into a beat-up, battered old Chevrolet and drove to Perino's, one of the most elegant restaurants in town. As I was seated, Howard said, "Excuse me for a minute." He disappeared into the kitchen . . . He finally reappeared, carrying a huge bowl of salad. "I mixed it myself. I never let anyone touch the food that I eat," he explained.

Ann Miller

❏

Jack Warner has oilcloth pockets so he can steal soup.

Wilson Mizner

❏

The sheer gutlessness of the people who make the decisions at the major Hollywood studios—and I want you to quote me—is terrifying . . . It makes one feel that to try to make a career in motion pictures is kamikaze work.

Kate Nelligan

❏

I had done some films for Metro I didn't like, and told Mr. Mayer I wasn't going to do any more poor scripts. He became furious and screamed, "You'll do what we tell you! Remember, we made you and we can break you!" I told him "God made me" and left Hollywood.

Luise Rainer

❏

Mr. Mayer may have had his other side—you know, the monster, the tyrant —but if he did, I never saw it. *He* was the one who wanted me in *Singin' in the Rain*; nobody else did. He was a great chief, and he knew how to build stars. But they got rid of him and Dore Schary took over. Dore only wanted to make message pictures, but he never got *my* message.

Debbie Reynolds

❑

Sunday lunch at Mr. Mayer's beach house was like an audience at the Vatican. Of course, it wasn't His Highness' ring you kissed.

Phil Silvers

❑

Much as I cared for Joe Kennedy, he was a classic example of that person in the arts with lots of brains and drive but little taste or talent.

Gloria Swanson

❑

Louis Mayer brought in Dore Schary as the crown prince at MGM, and the whole atmosphere began to change. This betting game started: Within seven years Dore Schary would ruin the empire—and the s.o.b. did it in *five*, which surprised us all.

Lana Turner

❑

Darryl Zanuck's proposition to me was a bit perfunctory, since the word was out that I was uncooperative in such matters, and my polite refusal was shrugged off. Even so, he got his revenge a short while later, at a dinner party held in a restaurant featuring the kind of banquette seating that makes escape impossible. Zanuck arranged to be seated between his wife and me, and throughout the dinner he pawed me under the table without saying a word, knowing I dared not make a scene in his wife's presence.

Ruth Warrick

❑

The problem with the men who run the studios in the '80s is they have no balls. MGM's Louis B. Mayer had balls. What he said went. But I saw the whole system come crumbling down before my eyes. The stockholders in New York ousted Mayer and put in Dore Schary, who didn't know what to do with movie stars. He was only interested in featured players. People like Nancy Davis.

Esther Williams

Esther Williams
Observed system's fall

Lauren Bacall
Just a working girl

228

❏

For God's sake, don't say yes until I finish talking!

Darryl F. Zanuck

Money

Lucy (Ball) was negotiating to star in Cecil B. DeMille's *The Greatest Show on Earth* at Paramount. At the same time she was having some trouble with Harry Cohn at Columbia. Harry had to pay her $85,000 for the last film on her contract, so he sent her a terrible script called *The Magic Carpet*. It was the kind they wanted you to refuse—a contract breaker. "All I have to do to get the $85,000," she said, "is appear. It only has a six-day schedule. I can't do the DeMille picture anymore because by the time Mr. DeMille is ready to go, I'll be so big with your child I won't be able to get away with it." She did the picture for Columbia. I saw DeMille about a month afterward, and he said, "Congratulations, Mr. Arnaz. You are the only man who has ever screwed his wife, Cecil B. DeMille, Paramount Pictures and Harry Cohn, all at the same time."

Desi Arnaz

❏

I have to work. I don't have any money. My movie money went to the U.S. government. Bogie left a sizeable estate, but it went to educate his children. It wasn't enough for us to live on the rest of our lives. It's funny how people get the idea I'm rich.

Lauren Bacall

❏

I suppose money and things have the proper perspective in my life today because I had so much—and lost so much. In a span of only four years, I lost my child, my mother, my father, my sister, my only uncle, my home and all my money. I learned real values the hard way.

Florence Bates

❏

To his agent:

Before God, I am worth $35 a week; before the motion picture industry, I'm worth anything you can get.

Ronald Colman

❏

I've got $10,000 in the Bank of Berlin, just in case that son-of-a-bitch Hitler wins.

W.C. Fields

❏

The cost of living has gone up a dollar a quart.

W.C. Fields

❏

Ronald Colman
His worth before God

I really don't know anybody in this business who has retired on the money he made from films. I have diversified business interests in international trade and investments ... real estate holdings out West ... in Montana, like that. Look at the really successful stars who become wealthy, like Bob Hope; it wasn't from their films, but from their other business investments.

Douglas Fairbanks, Jr.

Alan Hale was such a good actor that if he was with you in a scene he could take it away, whether standing behind you, beside you or in front of you. He was full of tricks. I got him and S.Z. "Cuddles" Sakall together one night. Sakall was a funny old guy, but most actors hated him. He messed up the English language so much that they couldn't get their cues. Hale couldn't stand him. Naturally I brought them together as often as I could, and on this night Hale hollered, "For Chrissakes, Sakall, ain't it time you learned to speak English? You been here long enough!" Replied Sakall, "And for vy I should spik Englich better, ven mitt dis Englich I em makin' more vot iss you?"

Errol Flynn

How do I reconcile getting a million dollars a film with my political views? I guess some people think if somebody has money, why should they care about somebody who doesn't? I don't know why but I just do. I'm not interested in people who are wealthy. I grew up with them. Look, they pay me this money. I'm not going to say to these studios, which are multi-national corporations, "Don't pay me so much money." They'll just go and waste it on something. So give it to me. I will take as much money as they are going to give me. How I spend it is another thing—that's been well publicized, too. I put my money where my mouth is, as my father says.

Jane Fonda

My father was not the kind of star who got five million dollars for a picture. The most he ever got was $250,000. He was embarrassed to ask for more.

Peter Fonda

(Bob) Hope is gorgeous! I drive him crazy. For instance, we did a show in New York a while back and he said to me beforehand, "For Christ's sake, during this interview don't start that shit about me having $150,000,000." So as soon as the interview started, I said, "Tell 'em about the $150,000,000 you got!"

Jackie Gleason

Actors are for Dr. Menninger. The ideal man is one who has $8,000,000 and no complexes. To such a man I could give security.

Paulette Goddard

I don't want to make a nickel on this picture (*The Best Years of Our Lives*). All I want is for everybody in the country to see it.

Samuel Goldwyn

Errol Flynn says he doesn't worry about money just as long as he can reconcile his net income with his gross habits.

Sheilah Graham

"How rich are you?" I resent that question, since it has been blown out of all proportion. One publication claimed I had $500,000,000. If I had all that, I would not have gone to Vietnam—I would have sent for it! Also, it's easy to have $500,000,000. All you have to do is save a million a year for 50 years. Of course I'm wealthy—but I'm not *that* wealthy.

Bob Hope

Writing is like the world's oldest profession. First you do it for your own enjoyment. Then you do it for a few friends. Eventually, you figure, "What the hell, I might as well get paid for it."

Irma Kalish

Alan Ladd
Sans grand illusions

I haven't any illusions about Hollywood. You see, I grew up here and pictures have no glamour for me. They're just a big industry—a tremendous business—in which people work very hard. Sometimes if they're lucky they make a great deal of money. I have no grand ideas about myself as an actor. I didn't go into acting to "express myself." I don't regard myself as a great artist. I went into acting to make money—because you can make more of that in less time in motion pictures than you can in any other business. Some day I'd like to be a director.

Alan Ladd

❑

I can only dish it out. I can't take it. I don't go to see my movies. Once I had a terrible fight with Jack Warner, who asked me what I thought of a picture I had done with Humphrey Bogart. I told him I didn't go to see it. Mr. Warner was furious. I said that I only get paid for making pictures. If he wanted me to see them, he'd have to pay me extra.

Peter Lorre

❑

If I were an inch taller, I'd make another $150,000 a movie.

Gordon MacRae

❏

Beverly Hills: It only goes to show what God could do if He had money.

Herman J. Mankiewicz

❏

When I got the part in *Gentlemen Prefer Blondes*, Jane Russell, the brunette in it, got $200,000 and I got my $500 a week, but that to me was, you know, considerable. She, by the way, was quite wonderful to me. The only thing was I couldn't get a dressing room. I said, finally—I really got to this kind of level—I said, "Look, after all, I am the blonde and it is *Gentlemen Prefer Blondes!*" Because they always kept saying, "Remember, you're not a star." I said, "Well, whatever I am, I *am* the blonde!"

Marilyn Monroe

❏

I'm not what you call a commercial actress. Even though the parts in the movie versions of *Summer and Smoke* and *Sweet Bird of Youth* were meaty roles, they weren't moneymakers. But I'd rather have people think I was a great actress than a bankable one.

Geraldine Page

❏

I don't know anybody worthwhile who you can talk about who doesn't want some money. Striking it rich? Hey, I saw my mother turn tricks for some dumb white man when I was a kid. I saw my father take the money, and I saw what it did to them. But they gave me righteousness—I'm a good person.

Richard Pryor

❏

I spent so much on my wife, I decided to marry her for my money.

Richard Pryor

❏

Part of the $10,000,000 I've made in my career went for gambling, part for horses and part for women. The rest I spent foolishly.

George Raft

It still boggles my mind how Andy and Betsy (Mickey Rooney and Judy Garland) transcended language barriers in the Andy Hardy series and those musicals I did with Judy. Alone, those grossed MGM over a *billion* and a half dollars around the world. That was at 30 cents a ticket! In today's box office terms, it would be over six billion!

Mickey Rooney

I was popular when it wasn't popular to be popular. So the press said, "Let's knock Mickey Rooney." They painted me as this guy who was always losing his money and his wives. They said I lost all my millions, which was impossible since at my peak I was earning only $200,000 a year. I was supposed to be a cocky kid, drinking, caring for nobody but myself. I tell you 80 per cent of the stuff written about me is lies. Of course, the other 20 per cent. . . .

Mickey Rooney

Money can't buy happiness. That's why we have credit cards.

Red Skelton

One thing I did learn: If you are going to be mentally ill it is like anything else, like the best country club or the best hotel. The most exclusive places are always the most desirable. I used up every cent I had earned as an actress.

Gene Tierney

Mr. Marlon Brando got, for an aggregate of 20 minutes on the screen in *Superman* and *Apocalypse Now*, more money than Clark Gable got for 20 years at MGM.

Billy Wilder

News

Occasionally some newspaper makes me pregnant. I don't know how many times I've been made pregnant by the press. It can get embarrassing.

Audrey Hepburn

In Hollywood the only reading material they consume willingly is a local newspaper called *The Hollywood Reporter*. Like all residents of small towns, they are tremendously impressed by its flattering references to themselves and exult in its edgy comments about their friends.

James Mason

I'm right on top of the news: I get *The Los Angeles Times*, but everything else I read at the newsstands—I take from them as they have taken from me.

Sean Penn

Nudity

Appear in the buff? No! Never! I just don't think it's right. I don't know if it's my upbringing or if it's just me, but I could never do it. Besides, I'm too skinny.

June Allyson

In *Roman Scandals* in 1933, I played a slave girl and all I wore was a wig and a G-string. But the wig covered up everything because the long hair came down to our knees. I had forgotten my wardrobe in that picture until years later when I was giving an interview and berating all the actresses tearing off their clothes in movies. I was really spouting off when someone asked me, "What about you in *Roman Scandals?*" They reminded me I had started out in a G-string and wig.

Lucille Ball

Gene Tierney
Only the best

June Allyson
No good nudes

237

I hear about that actor—what's his name? Oh, yes, Brando. Imagine, showing nakedness and sexual intercourse on the screen! What should be done about such people? I say shoot 'em. They're going to ruin the picture business.

Donald Crisp

When I'm cleaning the house I wear an apron, but nothing else. It makes my activities—dusting, washing—more interesting to my husband.

Nina Foch

Nudity on the stage? It is traditional when you run out of creative juices to go to the old "dropping the pants" routine. This, in such as *Hair*, is sadder because of the extreme youth so exposed by the promoter. I mean procurer. Please excuse; what I mean is the producer. *Producer????*

June Havoc

The new nudie films? I'm personally so tired of seeing all those breasts— I'm not tired of seeing cocks yet because there haven't been that many on the screen. I think that if (President) Nixon wouldn't be so stuffy, if pornography was a free and open market, all this trouble would be avoided. Repression breeds so much interest. By knowing that you're seeing something that you shouldn't be seeing you're going to want to run out to see breasts and cocks twice as fast as you would if no fuss was made at all.

Sally Kellerman

I've never undressed in front of a lens, never, never. I can't be mixed up with those little whores that undress at any moment. My father and mother would only allow me to see the films of Shirley Temple.

Gina Lollobrigida

Lucille Ball
A scandalous costume

Sally Kellerman
Tired of breasts

239

Young actresses are always telling me they can't go to an audition any more without undressing. The boys have to take their clothes off, too. It's too excessive, and it's getting boring, all this nudity. It'll be a shame if it upsets people so much that it brings the need for censorship. I hate censorship. But I'm afraid we're heading in that direction. There's no mystery! No privacy. And frankly, no sex, either. Most of the sex I've seen on the screen looks like an expression of hostility towards sex. I know mystery is a dirty word to the young people of today, but a suggestion of sex is much more interesting than actually showing it, don't you think?

Myrna Loy

A woman's ass is for her husband, not theatergoers.

Louis B. Mayer

In *The Jungle Princess* with Dorothy Lamour, she wore her sarong for the first time. I was supposed to be teaching native girl Lamour the art of Western kissing—she catches on fast, and when she begins to like it too much, I am supposed to run off down the beach, dive in—to cool off, I suppose. Dottie was to give chase. She did, diving in right after me—but instead of swimming my way, she kept right on going *out to sea!* For a moment I didn't know what had happened—until I got a look at her face ... a montage of shock, fury, amusement, bafflement. No explanations needed: when she hit the water, her sarong fell off.

Ray Milland

My impulse to appear naked and my dreams about it had no shame or sense of sin in them. Dreaming of people looking at me made me feel less lonely. I think I wanted them to see me naked because I was ashamed of the clothes I wore—the never-changing faded blue dress of poverty. Naked, I was like the other girls and not someone in an orphan's uniform.

Marilyn Monroe

What do I wear to bed? Why Chanel No. 5, of course.

Marilyn Monroe

Elliott Gould." To make it contemporary. I *like* Elliott Gould, but I *meant* Joel McCrea. It's not the same.

Maureen Stapleton

❏

The war had just ended, and the city was booming again. Almost overnight the orange groves and open spaces disappeared under the spreading blanket of suburbs. Light—that's my strongest impression of that postwar time. After the long years of blackouts and conservation, the city was adazzle with blazing bulbs, brilliant and glittering and fun. And the men were home. They seemed to catch your eye everywhere you went, like the first greening after a thaw.

Lana Turner

Permissiveness

I've finally figured out today's movie ratings system: "G" means the hero gets the girl; "R" means the villain gets the girl; and "X" means everybody gets the girl.

Kirk Douglas

❏

There wasn't one moment of reality in *Casablanca*. We weren't making art. We were making a living. Movies in those days were prevented from reality. Every leading man had to be a great sexual athlete. Every boy and girl had to "meet cute" and the girl had to dislike the boy when they met. If a woman committed adultery, she had to die. God said, "Get that woman!" Now the woman who commits adultery is your heroine.

Julius J. Epstein

❏

I don't go to see any of the new pictures, because I can't sit next to people in the dark and hear "Fuck you" and "Fuck off." I just can't take it. It's too vulgar now. Now, pictures are too realistic. The brutality and the nudity and the swearing . . . it's all too harsh.

Henry Hathaway

❏

I received a script recently about a 65-year-old woman being raped by an 18-year-old. It was a hideous use of old people and made fun of their arthritis and sex problems. I threw it right into the fire. For all I know the next script I receive will have a 92-year-old lesbian being raped by a fag—this whole business now is utterly gratuitous and done only for the money. I suffer for people whose day-to-day livelihood depends upon working. Fortunately I'm lucky and can fumble along and not work. Everything I've turned down has not been made with only one exception—Coral Browne's part in *The Killing of Sister George*. I just can't see sticking my tongue down Susannah York's whatever.

Deborah Kerr

❏

In *The Mask of Fu Manchu*, a terrible old movie in which I played Boris Karloff's evil daughter, I carried around a pet python and whipped a young man tied to a rack and all sorts of dreadful things. Now I had been reading

Deborah Kerr
Done for the money

a little Freud around that time, so I called the director over one day and said, "Say, this is obscene. This woman is a sadistic nymphomaniac!" And he said, "What does that mean?" We did it *all* before these kids today ever thought of it, and we didn't even know what we were *doing*!

Myrna Loy

❏

I walked down Broadway one day a few years ago and thought I'd go see a cowboy movie. So I stopped in to see *Midnight Cowboy*. That was sickening. That was the most sick thing ever in an American movie. Whoever made that movie doesn't give a hoot about the public or the family or the nation. When that boy started going down on that guy, I was slidin' farther and farther down in my seat and that was *sickening* . . . SICK! I'm not a prude; I've been around some in my day. But there are things that are sacred in American life. What are we supposed to do, just go . . . FUCK?

Roy Rogers

Phobias

Lew Ayres was under contract to MGM. He had some difficulty with the draft board about being a conscientious objector. Louis B. Mayer was head of MGM and, upon being told of this, allegedly said, "Lew Ayres has some kind of phobia about killing people."

Ralph Bellamy

❏

At eight, I was walking down the street in Pasadena when a flock of blackbirds swarmed over my head, then suddenly swooped down and pecked at me till I bled. From that time on, I was terrified of birds. Once, when I was visiting a friend in Bel-Air I had to refuse to enter the aviary that was the pride of his life. It was while I was working in *This Gun for Hire* that something happened which gave me a chance to free myself of the 20-year phobia. My name in the picture was Raven, and there was a raven being used on the Dorothy Lamour set next to ours. Someone thought it would be a good idea to bring the raven to my set as a good-luck gesture. Sort of have one raven meet another. The first day they brought the bird over, I couldn't bring myself to get close to it. But all week long that bird stayed on the set. Seeing it every day finally broke down my fear. I actually missed the darned thing when they took it back to its own set. That close association with the thing I subconsciously dreaded completely freed me from my phobia. I wonder how I could ever have been dominated by such a fear most of my life.

Alan Ladd

❏

Marilyn Monroe was always normal with me. She had the peculiar psychic condition where people are afraid of people and places. What's it called? Agoraphobia. She'd go to the hairdresser early in the morning, and then go home and not leave her home all day. They were always talking about her perfect complexion. God, it was beautiful, all right. Until the director said *action*, that is. Then she'd immediately break out in a rash. My theory is, she started to menstruate whenever the camera started to roll. She was that vulnerable.

Robert Mitchum

❏

I had a real phobia about flying until the 1950s, when I had to stump the country for General Electric and the only way to get quickly from place to place was by air. Finally, after a while, I grew used to flying and became more comfortable with it—sort of.

Ronald Reagan

❏

I'm frightened to death of the water, and yet it seems I'm always required to go into it on every one of my pictures. I can swim a little bit, but I'm afraid of water that is dark. I've always feared sharks, even before *Jaws* scared everyone else about them.

Natalie Wood

Politics

I don't want to go into politics. I want to do some good in the world.

Alan Alda

❏

I'm furious about Vanessa Redgrave's insensitivity over Israel. Just about everything she stands for—outside of her artistic life—seems to me not only
reprehensible but atrocious. She's calling for armed revolution; she wants to
kill me and my children. I think the first overt step she takes toward bringing
about that revolution should result in her being put in jail. But as long as
she doesn't break the law she should be free to practice her art without any
limits. I'd fight for her right to do that. I might add that I'd also like to be
the one who arrests her if she starts any trouble.

Alan Alda

❏

John Wayne, my leading man in *A Lady Takes a Chance*, was late to show his
political potential. If I had known then (1943) what I know now, I think I
would have shot him dead on the spot.

Jean Arthur

❏

The President has asked for severe cuts in aid to the arts and humanities. It's
Reagan's strongest attack on the arts since he signed with Warner Brothers.

Johnny Carson

❏

I remain just one thing and one thing only, and that thing is a clown. It places
me on a far higher plane than any politician.

Charles Chaplin

❏

I think actresses talking about politics is getting on very, very dangerous
ground. Whatever I'd say would alienate a certain group of people. I don't
want to do that. Why not? Because I'm controversial enough, for Chrissake!

Joan Collins

❏

Ronald Reagan? We used to call him "Little Ronnie Reagan." He did give one
good performance—in *Kings Row*. Of course, losing a leg does give an actor

Jean Arthur
Draws bead on Duke

Natalie Wood
Her prophetic phobia

248

Jane Fonda
Not crazy after all

❏

Dad and I would argue about what I was doing. Dad would say, "You're dead wrong," and I'd say, "No, I'm not." And he'd say, "If you can prove to me what you're saying is true . . ." And then I would bring home soldiers from coffeehouses who'd been in Vietnam, and have him listen to them. And Dad and I would fight. And he was worried. Obviously, he thought, "What foreign agent is manipulating my daughter?" Until slowly he realized what a lot of parents did: we weren't crazy.

Jane Fonda

❏

I was blacklisted from 1970 to 1975 in the same way as Jews during the McCarthy era.

Jane Fonda

❏

I wouldn't want to run for political office any more than I would want to direct. And for much the same reasons. In both instances you have to have real leadership qualities—the ability to remain objective, to keep people's morale up, to think strategically, to take an overview. I don't do any of those. I work best as part of a group where I can express myself, and if I'm wrong, people can say, "You're full of shit." I can accept that kind of criticism. I like working in committee, just like I like being married. I don't like being on my own.

Jane Fonda

I wanted to join the Communist party. I really did ... I tried. Hell, I'm a *joiner*. But they wouldn't let me in. Can you imagine that? They thought I was too dumb. They said I couldn't be trusted.

John Garfield

In the '30s, that wonderful era, actresses didn't go out and tell people what to do and who to vote for, did they? Who am I to tell people what to do?

Sharon Gless

If anyone accuses me of being a Communist, I'll hit them with my diamond bracelet.

Paulette Goddard

I will not go and see Vanessa Redgrave in anything at all. She is, frankly, a pain in the arse. Actors have opinions, they are not idiots; but to use the position which the public and the studio have given them to influence people's ideas is absolutely nauseating.

Stewart Granger

I was the only person to buy a yacht and join the Communist party in the same week.

Sterling Hayden

❏

I think politics is an Irish talent. Look at Jack Kennedy, whom I worked for some, and knew. He had the same gift as Reagan. Look at Tip O'Neill. Ted and Bobby Kennedy. Mayor Daley. That fire burned in each of them. But with us Scots, it's a different thing. We do things out of a dour Calvinistic sense of duty. We take no pleasure in it.

Charlton Heston

❏

Years ago during a particularly onerous Screen Actors Guild strike, when Ronald Reagan was President of the Guild, I spent a lot of time with him in all-night caucuses drinking cold coffee, sitting on hard chairs and sleeping on couches. You get to know someone real well under such conditions. I would come home near dawn and my wife would say, "How'd it go?" And I'd say, "Honey, we've got a real President!" Little did I know how prophetic that was!

Charlton Heston

❏

So many actors are thinking of running for President that they may put a marquee on the White House with "Now Playing" on it.

Bob Hope

❏

The terrible thing about being blacklisted as an actress was that even though, intellectually, you knew what was happening, you still always wondered whether you weren't being hired because you weren't any good.

Kim Hunter

❏

It was the Roosevelt era. Everyone was interested in making a better society. Hollywood set the fashion then, and the fashion was progressivism. Then came the death of Roosevelt. And almost the next day you could feel things change.

Howard Koch

❏

Ronald Reagan's a sheepish, 73-year-old farm boy. With him (as President), we'll have missiles in every hayfield.

Nancy Kulp

❑

Politicians, like the Chinese, all look alike.

Veronica Lake

❑

I don't believe in politics or politicians. In general, politicians are all unsuccessful actors. The only good politician I've ever met—the only honest one—is Barry Goldwater. The Kennedys weren't worth anything, especially poor Bobby who had a child for every election.

Robert Mitchum

❑

There are three times in life when it's useless trying to hold a man to anything he says—when he's madly in love, drunk or running for office.

Robert Mitchum

❑

I am concerned only with the character I am called upon to interpret. I have always avoided being brought in as a crusader. My politics is the business of acting. Nothing else matters. It may sound dull, but I'm not really concerned with the Depression, or Communism, or Capitalism. If Communism comes along, swell! If Fascism, it's all right with me. I'll take my chances. My work is the theater. I work in it like a scientist who works on an invention, not knowing whether his discovery will be constructive or destructive.

Paul Muni

❑

I have this dream that someday my son will become President of the United States. He'd still be messing up my life, but at least he'd be getting paid for it.

Ryan O'Neal

❑

When I was 16, I represented Czechoslovakia in the Olympics, losing by only a few points to Sonja Henie. I refused to give Hitler the usual "Heil" when I skated past his box. Nevertheless, he subsequently sent for me and asked me to skate under the flag of the Third Reich. I told him I'd never skate under his flag, but that I'd be very happy to skate over it. A short time later, when the Nazis invaded Czechoslovakia, my mother and I escaped on the last flight out of Prague.

Vera Ralston

In the late 1940s:

Politicians have asked me to run for Congress. Heck, I couldn't do that. If I did, I'd be the subject of criticism as a politician. I couldn't go around making speeches without feeling I was doing it for self-glorification. No, I don't want to have any ax to grind. Making good pictures is enjoyment enough for me. If I weren't really happy acting, I'd do something I really enjoyed, success or no success. But I must admit I do enjoy being a ham.

Ronald Reagan

Ronald Reagan
Enjoyed being a ham

❑

Washington makes Hollywood look like a class act in terms of being paranoid and concerned about its own image.

Robert Redford

❑

I am anti-Fascist, anti-imperialist and anti-Zionist. They are malignant catastrophes, and they must be overthrown. Everything must be done to make the world safe for the working people. For the safety of all, we must put an end to this system. The Zionists are part of it. The Jews and the Palistinians used to live in peace before the Zionist state was created and they can and will live in peace again. Zionism is based on racism. In the laws of Israel there are laws for Jews, laws for non-Jews. That's racist.

Vanessa Redgrave

❑

Everyone is curious about those monstrous times now, which is most amusing. I was called before the House Un-American Activities Committee, and I did refuse to testify before them. That was in April, 1951. What a season that had been: I did a flop play with Otto Preminger, my apartment was robbed, I was subpoenaed. Very soon after my testimony, at once, I was unemployable in films. It was imperative to find a way to go on. I began doing one-woman shows, readings for women's organizations, colleges, stock, anything to survive.

Anne Revere

❑

The difference between a conservative and a liberal is that a conservative believes in marriage and a liberal believes anything is okay behind closed doors—between three consenting adults.

Burt Reynolds

❑

Jane Fonda? She's a good actress, but mixed up. If a performer wants to get politically involved to that extent, he or she should do what Ronald Reagan did: get out of show business and run for office.

Ginger Rogers

❏

I am not a member of any organized party—I am a Democrat.

Will Rogers

❏

Actors in politics? Politics needs leaders. The actor's only experience in that line is leading a horse through a scene.

Robert Ryan

❏

I would never run for President. Some people have skeletons in their closets, but I have a graveyard.

Sylvester Stallone

❏

One day Hedda Hopper called and said, "I hear Bob (Taylor) is going to play a Communist in *The Conspirator*. I think that's disgraceful." So I said, "Who do you want to see in the role, Brezhnev or Vishinsky? Get off my ass, Hedda."

Barbara Stanwyck

❏

Acting is not the noblest profession in the world. There are things lower than acting—not many, mind you—but politicians give you something to look down on from time to time.

Spencer Tracy

❏

They'll never find a blacklist at Warner Brothers. Everything is done on the phone here.

Jack L. Warner

Progress

I came out here with one suit and everybody said I looked like a bum. Twenty years later Marlon Brando came out with only a T-shirt and the town drooled over him. That shows how much Hollywood has progressed.

Humphrey Bogart

Trained dogs who sniff out bombs could be valuable in Hollywood.

Raymond Burr

3-D movies? I like people coming out of the screen, but I prefer them coming out of that screen on their own personality.

Joan Crawford

People who think about the past have no future.

Hermione Gingold

We have all passed a lot of water since then.

Samuel Goldwyn

Let's show the movies in the streets—and drive the people back into the theaters.

Nunnally Johnson

❑

Fifty years ago when the Directors Guild of America was founded by King Vidor, such films as *San Francisco, Mr. Deeds Goes to Town* and Charlie Chaplin's *Modern Times* were popular. Today we have *Teen Wolf, The Goonies* and *Pee-wee's Big Adventure*—a half-century of progress.

Hal Kanter

❑

When I had been in Hollywood only a year, I went to a party and met Gary Cooper. He came over to me and said, "I've heard of you. How many pictures have you made?" I answered, "Two." Cooper asked, "Were they any good?" I said, "One was good and one was bad." Cooper's reply was, "You're way ahead already."

Gregory Peck

Psychiatrists

Why should I have to pay someone to tell them what I'm going to tell them anyway? Sooner or later, I always tell everybody *everything*, dahling.

Tallulah Bankhead

❑

I was seeing the psychiatrist every morning at six o'clock and was at the studio at seven. Then I'd see him for an hour at night after work. When I think of it now, no wonder I was strange. Imagine whipping out of bed, dashing over to the doctor's office, lying down on a torn leather couch, telling my troubles to an old man who couldn't hear, who answered with an accent I couldn't understand, and then dashing to Metro to make love to Mickey Rooney.

Judy Garland

❑

Tell your troubles to a bartender—who ever heard of a shrink giving you one on the house?

Jackie Gleason

❏

Any man who goes to a psychiatrist should have his head examined.

Lillian Hellman

❏

I told my female psychiatrist that someday we men were going to get revenge on all the strong women like her who were going into medicine and art and politics and trying to act like men. And she said, "What kind of revenge?" So I said, "We'll all turn into fairies." And she said, "That's a very symptomatic statement." And I said, "*Every* statement I make is symptomatic." And that finished my treatment with *her*.

Oscar Levant

❏

I went to a couple of Mama's (Judy Garland) analysts with her. She was so outrageous with them, because, well, she was an entertainer and would make up the most terrific stories to tell them. She would do it in the car going there. She'd say, "Now what's a good dream? What can I say I dreamt?" And I'd say, "Don't you think you should tell him what you really dreamt? Aren't you going so he can help you?" She'd say, "Yes, but he always looks so bored, and I can't stand to bore people." That's what drove my father crazy, because he was paying for all this stuff and found out she was making up all these stories.

Liza Minnelli

Publicity

You know, this "King" stuff is pure bullshit. I eat and sleep and go to the bathroom just like everyone else. There's no special light that shines inside me and makes me a star. I'm just a lucky slob from Ohio. I happened to be in the right place at the right time and I had a lot of smart guys helping me—that's all. I had a combination of the best directors, the best cameramen, the best make-up men, the best writers and the best goddamn publicity man in the world—Howard Strickling of MGM. Especially Strickling. Without him I'd probably be driving a truck or stringing telephone lines somewhere.

Clark Gable

❑

Hollywood—that's a place where love is viewed both pragmatically and philosophically in the saying, "Tis better to have loved and divorced than never to have had any publicity at all."

Ava Gardner

❑

Greer Garson and Clark Gable worked together in the disastrous *Adventure* with which I, thank God, had nothing to do. The best brains in the MGM publicity department pooled wits and produced the promotional catch line, "Gable's back and Garson's got him." A second choice was "Gable puts the arson in Garson." Greer objected to both. "They're ungallant," was her complaint. "Why don't you say, 'Garson puts the able in Gable'?"

Tay Garnett

❑

Howard Hughes was spending a part of his fortune to make a star of Jane Russell. It seemed that every 24-sheet in New York bore that famous, reclining figure and its beckoning bosom over the title *The Outlaw*. Walking down Broadway, George S. Kaufman and I counted five such billboards. "They've got the wrong title on that picture," George said. "They ought to call it *A Sale of Two Titties*."

Garson Kanin

Radio

Every other star in Hollywood was appearing on radio shows, but I'd turned down each offer. Mike fright was only part of it. My alarm had to do with the studio audience and no major broadcast was without one. To this day I've never accepted a stage part. We'd had a trial run on the Bing Crosby show with an audience of only 50. This was as big for me as a premiere. I'd planned my clothes, rehearsed my lines for a month. All I had to do was speak a few lines about music, but I was Joan Crawford, no character to hide behind. I was so nervous they nailed my chair to the floor, later we used a chrome bar like a towel rack for me to hang onto, and every line was printed on cardboard—paper might have rattled in my shaking hands. Carroll Carroll,

Bing's writer, actually held me up, and my husband and my doctor stood in the wings. Somehow we made it.

Joan Crawford

❏

Radio—we couldn't even say "Kate Smith's trying to get her moon over the mountain."

Bob Hope

❏

I caused a situation of national shock not to be matched till we dropped our first Atomic bomb. I was to appear as guest star on the Edgar Bergen-Charlie McCarthy Sunday radio program, and the news that I at last would be on the air caused workers to ask for the hour off to listen, while restaurants, bars and drug stores advertised that the broadcast could be heard in them. Church attendance dropped during the show. The trouble was caused by the Adam and Eve sketch I did with Don Ameche. Protests were hurled at NBC. To pacify some pious frauds among the radio audience, I was *persona non grata* on radio for several years. All I had done was ask Adam, "Would you, honey, like to try this apple sometime?"

Mae West

Rejection

After 200 or 300 rejections, it's hard to come back a human being. And I never wanted survival; rats survive, cockroaches survive. I want to live with dignity.

F. Murray Abraham

❏

That script? In two words—im-possible.

Samuel Goldwyn

❏

Joan Crawford
Acute audience fright

Bob Hope
The restraints of radio

Roddy McDowall told me, "All you get in the movie industry today is rejection. You're lucky you're out of it." What's funny to me is that everything I see today has Roddy McDowall in it. I don't know what he was talking about!

Gloria Jean

❏

I didn't quit movies. They quit me. Nobody wanted me. That was a terrible period of my life. I was 25 when I left MGM and it was the first time I had nobody to protect me. I didn't know anything about decisions or agents or income taxes. And the hardest thing in anyone's life is not being wanted. That hurt me more than anything in the world.

Jane Powell

❏

The only movie role I ever wanted really badly was the Donna Reed part in *From Here to Eternity*. Director Fred Zinnemann had his hands tied by Harry Cohn on that one. It was before Zinnemann *was* Zinnemann. Monty Clift and I worked on a scene, even. I went with Mr. Zinnemann and he introduced me to Mr. Cohn. And staring right at me, not looking at Mr. Zinnemann, he said, "Why are you bringing me this girlie? She's not even pretty." I *knew* I wasn't pretty, but I wasn't ready for that kind of artillery at that close range! I don't remember too much, but I did call him a pig or something.

Kim Stanley

❏

It's a funny thing about Hollywood—if you raise the roof and holler like crazy and you are wrong, then everybody tolerates you. They pat you on the head and thank you for your suggestions about how to play a role. But if you scream about something and you are *right*—brother, that's death!

Shelley Winters

❏

I think it's perfectly fair for a child to work if the family needs the money. When I was 12, my father couldn't work and the family depended on me. It's awfully difficult for an adult, much less a child, to accept rejection, however. Whenever I was sent up for a role and heard that I was "too short" or "too tall" or "too young" or "too old," I felt awful, as if I had let everybody down.

Natalie Wood

❏

Because I thought *The Men*, with Marlon Brando, would be an important picture, I agreed to do it for $25,000 instead of my usual $200,000. It was a financial disaster. I was now a $25,000 actress and soon found myself doing a Western called *California Conquest* and saying lines like "This gun isn't particular, mister." Cornel Wilde was in it, and one day the director came to me and said, "Now I want you to put on a bit of make-up." I never do. Then he went on, "It's because Cornel is prettier than you are." It was a real low point.

Teresa Wright

Religion

I hated school. The teachers were all anti-Semitic. A lot of ladies with blue-grey hair who'd keep the kids after class so they couldn't go to Hebrew lessons.

Woody Allen

❏

I was Jewish but became a Catholic when I married (producer) Mike Frankovich. I had to do it to please or shock Louella Parsons. Louella used to say to Mike, "Why did you marry that dreadful woman? A nice Jewish boy like you, marrying that dreadful English Catholic." She had it backward and never did get it straight. I was always "that dreadful woman who married that nice man, Mike Frankovich." She always called me Bannie, not Binnie. But I respected her. She was the best Hollywood columnist of them all.

Binnie Barnes

❏

You know, when *Going My Way* was first released, it couldn't play any Latin American countries for several years because the priest wore a sweatshirt and a baseball cap. To them, that was absolutely sacrilegious. But as for my own impact on the priest being recognized as a human being, well, I think it was coming anyhow. I was just kind of part of that movement.

Bing Crosby

❏

He never answered me, baby. He was never around when I needed Him. He did nothing but screw up my whole life since the day I was born. Don't tell me about *God*! I know all about that bugger!

Ava Gardner

I believe in God, Jesus, Life Eternal, people, luck, my voices, myself. Pan me, don't give me a part, publish everybody's book but this one, and I will *still* make it! Why? Because I *believe* I will. If you believe, then you hang on.

Ruth Gordon

I don't know about being a Catholic anymore, though I had a great romance with the Church. But its male hierarchy causes me pain and distress. So I can't really pay too much attention. When that encyclical from the Pope—the one about contraception—began "Dear Sons and Brothers" I figured it must be private mail and had nothing to do with me. So I didn't read it.

Joan Hackett

In *Come to the Stable*, I wrote a scene wherein the nuns put on a fund-raising pageant depicting the flight into Egypt. This, of course, involved a donkey and I could not resist describing the opening scene thus: "ENTER Sister Margaret on her ass."

Oscar Millard

I was an 18-year-old Jew headed for the oven, but the kick Hitler gave me in the ass that sent me flying out of Germany was the best stroke of luck in my life. I went to England, married Rex Harrison in 1943 and I've been a British citizen ever since. I never asked for financial retribution from the German government, as others have done, because I was grateful. I would never have had the career I've had if I had stayed in Germany.

Lilli Palmer

Little Darryl Hickman couldn't quite get the idea of having a Hebrew director and a mostly Jewish crew making a movie about a priest's activities (*Men of Boys Town*). He didn't say anything, but I could see that he, raised in the Catholic Church, was slightly puzzled. Finally, on the last day of shooting I persuaded producer Johnny Considine, a devout Catholic, to come on the set to watch. I brought Considine over to the child, and said, "Darryl, I want you to meet Mr. Considine. He's one of the finest gentlemen in Hollywood and the producer of our picture." Darryl looked up, impressed. "Glad to meet you, Mr. Conselstein."

Norman Taurog

In Hollywood you could make jokes about almost anything, including God and the Pope. But you could *not* makes jokes about Louis B. Mayer.

Ruth Warrick

The fact is that some of the worst of us make the happiest Christians. The further we've gone as sinners the more enlightened believers we can become. Some folks are so heavenly minded they ain't any earthly good.

Ethel Waters

Rumors

Marilyn Monroe's the biggest thing we've had at the studio since Shirley Temple and Betty Grable. With Temple, we had 20 rumors a year that she was kidnaped. With Grable, we had 20 rumors a year that she was raped. With Monroe, we have 20 rumors a year that she has been raped and kidnaped.

Harry Brand

I was playing a small-town lawyer in a picture called *Storm Warning* that teed off on the Ku Klux Klan. Some of our first scenes were shot at night in a small California town that is rumored to be the center of Klan activity here on the Coast. The studio was understandably nervous and halfway expected some kind of incident. About three o'clock one morning, shooting a street scene, I thought maybe the studio was justified in its concern. A little character sidled up to me and whispered out of the corner of his mouth, "I hear this movie is about the Klan." I allowed as how it was—getting ready to yell "Hey, Rube"—when his next line stopped me cold. He said, "Well, I'm in the local outfit and if you need to rent some robes, let me know."

Ronald Reagan

I was about 14, and there had been a rumor that I was to do a film called *Sally in Her Alley*. I was supposed to sing and dance in it, and Mother went up with me to ask Big Daddy (Louis B. Mayer) if it was true and should I begin to train. He sat behind his desk, looking at these two insects, and blew up. He used the most obscene language. He yelled at my mother, "You're so goddamned blankety-blank stupid you wouldn't even know what day of the week it is. Don't try to meddle in my affairs. Don't try to tell me how to make motion pictures. I took you out of the gutter." I sprang to my feet and said, "Don't you to speak to my mother like that. You and your studio can both go to hell!" And I ran out of the room, tears pouring down my face. I never did apologize, and I wasn't fired. I swore I'd never go back into that office, and I never did.

Elizabeth Taylor

Self-Improvement

The reason I come off being sexy and attractive—I still can't bring myself to say "pretty"—is because I have had myself re-built. I had the hair under my arms taken care of. And I had an operation to firm up my breasts. And I spend about $1,000 a week to have my toenails, fingernails, eyebrows and hair put in top shape. I'm the female equivalent of a counterfeit $20 bill. Half of what you see is a pretty good reproduction, and the rest is a fraud.

Cher

Some guys look at themselves in the mirror for 20 years, then decide they got to get a nose job or an ear lift or something. I don't know. I just couldn't see myself getting my knees stretched.

Danny DeVito

Shug Keeler, an electrician, is a guy who helped me stick it out in those early days. I remember one day I was pretty sore because they insisted on taping my big ears back. I groused to Shug that I was sick of it and I was going back to the stage where a man's ears weren't a major catastrophe. Shug said, "You stick around, kid; you'll get places." And the ears took care of themselves. One day, in a scene with Garbo for *Susan Lennox*, the tape snapped loose and one ear flopped in the breeze. That was the end of taping.

Clark Gable

I never jog. Love is still a better and more pleasurable sport.

Cary Grant

Clark Gable
Issue of ears

People have talked about my nose all my life. And I'm always getting people wanting to know who my plastic surgeon is. And my daughters say they don't mind anything else, but why didn't God give them my nose? So here I am, an old woman known for her nose. I really think it's what put me on the map. I was pretty, but I didn't have huge, fantastic eyes or marvelous cheek bones. Just this silly old schnozz. And no, I've never had my face lifted. I'd be afraid of coming out looking Chinese.

Deborah Kerr

My favorite exercises are grovelling, brooding and mulling.

Oscar Levant

I wasn't a pretty kid, but I sure grew up to be a much worse looking adult. There were all sorts of things wrong with me. I could have kept a plastic surgeon busy for a year just working on my faulty parts.

Liza Minnelli

I never diet. I was outside the Beverly Hills Hotel one day when I bumped into Gina Lollobrigida. She was going on the Johnny Carson talk show live that night and says to me, "How on earth do you keep that figure? Is it some special diet?" I tell her, "No, lady, by isometric farting." She went on the show that night and sure enough, the talk got around to diet. She's got no sense of humor, that dame, and she says, "I saw Robert Mitchum today, and he keeps his figure by isometric farting." Carson nearly fell off his chair.

Robert Mitchum

I bought all those (fitness) videos—Richard Simmons, Jane Fonda. I love to sit and eat cookies and watch 'em.

Dolly Parton

All those stories that have been written and rumored about my having had silicone injections to bring out my bust are totally false. They also say I had my nose fixed and even my ass lifted. I don't understand how those stories got started, except I do admit that when I first tried to get into show business I was a mess. I was underplaying my best parts and overplaying everything that was wrong with me. I wore so much make-up that it's amazing I didn't wind up round-shouldered from carrying all that weight on my face. I inadvertently played up my nose and down my chest.

Raquel Welch

At the time I had my face lifted, I was doing several pilots for TV series and, believe it or not, I blew one of them because I looked too young for the part! They tried the "aging" make-up and all, but it just didn't work. I did tell my doctor that I did not want that pulled look and to leave a few "laughing" lines here and there. The operation was a success, even though I did not get the series I thought was so important at the time. As it turned out, both series were cancelled after two showings, so I can laugh about it now.

Marie Windsor

I'm not overweight—I'm just nine inches too short.

Shelley Winters

Sex

Sexual harassment (in Hollywood) goes on right and left. I know a girl who went to see an agent and he closed the door by pressing one button. He pushed another button and a bed shot out from the wall. That's about as glaring as it gets.

Ed Asner

I don't know what I am, dahling. I've tried several varieties of sex. The conventional position makes me claustrophobic. And the others give me either a stiff neck or lockjaw.

Tallulah Bankhead

❑

I was dying to do *The Razor's Edge*, but Darryl Zanuck thought I was sexless and tested at least a dozen other girls from everywhere for it. Finally, my friend Gregory Ratoff, the actor-director, asked his friend Zanuck why he didn't sign me. When Zanuck replied that I was a cold potato, Ratoff, with an evil leer, answered, "Darryl, I have had it. *Marvelous!*" I got the part.

Anne Baxter

❑

I'm really a very square person. I've never smoked pot or seen a stag film. I don't drink. I'm really out of it. My idea of an orgy is watching three movies on *The Late Late Show*.

Carol Burnett

❑

Hollywood is different these days. Do you believe all the sex and violence in the movies today? Of course, at my age, sex and violence are the same thing.

George Burns

❑

There's nothing wrong with making love with the light on. Just make sure the car door is closed.

George Burns

❑

My doctor told my wife and me that we should enjoy sex every night—now we'll never see each other.

Chevy Chase

❑

I had an interview with a young girl the other day, and she talked about my "promiscuity." And I said, "Oh, you think I've been promiscuous?" And she said, "Yes." And I said, "How many men have you been to bed with?" And

Joan Collins
Topped by reporter

she said, "Between 50 and 75." And I said, "Well, I've been to bed with fewer men than that."

Joan Collins

❏

When I was 13, I was having sex two or three times before nine a.m. with the 20-year-old girl across the street. Joan Crawford wasn't the only older woman I had an affair with. There were a half-dozen friends of my mother, bored with their husbands. Before I was 18, I was having experiences a man doesn't get in his whole life.

Jackie Cooper

❏

Claudette Colbert became an instant goddess as soon as her first film was released. The real sign of puberty in a youth of my day was when he first fell seriously in love with Miss Colbert.

Sammy Davis, Jr.

❑

"And now," Darryl Zanuck once said to me, "we go into a tender love scene; he rams his tongue down her throat." I knew what he meant; it could be tender but not boring.

Philip Dunne

❑

They say that drinking interferes with your sex life. I figure it's the other way around.

W.C. Fields

❑

I had to decide whether to "use" the casting couch a couple of times very early in my career. I was in New York a couple of months, and not very savvy, let me tell ya. I really thought I was in those offices for honest reasons ... One of the great fears I had, when a man told me I'd be a big star and he'd take me to Hollywood, was whether that was for me. I'd go back to my little apartment with all the cockroaches and I would think, I don't know if I want that. I don't want to be public property. So I reacted to him as any 18-year-old would. I got hysterical. He said, "Go back home and marry a Jewish dentist because you'll never get anywhere." I said, well, if that's what I'm going to have to do, then I will. And I ran out. It was frightening.

Goldie Hawn

❑

It's really crotch time. I simply would have refused to play the parts that involve explicit sex scenes. As a woman, I wouldn't have demeaned myself by undressing, and having them photograph fornication. And the minute actresses refuse ... it would stop, wouldn't it?

Katharine Hepburn

❑

All love scenes started on the set are continued in the dressing room after the day's shooting is done. *Without exception.*

Alfred Hitchcock

☐

I've never been able to say of a girl, "Gee, we're great friends," and let it go at that. I've always had the urge to make love.

Dustin Hoffman

☐

There is a lot of "action" today, but very little love. Frankly, I think sex without affection is like life without breath. I have never been interested in making love with a man whose child I wouldn't want to bear.

Celeste Holm

☐

They're doing things on the screen today that I wouldn't do in bed—if I could.

Bob Hope

☐

I try not to rape my own feelings in my work. I try to act, not to act out. If you have a sex scene with somebody, you don't get erections. I mean, if I'm holding Kathleen Turner in *Body Heat*, I don't have time to think about sex. I have time to work as an actor . . . I get turned on by expressing other things in my work. I get turned on sexually at home; that's my private life.

William Hurt

☐

She descended from a long line her mother listened to.

Gypsy Rose Lee

☐

We didn't have too simple a time getting going—me and Clark (Gable)— because when we first started messin' around, he was tied up elsewhere and so was I. So we used to go through the God-damnedest routine. He'd get somebody to go hire a room or a bungalow somewhere. Like on the outskirts. A couple of times the Beverly Hills Hotel. Then the somebody would give him a key. Then he'd have another key made, and give it to me. Then we'd arrange a time and he'd get there. Then I'd get there. Or I'd get there, then he'd get there. Then all the shades down and all the doors and windows locked, and the phones shut off, and then we'd have a drink or sometimes not. After we were married, we couldn't ever make it unless we went someplace and locked all the doors and put down all the window shades, and shut off all the phones.

Carole Lombard

❏

Bedroom voice? I use this voice everywhere *except* in the bedroom. I never talk in the bedroom—except on the phone.

Marilyn Monroe

❏

I never understood it—this sex symbol—I always thought symbols were those things you clash together! That's just the trouble, a sex symbol becomes a thing. I just hate to be a thing. But if I'm going to be a symbol of something, I'd rather have it sex than some other things they've got symbols of.

Marilyn Monroe

❏

Sex is part of nature, and I go along with nature.

Marilyn Monroe

❏

To 10,000 Marines at Camp Pendleton, California:
    I don't know why you guys are so excited about sweater girls. Take away their sweaters and what have they got?

Marilyn Monroe

❏

Once, when Martin Balsam and I were on location in Arizona for *Hombre*, we had to wait hours for the wind to let up. To kill time, we decided to classify fucking. We got all the psychological classifications. There was sport fucking. There was mercy fucking, which would be reserved for spinsters and librarians. There was the hate fuck, the prestige fuck—and the medicinal fuck, which is, "Feel better now, sweetie?" It just goes to show you what happens when you're stuck on location on the top of a mountain.

Paul Newman

❏

My wife Vivien Leigh's dreaded (mental) illness always seemed to add mercilessly to my troubles just when my work was at its most exhausting. From time to time during this period of our anxious lives, I would put a last desperate arrow into my bow and, as at the end of *Lady Chatterley*, try "fucking" our love back into existence. It was successful. My prowess, so often failing from nervous premature ejaculation, had gained, through the practice given to me by my gentle, patiently bestowed few love affairs, a calmly confident strength.

Laurence Olivier

❏

If all those sweet young things in Hollywood were laid to end, I wouldn't be a bit surprised.

Dorothy Parker

❏

I never got anywhere that I was just because I was goin' to the couch or anything. People knew I was no dummy and I was not a slut just because I looked like trash.

Dolly Parton

❏

There is something very attractive about youth. I was always outrageously young-looking in my own youth, and I was always attracted by young and innocent girls. My friends, rather, had longings and desires for older women. They even treated me like a weirdo because of this. There's still a streak in me. I don't think there's anything vicious in it. For some reason, young girls like me as well.

Roman Polanski

❏

Paul Newman
Elevated sex talk

Laurence Olivier
Used medicinal sex

Errol Flynn was going through the Peggy Satterlee rape trial. He used to go to court in the morning and come back and report to us on the set (of *Edge of Darkness*) what had happened. Lewis Milestone (the director) and all of us used to gather around and start gurgling from the toes up at the reports of Old Dad Flynn. It was absolutely fascinating, the things this idiot child accused him of. I think what hurt him most was when she said he raped her with his boots on. He said, "My God, next she'll accuse me of wearing my top hat!"

Ann Sheridan

Explicit love scenes jolt me. I'm watching and suddenly I'm wondering, "There's Kevin Kline and look what he's doing to Bonnie Bedelia. Oh, they must have been uncomfortable doing that." But at 36 maybe I'm not so comfortable doing things I wouldn't have given a second thought in my 20s.

Sissy Spacek

My troubles all started because I have a woman's body and a child's emotions.

Elizabeth Taylor

Sex with love is about the most beautiful thing there is—but sex without love isn't so bad, either.

John Travolta

America is so puritanical and hypocritical and it seems that anything to do with sex is taboo. Should I pretend that I am scandalized about playing a prostitute or pretend that 224 million Americans don't have orgasms? Good sex belongs in the cinema just as much as a good gag.

Kathleen Turner

I might as well confess that I was not a great companion in bed. Sex was never, with any man, the first thing on my mind, and if I didn't make love

Sissy Spacek
Position in life ...

Lana Turner
Fourth favorite thing

for weeks I was content. No, I wasn't frigid. But I hated the public notion that I was constantly picking up men. Sex was so much what I symbolized, so much of my image, that I closed myself off to the pleasures of the act. Holding hands, cuddling, being close together in bed, all those intimacies I enjoyed more than the actual sex.

Lana Turner

I adore younger men—they can go on forever. Besides, I don't want any sagging tummies hanging over me.

Brenda Vaccaro

It has often been said that sex, not silver nitrate, is the chief ingredient of motion picture film.

Jerry Wald

Graphic sex on the screen? When you get hairy, sweaty bodies in the foreground, it becomes distasteful, unless you use a pretty heavy gauze. I can remember seeing pictures that Ernst Lubitsch made in the '30s that were beautifully risqué—and you'd certainly send your children to see them. They were done with *intimation*. They got over everything these other pictures do without showing the hair and the sweat. When you think of the wonderful picture fare we've had through the years and realize we've come to this shit, it's disgusting. If they want to continue making those pictures, fine. But my career will have ended. I've already reached a pretty good height right now in a business that I feel is going to fade out from its own vulgarity.

John Wayne

It's never satisfactory. Either the man is able to keep you happy sexually, and he has no intellectual quality; or he's very intellectual and not good at carrying on a satisfactory sexual relationship.

Tuesday Weld

John Wayne
Slow fade to vulgarity

Mae West
It felt divine

It's better to be looked over than overlooked.

Mae West

❏

I've been gettin' a lot of letters from women these days. Women askin' me my advice on how to hold a man. "There's only one way to hold a man, honey," I tell 'em. "In your arms, of course!"

Mae West

❏

To err is human, but it feels divine.

Mae West

❏

When a girl goes bad, men go right after her.

Mae West

❏

The sexiest thing in the world is to be totally naked with your wedding band on.

Debra Winger

Sports

Of the recreation sports in Hollywood, tennis or whatever, I can't think of anyone who runs like I do. I am a world-class runner in my age group at 800 meters, about half a mile. That takes about eight miles of training a day, so you're running 55 miles a week. I figure I've run 105,000 miles in my lifetime, about four times around the world.

Bruce Dern

❏

This guy went to Vegas, met this girl, got drunk and married her. In the morning, he said, "Honey, I've got a little surprise for you. You won't see me all day, because I'm a golfer, and I'll be on the course." And she said, "Well, I have a surprise for you, too. I'm a hooker." And he said, "Well, don't worry. Just take your right hand and put it over the club like that, and you'll be fine."

Bob Hope

❑

What would happen if someone were to cast a (skating) picture with me, Sonja Henie and Barbara Ann Scott? Ha! They'd have to lock us in separate cages—like tigers! Believe me, those Figure Eight Girls play for keeps! I'm not anxious to go back to skating pictures *at all!* Why? Well, you just don't know ice skaters, Dollink. For instance, a girl in the (1936) Olympics was jealous of me and put laxative in my food. In New Haven, Connecticut, I saw one star pull a knife on another and guess who was right in the middle? Me! They put needles in your skates, they foul up your zippers, they take nickels and dull your blades so that you'll break a leg, maybe. Everything goes— yes, even spiders in your underwear! O-h-h-h, it's Hades, Dollink! Ha! I will tell you how one star toasts another backstage at an ice show. You lift your glass and you say, "Here's to So-and-So. May she drop dead in the middle of her big number!" Nice, huh? Dollink! I used to skate around at rehearsals with a Bible in my hand. It's a terrible thing to be an ice queen. A bobby pin or a cigarette butt on the ice can make you fall and break every bone in your body.

Vera Ralston

Stage

When I was touring in *Hamlet*, a local reporter asked me if I thought Hamlet had ever had sexual relations with Ophelia. "Only in Chicago," I replied.

John Barrymore

❑

My view of the theater is that you have nothing to do all day and just when it becomes interesting, you have to go to work.

Michael Caine

Michael Caine
A theater critic

❏

I've made 58 movies and I hate every one of them. All those films—and I don't remember one with any special fondness or satisfaction. If I had my time over, I'd never make a film. I'd stick to the stage and starve if I had to.

Lee J. Cobb

❏

I really love doing movies. You don't have to say "I love you" to 1100 people in a Broadway house. I mean, that's not natural.

Jeff Daniels

❏

I hate the theater and never intend to do it again. I hate the hours and the life, and half the New York audiences are not worth your time anymore.

Bette Davis

❏

Theater is reality—cockroaches in the dressing rooms, dust on the floor. No one edits you.

David Dukes

❑

The stage? No. I've got no great message for the world. This (films) is what brings in the groceries, and that (the stage) is *work*. Sure, this is work, too, but it's broken up. You get a day off now and then. You get time between. If a stage show's a hit you're in for the duration. Not for me, brother!

Clark Gable

❑

Years ago, people would say, "Los Angeles? There's no theater, only touring companies." Now there are no touring companies, but lots of theater. The potential is enormous. When I used to think of theater, it was New York. Now producers almost can't afford to do it and people really can't spend $40 and $50 for a ticket. That's not theater anymore. It's something else.

Julie Harris

❑

I tried the stage—the Las Vegas production of *Mame*—but that was only because Martin Rackin insisted. I could not wait for the run to get finished. Talk about being bored! The same old lines, the same old songs every night. Not for me, Baby, not for me.

Susan Hayward

❑

On returning to the stage:
We've done the political thing, and now a little tits and ass won't hurt. We're going through so much shit in the world, a little laughter won't hurt now. I'd like to go out and really have the audience jump and laugh and carry on and learn a little more about me!

Shirley MacLaine

❑

Stage fright, me? Never! I figure if those people out there in the audience could do what I do, they'd be up there on the stage instead of me.

Ethel Merman

❏

I think *Sugar Babies* really remade Mickey Rooney again. I was a famous has-been before this show. Now it's given me the security and the opportunities that a man of theater stature gets.

Mickey Rooney

❏

Richard (Burton) is so discriminating he won't see a play with anybody in it but himself.

Elizabeth Taylor

Stardom

The words "movie stars" are so misused they have no meaning. Any little pinhead who does one picture is a star. Gable is a star. Cooper is a star. Joan Crawford, as much as I dislike the lady, is a star. But I don't think the so-called others are. To be a star you have to drag your weight into the box office and be recognized wherever you go.

Humphrey Bogart

❏

A star is when someone says, "Let's leave the dishes in the sink and go see Joan Crawford."

Clarence Brown

❏

I hate the word "superstar." Who hung it on the business? I have never been able to think in those terms. They are overstatements. You don't hear them speak of Shakespeare as a superpoet. You don't hear them call Michelangelo a superpainter. They only apply the word to this mundane market.

James Cagney

❏

You know, because of the studios, we were like pieces of merchandise—soap or Jello. They'd build us up and we'd be known all over the world. There are stars today like Beatty, Jane Fonda, Brando, Newman, Redford, Hoffman, but it's not exactly the same. Glenda Jackson and Anne Bancroft are marvelous actresses, but they don't draw the same way. In my day, people would go to see the star; they didn't care about the story like they do now. Faye Dunaway, another fine actress, may take several months to find the right script. Which I envy. I was made to do pictures I really didn't want to do.

Claudette Colbert

❏

I always called Betty Grable princess 'cause that's how I felt about her. Betty was class. She was a true star. She could light up before the camera. If she had wanted she could have become a great dancer. I'd be suggesting new routines and she'd holler, "Who are you, the director?" She was lazy, I guess. Loved that racetrack. But great for the business and wonderful to work with.

Dan Dailey

❏

I had no great talent, and I never wanted to be a movie star. But my mother had always wanted it for herself, and I guess she projected through me. I was going to become a movie star or Mom was going to bust in the attempt.

Linda Darnell

❏

I find what men like Nicholson and Brando say about me flattering. But I don't want to be an old-fashioned movie star in the true sense of that term. A Hollywood "star" is death as far as real acting is concerned.

Robert De Niro

❏

James Cagney
Shakespeare a superstar?

Linda Darnell
Mother knew best

291

Some actresses will sacrifice *anything* to become a star. I just don't want the gold ring on the merry-go-round that much. All I want is for the merry-go-round to play *my* song.

Joan Hackett

❏

Years ago, I was sitting with George Peppard and a kid approached our table. He asked George if he was a movie star and George replied, "No, I am an actor." The kid turned to me and asked, "Are you also an actor?" I said, "No, I'm a movie star."

George Hamilton

❏

Celebrity scars you. You live in a different world from other people. For example, I know that Sinatra goes to the Dodger games, but he sits in a (private) box. I go to tennis matches because the crowds are controlled, but I wasn't able to take my kids to Disneyland. The downside of celebrity is the damage to your character—you start believing your press clippings. You have to think of the Roman emperors, who lived in such splendor. Girls walked in parades, showering them with rose petals, whispering, "You too shall die!" You survive it by saying to yourself, "You too shall die." Still, celebrity is a corrosive condition, and I think I was lucky that it came to me slowly, so I could adapt.

Charlton Heston

❏

After a taste of stardom, everything else is poverty.

Hedy Lamarr

❏

I was a movie product, pushed up as a star without any foundation. I ate flowers for publicity. They wanted my cute, 18-year-old pout and kiss when I was 25. I went to classes on the (Universal) lot, even wore spike heels with my mortarboard when I got my diploma. As I look back, it was a tragic-comic affair. When I left in 1957, I left a good contract which the next year would have given me $2,500 a week. But I couldn't stand it one minute more. I thought it would kill me or I would kill someone.

Piper Laurie

❑

Maria Montez became a star by being seen at Ciro's. She had a little trick she'd pull to make sure she was seen. She always sat at a table as far away as she could from the washrooms. Then she would make five or six trips a night clear across the room to go to the john, and always flouncing herself sexily as she went by all the tables, intending for every male in the room to notice her. Which they did. Some of those males were important producers and directors. Miss Montez also sometimes bumped into more males emerging from the men's room. She always said she was going to be a star some day and word got around that she finally made it by going to the john at Ciro's. I'll bet a lot of people just thought she had bladder trouble.

Ann Miller

❑

I am very easy to get along with, I am very nice. I have changed a lot during this last year. I have outgrown my old publicity. I used to do and say things that shocked people. That was how I became famous, but now it is different. First the public likes you because you are spectacular. But after it thinks you are a star, it wants you to be nice. Now I am a star. Now I am nice. I am more ladylike—and I don't like it!

Maria Montez

❑

A star is not a manipulated image. Only that audience out there makes a star. It's up to them. You can't do anything about it, or I never would've got anywhere. Stars would all be Louis B. Mayer's cousins if you could make 'em up.

Jack Nicholson

❑

There are three ways to make it in Hollywood. You can become an "actor"—a guy with things standing out in his neck—or you can become a personality, or you can become a star. I always wanted to be all three. I think, I think I may have made it.

Burt Reynolds

❑

It is a strange business. There's no way to know whether you'll succeed. There's no rhyme or reason why some talented people have a difficult time working consistently while some other people who can't act a lick are stars.

Kurt Russell

◻

In 1949 I was loaned to Metro. I was there to do a picture with Gable, and Audrey Totter told me about a meeting she once had with (Louis B.) Mayer. He asked her if she knew whose name on a marquee, on its own, would draw people into a theater. And she said, "Gable?" He shook his head. "Crawford? Greer Garson? Robert Taylor?" And he said, "No, there's only one: Wallace Beery." It's really a funny and strange business.

Alexis Smith

◻

You make a star, you make a monster.

Sam Spiegel

◻

The depressing thing about Hollywood in 1966 is that there are no movie stars. I don't know what's happened. Bogart and Gable were stars, and let's not forget it. Women dreamed about making love to them, and men felt they'd like to have a drink with them. There's only one movie star in the world today, and that's Elizabeth Taylor. I don't think that's right. Look, I've got as big an ego as anyone, but I don't let my name stand alone on the marquee. It can break a picture. After all, people see me and say, "Oh yeah, that guy. That's Rod Steiger. Or maybe Rod Serling."

Rod Taylor

◻

The difference between just acting and being a star is that as a star everyone looks to you to set the tone on the set. If it's 120 degrees and you're going around smiling and telling the crew, "C'mon, guys," they'll work harder to make sure they don't let you down.

Kathleen Turner

Alexis Smith
All about audiences

Kathleen Turner
All the difference

295

Status

We (the Dead End Kids) went to "The MGM of the South," Monogram Studios. When you landed there, you were finished. It was the Foreign Legion—even the unemployed actors at Schwab's drugstore wouldn't talk to you. The meat . stamp was on you—D.O.A., Dead on Arrival. Suddenly it hit me that I was a primitive, an actor by accident. I decided to go back to New York and study with Lee Strasberg.

Gabriel Dell

❑

There were no overt problems with Maureen O'Hara on *Sinbad the Sailor*. But she *was* the leading lady. I played her handmaiden, and day by day I noticed the veil covering part of my face getting thicker and thicker. Finally, you could see only my eyes. I begged the make-up man to make me up only to the nose, since no one would see the lower half of my face.

Jane Greer

Jane Greer
Veil of mystery

❏

Beverly Hills has got a slum area, and it's called the rest of the world.

Bob Hope

❏

Please accept my resignation. I don't care to belong to any club that will have me as a member.

Groucho Marx

❏

How was jail? Just like Palm Springs—without the riff-raff, of course.

Robert Mitchum

Success

Louis Mayer told me he sat there and said, "I don't know what she's got, but something makes me interested." Then they sent me to the voice teacher to learn how to speak like a girl, and I was expelled because I couldn't learn that. They sent me to an eye teacher to learn how to smile with my eyes open, and I couldn't do that. They sent me to the dentist to see if they could get rid of my lisp, and the dentist said my teeth were fine. So they sent me back to L.B. Mayer just the way he threw me out. And he said, "OK, we'll chance it." And that was the film (*Two Girls and a Sailor*) that worked.

June Allyson

❏

I had an agent who was very nice to me. He had two protégées—me and Shirley MacLaine. It wasn't obvious to me which of us was going to make it —because when I first met Shirley, I thought, "What a poor, plain girl"— but it was obviously apparent to him.

Claire Bloom

❏

My part in *Boy Meets Girl* was to say, "Once more!" Period. They paid me for a week's work. In *Boom Town* I was a tailor. I slapped Spencer Tracy on the cheek and told him to stand still. In *The Amazing Dr. Clitterhouse*, I was the gangster who remarked in awful tones, "The Updyke jewel!" In *Casablanca*, I picked a pocket and had four words: "Vultures. Nothing but vultures." In *Cover Girl*, I yelled, "I quit!" Terrific parts, all of them! Bitter? How can I be? My name may not be in lights in America, but I can thumb my nose at the Hitler boys. That's worth all the billing in the world!

Curt Bois

❑

I was down the tubes not long ago. I always made a living, but I wasn't . . . sought after. You could see it on the faces of the air hostesses; you could see it when you rented a car; you could see it when you walked into a restaurant. If you've made a hit movie, then you get the full 32-teeth display in some places; and if you've sort of faded, they say, "Are you still making movies? I remember that picture, blah, blah, blah." And so it goes. The point of all this is, people are interested in people who are successful.

Marlon Brando

❑

Y'know, I think I've got a chance to really make it because in this hand I'm holding Marlon Brando saying "Fuck you!" and in the other hand saying "Please forgive me" is Montgomery Clift. "Please forgive me." "Fuck you!" "Please forgive me." "Fuck you!" And somewhere in between is James Dean.

James Dean

❑

If at first you don't succeed, try, try again. Then quit—there's no use making a damn fool of yourself.

W.C. Fields

❑

A truly successful man is one who makes more money than his wife can spend. A truly successful woman is one who can find such a man.

Glenn Ford

❏

After *Teen Wolf*, producers began thinking, "Hey, this guy can even make money in bad pictures!" And I thought, "Hey, what does a guy have to do to fail around here?" I really have been lucky. I'm the sort of guy who falls through the ice in a river and the water is only two feet deep. I'm still waiting for the inevitable disaster.

Michael J. Fox

❏

There are a dozen girls I know who can sing better, dance better and act better than I. I can do a little of all three and I suppose that's why I get by.

Betty Grable

❏

I was totally unaware of the Depression. I kept thinking, "What is *wrong* with everyone?" I was in Hollywood making movies, and lucky lucky lucky.

Katharine Hepburn

❏

The first time I saw George Burns on stage I could see that he had what it takes to become a big star: Gracie Allen.

Bob Hope

❏

"The Perfect Wife." That was a role no one could live up to, really. No telling where my career would have gone if they hadn't hung that title on me. Labels limit you because they limit your possibilities. But that's how they think in Hollywood. All I can say is, if you're successful at something, God help you!

Myrna Loy

❏

These success stories full of misery! Really! I've got a life story I could write a book about. Just before I came out here, I had gotten off a chain gang. How do you like that? I'm serious. I'm not kidding. They just threw me in the can

Myrna Loy
The perfect label

Betty Grable
Triple-threat champ

300

down in Georgia. No means of support. Imagine, a kid of 15! So they tell me their hard luck stories: "How I starved to become a star"! What's wrong with a little honest starvation? It makes you appreciate steak!

Robert Mitchum

❏

Hollywood is very seductive in that a lot of people make a lot of promises —limos, parties, money ... but it's all a distortion, because if you don't succeed, all these promises will quickly be taken back. People in Hollywood get interested in you very easily, but they get *bored* with you very easily, too.

Tyrone Power, Jr.

❏

There is no formula for success. But there is a formula for failure and that is to try to please everybody.

Nicholas Ray

❏

It's very hard to climb the ladder, and it's very easy to go down the slide.

Debbie Reynolds

❏

Most of the Hollywood actors I meet are slick industry types—self-consumed Dorian Grays. I've *always* fought to avoid the trap. It's that feeling that a lot of actors have that certain things are necessary accoutrements to success— like the chocolate brown Mercedes, the Jacuzzi, one good piece of turquoise, the *best* table at the Palm Restaurant and the Star of David around your neck because you're suddenly proud to be a Jew.

Peter Strauss

❏

The principal difference between a dog and a man is that if you pick up a starving dog and make him prosperous, he will not bite you.

Barbra Streisand

❏

I got into *Tarzan* by accident. Since I was a well-known swimmer, I'd gotten to know Clark Gable, and he invited me to come out to the studio and visit him on the lot. Well, one day I decided to do that, but when I got to the gate the guard wouldn't let me through until somebody mentioned they were testing for *Tarzan*. The guard said, "If you'd like to go test, you can, and you'll get a free lunch whether you get the part or not." So I went on out, and from 75 men, they picked me.

Johnny Weissmuller

Superstition

This casting director imported for his very own a very well-endowed lady from South of the border (who) became well known not only as an actress of the "tits and sand" variety, but for other quirks. On the back lot location, the studio provided the actors with a group of tentlike structures, hotter than Hades, with no facilities for answering nature's call. The lady in question found a simple solution. Perhaps partially in protest against the shabby dressing room and partially because she was too lazy to walk half a mile to tinkle, she answered nature's call in the natural way. After about a week of this and several unanswered complaints, the gent in charge of her dressing room came up with an ingenious answer: he decided to sprinkle the floor with quicklime. The following day, the quiet was shattered by a scream of which Medea could have been proud. This time when the lady let fly, a cloud of sulphurous smoke engulfed her and flames began licking at her feet. Those of us who were in on the plot tried to convince her that it was a supernatural manifestation, the god of Universal's back lot striking back.

Robert Stack

Tardiness

I was making *The Sundowners* for Fred Zinnemann in 1960 in Australia in such heat as you can't imagine. It was a 75-mile drive to the location. One went to make up in a tent that was absolutely boiling. On this particular day, after the long drive and the unpleasant tent, I was 10 or 15 minutes late on the set. Mr. Z., usually so amiable, was stony-faced. He informed me that I'd held up production. "How *dare* you!", I told him. I did really shout at him and I made sure everyone heard. "If Ava Gardner were playing the part, you'd be lucky if she were only three hours late!"

Deborah Kerr

It makes something in me happy to be late. People are waiting for me. People are eager to see me. I remember all the years I was unwanted, all the hundreds of times nobody wanted to see the little servant girl, Norma Jean—not even her mother. And I feel a queer sensation in punishing the people who are wanting me now. But it's not them I'm really punishing. It's the long-ago people who didn't want Norma Jean. The later I am, the happier she grows. To me, it's remarkable that I get there at all.

Marilyn Monroe

Marilyn Monroe was never on time, never knew her lines. I have an old aunt in Vienna. She would be on the set every morning at six and would know her lines backwards. But who would go to see her?

Billy Wilder

Television

I've decided I know why they call television a medium. It's because nothing in it is well done.

Fred Allen

There are no writers on TV, and the directors are nothing at all. "Walk in the door," my director kept saying to me, "turn right, face the camera and start talking." Finally, I said, "Look, if you say that to me one more time, I'll knock your teeth out!"

Jean Arthur

Good heavens, television is something you appear on. You don't watch.

Noel Coward

They keep the television in the living room, and it's just a garbage box. And so if you keep the garbage box in the living room, it will smell, and you will begin to smell like it.

Katharine Hepburn

Television has brought murder back in the home—where it belongs.

Alfred Hitchcock

I probably will be a has-been in a couple of years and I'll start doing television. It's a graveyard for old actors and aspiring young actors.

Walter Matthau

Thought

Acting is not a profession for a thinking man. I am not an actor but a reporter of contemporary emotion. To be an actor, you have to be either callous or talented. I'm neither.

William Holden

William Holden
Thinking man's actor

A smart girl is one who knows how to play tennis, golf, piano—and dumb.

Marilyn Monroe

❏

Even when I was a waiter, I liked to keep things clean. When I was in Europe I read nothing but stories about Al Capone in the papers. It was the same with the American movies I had to sell—gun molls and gang massacres. I was determined to make my movies about all the nice Americans who had been left out, and I did. I've got another line I used a lot: Never make an audience think. It always worked for me.

Joe Pasternak

❏

We could talk about how movies can change our way of thinking, and how MTV may change our way of not thinking.

Lily Tomlin

Thrift

Hollywood is a place where the only thing an actor saves for a rainy day is somebody else's umbrella.

Lynn Bari

I make $2 bets at the track because they won't take $1.50. I've tried.

Cary Grant

I used to telephone Clark Gable each Christmas and say, "Did you get any monogrammed stuff you don't want?" If he said yes, I'd hurry round and we'd exchange initialed presents.

Cary Grant

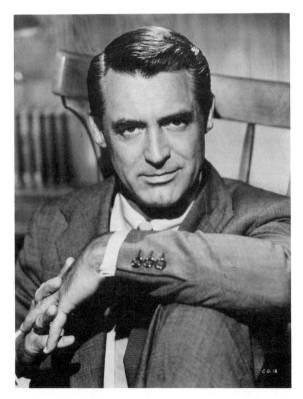

Cary Grant
The gift of thrift

Travel

I don't know how people do it, living in the country. To me, a vacation is a trip to Stockholm, Paris, Rome. Robert Redford has this film festival out in Utah, he likes to look at the mountains. Not me, I'm into looking at bridges, waterfronts, bars, the metropolitan reality. When I played Tahoe years ago, they were driving me up in the snow, and they stopped and said we were at the most beautiful place in America. All these mountains and lakes. I couldn't wait to get out of there and feel concrete underneath my soles.

Woody Allen

❏

For the first 20 years I was in Hollywood, I hardly left the sound stage. Never went on location, never. If they wanted a particular background for you, they built it. They'd have built the Nile for you and you'd never have known the difference. Nowadays, it's all different. Films have become travelogues. And actors stuntmen. I mean, look at the deep sea thing they made recently. Jackie Bisset going down to the bottom of the ocean. What's that got to do with acting?

Bette Davis

❏

I flew to the premiere of *That's Entertainment, Part 2* with Fred Astaire, Gene Kelly and Donald O'Connor. Four hoofers all on the same trip. I turned to Astaire during the flight and said to him, "Do you know if this plane crashes, Ken Berry will be the biggest song-and-dance man in America?" We all laughed.

Bobby Van

Trust

There's only one person in the world I can trust. Me.

Ava Gardner

❏

Nobody trusts anybody—or why did they put "tilt" on a pinball machine?

Steve McQueen

Typecasting

Playing a skin diver washed up my career as an actor. The public has viewed me as an underwater superman. It's a stereotype that I've never been able to break. Four years of *Sea Hunt* on TV ruined my chances of ever achieving success as a straight dramatic actor. Four years of saying lines like, "Toss me a fin," and I was finished. No one wanted me wearing a regular suit—just a wetsuit.

Lloyd Bridges

❏

You know, the curious thing about Margaret Dumont, in all the years we played together she never seemed to vary. She was always the austere, dignified dowager that we presented in pictures. That was part of her charm. She actually didn't understand any of the jokes. I'm serious—there was a joke in *Duck Soup* which was at the finish of the picture. There was a war and we were in a small cottage—Margaret and myself. She said to me, "What are you doing, Rufus?" I said, "I'm fighting for your honor, which is more than you ever did." And later she asked what did I mean by that.

Groucho Marx

❏

Boston Blackie helped me to decide to leave Hollywood. I liked the character—he was a forerunner of James Bond, except that my girls weren't as sexy and had more clothes. But Blackie's pictures were always in the "B" class. Before they were ever made, they were pre-sold to movie houses. Exhibitors had to accept them as the second half of the bill to get a picture with someone like Fred Astaire and Ginger Rogers. Contractually, I was bound for nine years to do four Blackies a year. After that a producer wouldn't put me in an "A" movie even if I paid for the privilege. The only thing I could do was get out and go back to the theater.

Chester Morris

❏

I seemed to be locked into playing heavies in episodic TV. The road to oblivion, being underpaid and overexposed. People didn't know my name but they knew my face, and they looked at me suspiciously—as if they'd seen my pictures on some post office wall.

Robert Loggia

❏

I played Sherlock Holmes for seven years, and nobody thought I could do anything else. When I would come onto a set or into a radio station, it was never "Hello, Rathbone." It was always "Hello, Holmes." I simply threw away the pipe and hat and came back to Broadway. It was a simple question of survival—Holmes or Rathbone.

Basil Rathbone

Basil Rathbone
Here comes Holmes

❏

I wasn't going to cast Natalie Wood in *Rebel without a Cause* because she's a child actress, and the only child actress who ever made it as far as I'm concerned was Helen Hayes. Then Dennis Hopper and Natalie were in a car accident. Hopper called me, said there had been some trouble and that he thought Natalie had a concussion. When I arrived at the police station, the doctor was just leaving and said Natalie was all right. Natalie was lying down, and she grabbed me and pulled me close and whispered, "You see that son-of-a-bitch?", and she pointed to the precinct doctor. "Well, he called me a juvenile delinquent. *Now* do I get the part?"

Nicholas Ray

❏

I once counted. I made 23 of those pictures (playing women executives), most of them at Columbia. We had a standing set for my office. Always the same desk, always the same window cutout behind me of the skyline of New York. I remember starting a picture once and telling the prop man, "Joe, would you move the Empire State Building? In the last picture, it looked like it was growing out of my head!"

Rosalind Russell

❏

I made a much better adjustment to (villainous roles) than did our poor late-lamented Laird Cregar, an actor of great talent virtually assassinated by Hollywood. Since Laird's physique was rather too robust, his eyes curiously slanted and his general features inconsistent with the general mold of the fashionable leading man, he was invariably cast as a fiend. In the preamble of every script, there is a description of the leading characters. In the case of Laird's roles, the description would always be that of a subhuman monster. Time and time again, Laird would go in and ask the chief make-up man what fantastic distortions of his face would be required. The make-up man would invariably answer, "We want you just as you are, Mr. Cregar."

George Sanders

❏

Every Maisie film cost under $500,000 and made two to three times that back. Sure I felt she was a millstone around my neck at times. When fans started demanding I sign their autograph books as Maisie, I knew she was strangling me. But I can't ever complain about how MGM treated me. The lighting was always meticulous. I got Greta Garbo's old dressing room when she left—Lana Turner was right below me, and what a racket her parties always made! When you went in they made a mannequin of you, and that became your measurements forever. If you put on a pound, you had to go to the front office.

Ann Sothern

❑

My first important role had been in *The Wedding March*, with Eric von Stroheim, a film rich with sensitivity. Naturally, I had hoped for a continuation of the particular values I found in such filmmaking. Instead, because of the enthusiastic reception given *King Kong*, more horror films were offered me. By the time I had finished *The Mystery of the Wax Museum* and *The Vampire Bat*, I was desperately in need of escape and welcomed an invitation to go to England to make pictures. It seemed an irony to be met by a representative of the BBC who asked that I come to their studios and broadcast a sample of my scream. Later, when I was walking in Hyde Park and overheard a Cockney woman threatening her tiny child with "If y' don't behive I'll have Fye Wrye get King Kong after yer!", I did feel like screaming—at that mother!

Fay Wray

❑

I thought I'd never get out of those wise-cracking heroine's chum roles I'd been playing for years. Then one day Billy Wilder told me he'd like to see me for *The Lost Weekend*, which he was co-writing and would direct. The book was a best-seller, and I rushed out and bought a copy. I thought Billy was crazy: darned if I could find the sort of light chippie role I was used to. I mentioned this to Billy, and he said, "Oh, you'd play the *heroine*, the loyal fiancée of the alcoholic." Billy'd been impressed by a serious scene I had just played in the comedy *Princess O'Rourke* and felt I could do it. So I got *The Lost Weekend*, and then came *The Yearling*, *Johnny Belinda*, *The Glass Menagerie*, *The Blue Veil* and *Magnificent Obsession*. I'll always be grateful to Billy Wilder.

Jane Wyman

❑

We were about to sign Joan Crawford for the captain's wife (in *From Here to Eternity*) when Deborah Kerr's agent called and said, "What about Deb-

Jane Wyman
No more chippies galore

Ann Sothern
MGM's Millstone Maisie

orah?" I found the idea fascinating, because up to that point, Deborah had played very cold, remote characters, and so I thought, if you hear two soldiers at the post saying she sleeps with everybody, you look at this woman and you don't believe it. She's a lady. So, therefore, the audience is curious to know how this comes about. You get a new facet to the character. Whereas with Joan Crawford, if you looked at her, with all due respect, you wouldn't find it impossible to believe she sleeps with everyone. You just accept it and say, "What else is new?"

Fred Zinnemann

Violence

Many psychologists have said that the United States is the most violent country is the world. We kill more people in New York City than in the whole of England in one year! I was watching *The Godfather* and people were talking about the horror and violence in it. The horror to me was the enjoyment the people in the audience got when they were garrotting the guy—they were really enjoying it! I was absolutely appalled that people enjoy seeing death and murder.

Dana Andrews

❏

Nude scenes? I wouldn't take off my clothes. There's enough violence in the world.

Carol Burnett

❏

They call me the fascist right-winger of the *Follies* cast. One day Hal Prince and Alexis Smith and I were talking about how expensive things could be. I said I knew what they meant because I was buying a box of Luger bullets in Virginia City, and I was amazed at how expensive they were. There was this shocked silence. I love to shoot, a lot of people do; so what? It's just target practice. I would never shoot an animal. Only targets—or people if they were attacking my house.

Yvonne De Carlo

❏

Violence doesn't distress me. I enjoy the healthy shooting in pictures. It has nothing to do with the way I feel in real life. After my movie *Hang 'Em High*, a critic implied that we might actually be inspiring some of the assassinations that were taking place and contributing to the violence of our era. That's a lot of bunk. When I was a kid, I'd go to the shoot-'em-ups at the movies every Saturday afternoon and come out laughing.

Clint Eastwood

❑

I think films have gone too far with violence and graphic sex. I would never again portray violence in a graphic way in a film. I've come to believe that it does do harm. Television's restraints in these areas are good discipline for a filmmaker. Movies have gone too far and freedom has been abused.

William Friedkin

Clint Eastwood
Violently answers critics

❑

I have a lot of respect for what Sylvester Stallone has accomplished, and I read something about Chuck Norris that made me think he's a decent guy. But they must take more responsibility for what they do! The people who make the money won't change them; they have to take it on themselves. They can't make it seem that bullets don't hurt! When you stand up and spray 20 of the enemy with bullets to rescue a couple of guys and nobody gets hurt, that's a fucking lie! We need heroes, they say, and I agree. The question is, what kind of heroes? The hero that sprays the village with bullets and people topple over like cardboard figures experiencing no pain? We must depict the suffering and the horror of that reality in order to grow a real hero. We don't need those heroes—those are *lies!*

Harvey Keitel

❑

After *Rambo*, I expect pretty soon to go to a theater and see them linking 500 bridges together and blowing them up one after another for an hour and a half and that will be it. I mean, I'm telling you, the social habits of the American public have been reduced to something between Attila the Hun and an ape up in a tree someplace.

Gordon Willis

Virginity

I'm as pure as the driven slush.

Tallulah Bankhead

❑

Good original screenplays are almost as rare in Hollywood as virgins.

Raymond Chandler

❑

When did I lose my virginity? When I married my first husband. It was *hell* waiting!

Bette Davis

I have the unfortunate reputation of being Miss Goody Two-Shoes, America's Virgin and all that, so I'm afraid it's going to shock some people for me to say this, but I staunchly believe no two people should get married until they have lived together. The young people have it right.

Doris Day

When I was making *Hello, Frisco, Hello* at Fox, they were starting *The Song of Bernadette* there with a new actress named Jennifer Jones. She had been chosen to portray the virginal French peasant girl who became a saint because—we were told—she was "a gifted young virgin herself." Then we learned she had two children! Jack Oakie, who was working with me and was always clowning, said, "Boy, I gotta get over to that set. This virgin I gotta see!"

Alice Faye

I knew Doris Day before she became a virgin.

Oscar Levant

L.B. Mayer signed me to a new contract. I got a Lana Turner picture called *Diane* to direct, but there were days when we'd sit around wondering how we could show her as a virgin. I said, "Oh, give her two left breasts!" and walked out and told Mr. Mayer I needed more time to adjust.

David Miller

I used to be snow white, but I drifted.

Mae West

War

After *Two Girls and a Sailor*, Van Johnson and I did so many war movies together that the studio joke was that no one would ever know how many missions Van had flown over my dressing room.

June Allyson

❑

I wasn't an actor at all. I was a banjo player. But they wanted an unknown for the part (in *All Quiet on the Western Front*) and I was certainly that. Well, when I read the book and then the script, I knew darn well I couldn't *act* it. I didn't have the ability or the training. So the only answer was to *be* that boy. While we were making the picture I came to know how horrible war was, how useless, how degrading for everybody. I came to believe that nothing justified killing your fellow man. That part did things to me.

Lew Ayres

❑

I don't know why we're in Vietnam. I can understand why we fought Hitler ... but I can't understand these piddling little things. It's not really explained to us what's going on there ... why 18- and 19-year-olds have to get shot at, why we always have to move into other countries' problems.

Lauren Bacall

❑

We (Germans) knew about the gassed children. We knew. It didn't require great courage to decide on which side to be.

Marlene Dietrich

❑

A Frenchman came up to me one day and said, "Well, how do you think your country is doing now?" The papers had just reported that famous incident where we had bombed a Vietnamese village in order to "save" it. I became very defensive. At the same time, there was the anti-war movement going on in America, and I could watch French television and see hundreds of thousands of Americans protesting the war. It made me think that something was going on that I didn't understand. So I began to study and to read. When I began to learn what was going on in Vietnam, I couldn't believe it. I started talking with soldiers who had been in Vietnam, and my reaction to what they told me was one of anger; I felt that I had been deceived and manipulated by a lot of government propaganda. I wasn't a young student anymore. I was 32. And I said, "Okay, half of my life is already over and I want to go back to the United States and participate with other people to expose what is going on."

Jane Fonda

When asked by a reporter, following her trip to North Vietnam, if she were being used for propaganda:
Do you think the Vietnamese blow up their own hospitals? Are they bombing their own dikes? Are they mutilating their own women and children in order to impress me? Anyone who speaks out against the war is carrying on propaganda—propaganda for peace, propaganda against death, propaganda for life.

Jane Fonda

I'm leaving this turmoil (Hollywood) for the tranquility of war.

Sterling Hayden

I was the all-American hero for all those years. In fact, I'm convinced if it wasn't for my on-screen heroics, we would never have won the war.

Van Johnson

And then there are the War Years. My God, looking back at the array of photos from that period, I realize Rambo was a piker next to me. Did he ever launch a ship? Sell a War Bond? Lead a military band and don a gas mask? (You can't be too ready.)

Evelyn Keyes

Evelyn Keyes
War is obscenity

© C.P. CORP. EVELYN KEYES #95

Someone asked me to define obscenity. I said: "Obscenity is blowing up people. It's a war. It's that chief of police in Saigon blowing out the brains of his prisoner. It certainly isn't consenting adults."

Evelyn Keyes

❏

Warner Brothers had guts. They hated the Nazis more than they cared for the German grosses. MGM did not. It kept on releasing its films in Nazi Germany until Hitler finally threw them out. In fact, one MGM producer was in charge of taking anyone's name off a picture's credits if it sounded Jewish.

Joseph L. Mankiewicz

❏

319

I would defend my home—about my country, I'm not sure. If 25 Russians landed on my front lawn today, I'd say: "Do you guys want a drink, or a cup of coffee?"

Lee Marvin

I can't remember one war that was ended by guitar playing.

Martin Mull

I'm something of a super-patriot, but these (Vietnam) aren't real wars we're fighting these days, except that boys really are being killed. These wars are morally wrong. No country has the right to ask young men to give their lives in wars they can't win.

Audie Murphy

I can't say I'm flatly against killing under any circumstances. I would kill in defense of my own family. I could kill in self-defense, I suppose. And I could kill if somebody invaded my country. But to kill Vietnamese, to slaughter them wholesale, in an undeclared war against other Vietnamese halfway around the world, at the request of a corrupt puppet regime that doesn't reflect the will of its own people—that I couldn't do. That kind of war I consider not only illegal but immoral.

Paul Newman

Maybe I'll go into the air force and drop Goldwyn pamphlets over Germany. You know, it wouldn't be such a risk since Goldwyn has ordered Hitler to shoot around me.

David Niven

My opinions do differ from those of Bob Hope (with whom I made the first entertainers tour of Vietnam in 1964). But I think by now (1970) even Robert wants this war over. I don't think anyone has the right to use indiscriminately anyone else's life. The ones who call for us to wage this war ought to be fighting it. I'll probably be blasted out of California for what I just said.

Janis Paige

I believe in fighting. Lately I've been asked by interviewers, "Aren't you afraid you'll hurt your career by being politically active and speaking out on things like nuclear disarmament?" That makes me laugh. If there is a nuclear war, I tell them, what sort of career would I have anyway?

Susan Sarandon

I go by instinct—I don't worry about experience. I mean, if there had been only one war, then you could listen to people who say they know about things, but experience hasn't counted for very much, has it?

Barbra Streisand

I'm neither a hawk nor a dove. I'm an owl. I feel if I am elected to Congress, I cannot do much about this war, but I can do something to prevent the next Vietnam developing.

Shirley Temple

Rings on Her Fingers was my first comedy part. But it was not a good time for comedy, the final weeks of 1941. On Sunday, December 7, we were filming on Catalina Island; we had just set up our cameras when an assistant came racing down the beach. "The Japanese have bombed Pearl Harbor!", he yelled. "We're gonna be at war. We've got to clear out for the mainland right away!"

Gene Tierney

Now, these women who write to me and want a few tips about men and love, they keep wonderin', since most of them are workin' for the duration, what they should do when World War II stops. Should they go right on supportin' themselves—and the home? I tell 'em I think a woman may owe a man a good lovin'—but not a livin'. If they want to hold their men, they can think that over!

Mae West

❏

The whole world was battling bravely for its soul, but somehow, no matter how hard the (second world) war effort was, in Hollywood it all appeared like a musical comedy war at the studios; not one good realistic war film was made. Even the men in uniform lived often in Beverly Hills and reported daily to Fort Roach, a film studio converted into the making of official films.

Mae West

Women

I always referred to the great women stars as the Monsters, and monsters indeed most of them are, but if I have not admired their characters it has not meant that I have been insensible to the charms which affect the rest of the world. I even found Bette Davis attractive, when I played Maximilian to her Carlotta (in *Juarez*) and, brilliant actress though she is, surely nobody but a mother could have loved Bette Davis at the height of her career.

Brian Aherne

❏

Daddy warned me about drinking and men, but he never said anything about women and drugs.

Tallulah Bankhead

❏

The way to fight a woman is with your hat—grab it and run.

John Barrymore

❏

Tallulah Bankhead
A father's warning

I think that the most important thing a woman can have, next to talent, is her hairdresser.

Joan Crawford

❏

Horses are like women. Some of them don't like you.

William Devane

❏

I find it easier to get on with women than with men. And if things are not working out on the set and everything else fails, I will look them up and down and flirt with them.

Michael Douglas

❏

Joan Hackett
The thighs have it

The practice of putting women on pedestals began to die out when it was discovered that they could give orders better from that position.

Betty Grable

❏

I'm trying to figure out why women (in Hollywood) are so dedicated to the way they look. It's crippling their minds. The general attitude out here is not "How good an actress are you?" but "How are your thighs?" It's an unfortunate handicap and it's crippling California women. If they're so involved in paying attention to how they look, they haven't the time to think about doing anything else with their lives. There are real women across America doing great things. Here, and I'm talking about Beverly Hills primarily, they all look and act like princesses. We can't even put real looking women on screen. They have to look polished, perfect, unreal.

Joan Hackett

❏

I'm cursed with being a man. You're constantly in competition with women because you can't give birth.

Dustin Hoffman

❏

Woman's movie: where the wife commits adultery throughout and at the end of the picture the husband begs her forgiveness.

Oscar Levant

❏

I like to see a woman walk down a street with no girdle or bra. If the buns don't move, it's like a TV dinner—it's just dead.

George Maharis

❏

Men react as they're taught to react, in what they've been taught is a "manly" way. Women are, by comparison, as if assembled by the wind.

Joseph L. Mankiewicz

❏

Women exist for men. Any woman who tells you different is a liar or—well, you know, something wrong.

Marilyn Monroe

❏

People talk slower to blondes—they just seem to think they aren't as bright.

Deborah Raffin

❏

Women aren't worth dating until they're at least 35.

Burt Reynolds

❏

Being adored by a woman is a nuisance. Women give us the gold of our lives, but invariably they want it back in small change. And when they have become stout and tedious and you meet them years later and long after the romance is over—they go in for reminiscence. That awful, long memory of women.

George Sanders

If there hadn't been women we'd still be squatting in a cave eating raw meat, because we made civilization in order to impress our girlfriends.

Orson Welles

Women's Lib

I'm not nutty about the Libs. They're so masculine they scare me. But there's one healthy thing about the movement. More and more women are aware they have a choice about the route they take. The idea of a "woman's place is in the home" has been beaten down.

Lauren Bacall

It is a ridiculous idea that a woman must stay at home because she is married. If an unmarried woman can be a successful author, or painter, or sculptor, or musician—as so many are—nobody objects. But let a married woman take a job as a secretary, a teacher—even a clerk—and she finds herself, very definitely, a storm center.

Madeleine Carroll

I believe in that women's lib cliché thing—you know, equal pay for whatever—but I'm against all the other nonsense. I hate the fringe types—the ones who tell you to throw away your bras. I mean, as far as I'm concerned, no woman ever wore a bra for a *man*. They'd just as soon you *didn't* wear one, right?

Claudette Colbert

❑

Women who are strong and dominant are often called bitches for the want of a better word. But a strong, dominant man is never called a bastard.

Joan Collins

❑

Sometimes, when you look at successful and attractive career women who haven't given their career up yet for anyone, it is not that they wouldn't if they got the chance, it's simply that they haven't met the right man. When they do, the devil with a career!

Helmut Dantine

❑

If a man does something silly, people say, "Isn't he silly?" If a woman does something silly, people say, "Aren't women silly?"

Doris Day

❑

Women are superior to men. You see a lot of smart men with dumb women, but you don't see a lot of smart women with dumb guys. A lot of guys will go out with a bimbo, but women who are smart don't do that.

Clint Eastwood

❑

No one should have to dance backward all their lives—this women's movement is as important as antislavery was in the 19th century.

Jane Fonda

❑

These women who go around saying, "Freedom now! Liberty for women! Equality!" Fine. Give them a gun and send them to Vietnam.

Peter Fonda

❑

Women's liberation as a movement makes some valid points. But in the final analysis, it doesn't matter who wears the pants—so long as there's money in the pockets.

Ava Gardner

❏

For most women, a career alone would not bring happiness. Your career should be your avocation and your life your vocation, whether it's your home life or what-have-you. Home life should come first, ahead of careers.

Paulette Goddard

❏

It's all a joke—women on Fifth Avenue whose husbands make $10 million a year, and they decide they want to be free. How can we have equality if we have capitalism? How can you say women should make as much as men for doing the same rotten thing? Even the prostitutes want equal time. We got the prostitute's movement, the men's movement, the children's movement and America's *still* constipated.

Richard Pryor

❏

The only thing wrong with women's lib is men. Men are so panicked, and feel so threatened themselves, they make women act more fanatical to get their rights. Men should just mind their own store.

Robert Redford

❏

Men have proven themselves supreme in all the arts and crafts; therefore I see no reason why women should presume to equality with us. Women often advance the specious argument that they are the "power behind the throne." They mean that many great men would not have been so great had they not had brilliant and enterprising women back of them. Granted. But the women in back of them were just that—back of them, where they belong.

George Sanders

❏

I'm all for equal rights, but I want it to stop right there. I don't want women to grow hair on their chests, and men will never have children.

Gloria Swanson

❏

A man has to be Joe McCarthy to be called ruthless. All a woman has to do is put you on hold.

Marlo Thomas

❏

When a woman writes her memoirs—like Candice Bergen, Lauren Bacall or Simone Signoret who wrote about Yves Montand's affair with Marilyn Monroe—it's okay. But when I did, the reaction was, "How can you do that?" Please don't talk to be about equality and then tell me to act differently.

Roger Vadim

Work

When I get the idea for a film and I'm just walking around flushed with the idea, it's magic—it's Renoir and Fellini. It's just great. Then I start to make the film, and the truck rolls in every day with fresh compromises. You can't get the actor you want, and you don't have enough money to do this, and you're not as good as you thought. And by the time the film is finished, it's 50 or 60 per cent of what I had envisioned.

Woody Allen

❏

People will come up to me and say, "Boy, it must have been fun making those old MGM musicals." Fun? I suppose you could have considered them that—if you liked beating your brains and your feet out.

Fred Astaire

❏

These kid actors today got it made. They've got tutors, limos, only work four, five hours a day. They have no idea what it was like, man, no idea. I can't watch any of those *Our Gang* comedies. It's too painful. My knees were destroyed. I was working in pain.

Robert Blake

Why do I make so many lousy pictures? Because I want Jack Warner to have to look at my sour puss for the rest of his life.

Humphrey Bogart

Burlesque was a marvelous training ground. It was great for my timing, my delivery and my eyes.

Red Buttons

Humphrey Bogart
Behind his prolificacy

❏

Recalling lunches at Paramount Pictures' writers table:

I remember Harry Tugend's wonderful crack about an actress when Tugend was trying to be a producer. He said: "This is a lousy job. You got to sit and talk to that birdbrain seriously about whether or not this part is going to be good for her fucking career and at the same time you got to keep from being raped." Whereat a rather innocent young man piped up: "You mean to say she's a nymphomaniac?" Harry sighed, "Well, I guess she would be if they could get her quieted down."

Raymond Chandler

❏

The next time I send a damn fool I go myself.

Michael Curtiz

❏

My favorite role? I'm like a pregnant woman; any baby I get is the most beautiful.

Fritz Feld

❏

I see about one fifth of the pictures I make. I would be embarrassed to see most of them.

Henry Fonda

❏

Working in Hollywood does give one a certain expertise in the field of prostitution.

Jane Fonda

❏

The kind of films that made you want to be an actor aren't being made anymore. Cars that eat bicycles or kids going to the moon—those are the kinds of plot they like nowadays. It makes you want to do a TV series.

Frederic Forrest

❑

I won the role of Alex in *Family Ties* mostly by being more obnoxious than the other kids. If you went to a Hollywood audition you would see these kids who are superfriendly, totally insincere and dropping names like crazy. I went the other way and put down everybody, which is what the character was all about. It worked.

Michael J. Fox

❑

The other day I was thinking I should have taken all the movies they offered me when I was in my 30s and 40s . . . I turned down a lot . . . like *Sweet Bird of Youth* . . . *The Graduate* . . . a lot. I even went on suspension so I wouldn't have to do *Love Me or Leave Me*, which Doris Day did. I don't remember why I turned that one down. Maybe I was having a love affair at the time.

Ava Gardner

❑

Work edict:
    No mamas, no murderesses.

Greta Garbo

❑

During the filming of my first Hollywood picture, *Julius Caesar*, I was waiting to go on the Rome street set with a whole menagerie of sheep, dogs and pigeons which had been brought in to make the city look more lively. One of the pigeons perched on a pillar suddenly jumped off and began walking around the floor of the studio. A hefty cowboy who evidently looked after all the animals dashed up and yelled at the bird, "Get back, get back, don't you want to work tomorrow?"

John Gielgud

❑

During the filming of *Two-Faced Woman*, Garbo and I were supposed to make a sedate entrance together. Director George Cukor was dissatisfied with the first three takes. I leaned close to Garbo and said, "Will you try to get it right this time? If you don't he's going to blame me." Garbo laughed so

When an actor says, "I shouldn't do that part"—it's vanity. It's just work, like any other work. Our work is acting. It hurts you to make it so important. It should be more a matter of daily bread. The star system is destructive when an actor says, "I can't do that part, I'm a star." You should act, period. And shut up.

Viveca Lindfors

On *Samson and Delilah*, Cecil B. DeMille, the director, wanted me to put my head in the lion's mouth. I said I really wasn't very enthusiastic about that. DeMille said, "*Victor*, don't worry; it's an old lion named Jackie whose teeth have all been pulled." I said, "Mr. DeMille, I don't even want to be gummed a little!"

Victor Mature

Why am I still acting? How else would a no-talent guy like me make this kind of dough? Besides, it keeps me off the streets. The thing I like best about acting is talking about it. What I enjoy the most are the days off. Fact is, actors receive more respect than they deserve, me for one. I'm the oldest whore in the business. I've got the same attitude I had when I started. I haven't changed anything but my underwear.

Robert Mitchum

Did you see me in *Cobra Woman*? That *Cobra Woman* was a *steenker*. I never liked my pictures. I have quit 148 times. Every time I begin to emote I look up and there is a horse—stealing my scene.

Maria Montez

When Jennifer Jones was married to David Selznick, they'd shoot a scene 40 times just to make sure Jennifer looked good in the take. Whenever I made a film, if the horse didn't ... you know what ... in the middle of a shot, it was a take.

Maureen O'Hara

❏

I'm a workman. I have to work to live. If I stopped working, it would be because I stopped breathing.

Laurence Olivier

❏

The picture was so bad they had to do retakes before they could put it on the shelf.

King Vidor

❏

At USC, I took Latin and Romance Languages and mathematics through calculus. And when I started in movies, they had to teach me to say ain't.

John Wayne

❏

I'm the girl that works at Paramount all day and Fox all night.

Mae West

❏

My old films? I want to climb up there and change everything. It's like meeting a girl you slept with 15 years ago. You look at her and you think, "My God, did I go to bed with *that*?"

Billy Wilder

❏

Now (1986), Hollywood studios are nothing but the Ramada Inn: You rent space, you shoot and out you go.

Billy Wilder

❏

Of course there must be subtleties in filmmaking. Just make sure you make
them obvious.

Billy Wilder

❑

What about the software? Who will write, direct, act? It's a human fact: a
microchip can't replace a human brain. So let's relax and tell the picture-
makers we are not expendable. The bigger they get, the more irreplaceable
we are. Theirs is the kingdom, ours is the power and the glory.

Billy Wilder